CW01082207

REGULATING SEX IN
THE ROMAN EMPIRE

REGULATING SEX IN THE ROMAN EMPIRE

IDEOLOGY, THE BIBLE, AND

THE EARLY CHRISTIANS

David Wheeler-Reed

Yale

UNIVERSITY PRESS

New Haven & London

Published with assistance from the foundation established in memory
of Henry Weldon Barnes of the Class of 1882,
Yale College.

Yale University Press books may be purchased in
quantity for educational, business, or promotional use.
For information, please e-mail sales.press@yale.edu
(U.S. office) or sales@yaleup.co.uk (U.K. office).

Set in Baskerville and Bulmer type by IDS Infotech Ltd.,
Chandigarh, India.
Printed in the United States of America.

Library of Congress Control Number: 2017936735
ISBN 978-0-300-22772-7 (hardcover : alk. paper)

A catalogue record for this book is available from the British Library.

This paper meets the requirements of ANSI/NISO
Z39.48-1992 (Permanence of Paper).

10 9 8 7 6 5 4 3 2 1

For Fitz, without whom none of this would've been possible

CONTENTS

CONTENTS

ACKNOWLEDGMENTS

It's rare in life to have a mentor. What's even more rare is to have three. Of all the people who have helped me complete this project, three stand out. First, there's L. Ann Jervis, who was my dissertation supervisor at the University of Toronto. She was the first person who encouraged me to think openly and critically about the Augustan marriage legislation and its possible effect on early Christianity. Additionally, she taught me the value of asking probing questions that consider all sides of an issue. I've never met a more genuine and thoughtful person in my life.

Second, there's John T. Fitzgerald. Fitz, to whom this book is dedicated, has become my intellectual father. He saw potential in me that I didn't see myself. And when I wanted to give up, he encouraged me to continue the struggle. If there ever was a "scholar and a gentleman," it's John.

Finally, there's Dale B. Martin. Nothing I could say or do could ever express how much Dale has meant to me and to my work. Some of the best discussions of my life have occurred around his fireplace with glasses of bourbon. The best thing I can say about Dale is that, beyond being a mentor, he has become one of my best friends.

In addition to these three mentors, I also thank Jennifer Wright Knust. Jenny has spent countless hours with this project. She has helped me sharpen my arguments and has been one of the best resources for discovering important books on gender and queer theory. Additionally, my editors at Yale University Press deserve praise. Without Larry Welborn, Heather Gold, and Jennifer Banks, this project never would have seen the light of day.

Furthermore, I thank Yale Divinity School for accepting me as a Visiting Fellow during Fall 2014. While there, I had the opportunity to discuss my work with Harry Attridge, Greg Sterling, Judith Gundry, Michel-Beth Dinkler, Andrew McGowan, and the many doctoral students enrolled in the Religion Department at Yale University. Each individual contributed in many ways to this finished project.

Outside of academia, many friends and family members supported me through this project. In particular, I thank Tom Jacobs, Scott Russell, John Inglis, Mike Schwab, William Gracie, Elliot Winks, Anne Kilbride, Matthew Waggoner, Jeremiah Coffey, and Peggy DesAutels. Additionally, my students at Albertus Magnus College deserve special mention since they suffered through much of the material in this book during a course I taught there titled "Issues in Sexual Morality." I also thank my parents, Robert and Linda Reed. My father has been my biggest fan, and my mother taught me to stand up for the oppressed. I would be nothing without the two of them.

Finally, I thank the most important person in my life, Kari Wheeler-Reed. It's an amazing thing to spend more than a decade and a half of one's life with such an incredible person. As someone once said, "If I had a flower for every time I thought of you, I could walk through my garden forever."

INTRODUCTION

By way of a preface let us say that on none of the matters to be discussed
do we affirm that things are just as we say they are: rather, we report
descriptively on each item according to how it appears to us at the time.
—*Sextus Empiricus*

This book isn't a work of history but is a study of ideologies.[1] In other
words, though I deal with historical material throughout, I don't sub-
scribe to the notion that suggests, "All valid interpretation of every sort is
founded on the re-cognition of what an author meant."[2] In some cases, I
don't believe it's possible to recover what an author meant. Often, the
crucial pieces are missing, and when they're not, historians seldom agree
on what the pieces mean. As any honest historical critic knows, many
times we don't even know the identity of the author of a text.

I use the term "ideology" throughout this book to refer to discourses,
which are made up of language and social structures of power. I'm not
thinking of the Marxist idea of ideology as "false consciousness"; instead,
I'm using it as, in Miriam Griffin's words, "a kind of collusion of belief
and expression, not altogether conscious, between those above and those
below."[3] My goal is to compare different ideological systems that deal
with the same themes. Specifically, I compare discourses from the Roman
Empire, Judaism, early Christianity, and modern America that attempt to

regulate marriage, procreation, and sexuality. Studying these discourses as ideologies of the family raises questions about "the connections between language and social power relations, about the actual or potential consequences of linguistic events, about who wins and who loses given the possibility of triumph of one position over another."[4]

In an ideological study, language becomes what it has always been, namely, rhetoric. But that doesn't mean that all ideologies are oppressive. Since I don't equate ideology with "false consciousness," I do believe that some ideologies—particularly counterideologies—can be liberating. I'm also convinced that counterideologies exist only because of the ideologies that oppress. In other words, liberating ideologies need their oppressive counterparts; the two live in a strange symbiotic relationship, as do so many things. As Susanna Drake maintains, "The site of injury can become the site of resistance."[5]

I'm also indebted to the work of Louis Pierre Althusser (1918–1990), who employed French structuralism to elaborate a new Marxist theory of ideology.[6] Althusser distinguishes between diachronic "ideologies" and synchronic "Ideology." In essence, he asks, "Why do people obey the unjust laws of oppressive governments, when it isn't in their best interest to do so?" In answer to his question, he describes two primary mechanisms by which people are coerced to live according to the oppressive laws of the state. He terms the first mechanism the "repressive state apparatuses," whereby the state enforces behavior directly through repressive measures such as the police and incarceration. The second mechanism Althusser terms the "ideological state apparatuses," which are institutions that influence behavior indirectly (e.g., the justice system, the media, banks, the military, churches, advertising agencies) by producing "ideologies" that individuals internalize.[7] Typically, ideological state apparatuses function "by violence—at least ultimately (since repression, e.g. administrative repression, may take nonphysical forms)."[8] As B. H. McLean notes, "Such institutions make the dominant ideology of a society . . . natural, whereas ideologies that differ from this norm are made to appear radical and unnatural."[9]

Next, Althusser explains the mechanism through which people internalize these ideologies by distinguishing between "ideologies" and "Ideology." The former enumerates actual systems of distorted thought, such as specific instantiations of capitalism and patriarchy. The latter is structural with no specific context. "Ideology" is an ontological structure, which can be filled out by many different local and culturally specific ideologies. This is why Althusser declares that Ideology has no history.[10] As he states, "On the contrary, if I am able to put forward the project of a theory of ideology *in general,* and if this theory really is one of the elements on which theories of ideologies depend, that entails an apparently paradoxical proposition which I shall express in the following terms: *ideology has no history*" (italics in the original).[11] Ideology, then, is an *omni-historical* reality. Its content is universal content, which varies according to specific social, political, and historical contexts.

According to Althusser, people internalize the ideologies they encounter in two ways. The first is what he calls the "conspiracy theory," which he deems incorrect. This way declares that the powerful in a society have deceived everyone else into accepting a false conception of reality, which is more what Marx meant when he defined ideology as "false consciousness." Althusser's alternative maintains that human beings are predisposed to generate false representations (ideologies) of themselves, by virtue of the ontological structure of "Ideology." Becoming a "subject-In-Ideology" has three forms: (1) each of us is born into subjecthood: we are "always-already" subjected to the power of others; (2) we always-already inhabit culturally specific ideologies that appear to us as natural and self-evidently true (in the modern world, an example would be the ideology of heteronormativity); and (3) the structure of Ideology actually "interpellates" individuals into subjecthood.[12]

"Interpellation" is a kind of naming, or a calling, or a hailing, of a person into subjecthood. Althusser writes, "As a first formulation I shall say: *all ideology hails or interpellates concrete individuals as concrete subjects,* by the functioning of the category of the subject" (italics in the original).[13] When ideology beckons to us, we reply, "Are you speaking to me?" As McLean suggests, "We always reply because each of us possess [*sic*] our own internal structure of Ideology."[14] Presidents, prime ministers, political candidates, and evangelists often employ, for example, an implicit or explicit "you" in their messages. This is what Althusser means by interpellation. The "you" makes the hearer feel personally involved, even though the "you" could be meant for anyone. It's our capacity to feel individually addressed by ideology that Althusser claims is an inherent part of our composition as human beings. This is why ideologies have so much power over us, since, as Michel Pêcheux points out, "They conceal their own existence within their operation by producing a web of *'subjective' evident truths,* 'subjective' here meaning not 'affecting the subject' but 'in which the subject is constituted.'"[15]

All the discursive ideologies of the family I examine in this work are about strategies of power that seek to regulate and control.[16] When I speak of power, I'm thinking of a quotation from Gilles Deleuze:

> Power is a relation between forces, or rather every relation between forces is a power relation . . . Force is never singular but essentially exists in relation with other forces, such that any force is already a relation, that is to say power: force has no other subject or object than force . . . It is "an action upon an action, on existing actions, or on those which may arise in the present or in the future"; it is "a set of actions upon other actions." We can therefore conceive of a necessarily open list of variables expressing a relation between forces or power relation, constituting actions upon actions: to incite, to induce, to seduce, to make easy or difficult, to enlarge or limit, to make more or less probable, and so on.[17]

Power, then, maintains a relation between the "sayable and the visible."[18] Furthermore, a lived hegemony is always a process. As Raymond Williams notes:

> It [lived hegemony] is not, except analytically, a system or a structure. It is a realized complex of experiences, relationships, and activities, with specific and changing pressures and limits. In practice, that is, hegemony can never be singular. Its internal structures are highly complex, as can readily be seen in any concrete analysis. Moreover (and this is crucial, reminding us of the necessary thrust of the concept), it does not just passively exist as a form of dominance. It has continually to be renewed, recreated, defended, and modified. It is also continually resisted, limited, altered, challenged by pressures not at all its own.[19]

In a lecture Michel Foucault gave in 1980 at New York University, he made the following point about the sexual discourses of early Christianity:

> But the so-called Christian morality is nothing more than a piece of pagan ethics inserted into Christianity. Shall we say then that Christianity did not change the state of things? [I propose that] early Christians introduced important changes, if not in the sexual code itself, at least in the relationships

everyone has to his [or her] sexual activity. Christianity proposed a new type of experience of oneself as a sexual being.[20]

In this book, my task is to demonstrate that Foucault was essentially right. Christianity borrowed much of its moral strategies from Latin and Hellenistic literature and then created new ideologies, which still affect us in the twenty-first century. Or, as Peter Brown once stated to Foucault, "What we have to understand is why it is that sexuality became, in Christian cultures, the seismograph of our subjectivity."[21]

Throughout this book, I'm not interested in total history but in general history. As McLean trenchantly observes, "Actual history is not a linear narrative: history is naturally *polycentric*."[22] I'm not interested in looking for "overarching principles that govern the development of an epoch."[23] If I were, I would spend most of my time trying to uncover authorial intention. Since I'm interested in comparing different ideologies, the people or group using an ideology doesn't need to be aware that they're using it. Instead, I concentrate on describing differences, transformations, continuities, mutations, and so forth.[24] This is what general history does, because it's nonreductive, nontotalizing, specifies its own terrain, the series it constitutes, and the relations between them.[25] My task is simply to open up "attention to detail, grain, and complexity, and the specification of form of relation which is indispensable if [we are] to move beyond caricatures of historical periodisation passing for a science of social development."[26]

Not everyone will agree with me. Kathy L. Gaca, for example, argues that there are two basic camps when it comes to the study of ancient Christianity, the Greco-Roman world, and sexuality. She claims that one camp downplays the idea that a "sharp difference separated Christian sexual codes and related normative themes from those in Greek philosophy and Greco-Roman culture at large."[27] The individual at fault for this way of thinking is Foucault, who once said, "We are not talking about a moral rupture between tolerant antiquity and austere Christianity . . . the codes in themselves did not change a great deal . . . [and] the themes are the same."[28] She also points out Foucault's inconsistency, since in *The Use of Pleasure,* he writes that it's "a mistake to infer that the sexual morality of Christianity and that of paganism form a continuity."[29] Gaca also knows that Foucault prefers a "thesis of continuity" over and against one of "discontinuity."[30] But she seems unaware of Foucault's belief that Christianity did in fact introduce changes into the sexual code and in the relationships everyone has to his or her own sexual activity.

Acknowledging that many scholars of the New Testament and Christian origins have followed Foucault, Gaca singles out Elizabeth Clark and Dale Martin as among some of the top scholars who regard Hellenistic moral philosophy as the "austere prescription-generating substratum of Christian sexual morality."[31] Clark, for example, stresses "continuities of theme beyond those Foucault himself had recognized," though Gaca readily admits that it's odd for Foucault to have considered few, if any, Jewish writings in his study. Martin maintains that "Christianity has sometimes been considered . . . as playing the role of the oppressive mother superior to the gay and sexually liberated pagan culture of Greece and Rome. Most recent works on sexuality in the ancient world, however, have shown this to be an oversimplification, if not totally inaccurate." In contrast, Gaca, a classicist, wants to argue for uniqueness and discontinuity between the Greco-Roman world and Christianity—particularly Christianity during the patristic period: "My argument, however, is that encratite sexual renunciation and the ecclesiastical sexual program, as exemplified by Tatian and Clement, respectively, differ radically from their counterparts in Greek philosophy and from marriage practices in Greek society at large, both in terms of their code of sexual rules and in the other facts of ethics that Foucault delineates."[32]

We've seen Gaca's story before, which Kyle Harper recently took up in his monograph *From Shame to Sin: The Christian Transformation of Sexual Morality in Late Antiquity.*[33] Both Gaca and Harper want early Christianity to be "unique," "unprecedented," and "revolutionary." What they fail to understand is that at the very moment they compare and contrast Christianity with any other movement in the ancient world, it stops being "unique."[34]

In his overview of Christian comparisons of early Christianity and Greco-Roman mystery religions, Jonathan Z. Smith demonstrates that Protestant anti-Catholic apologetics and Protestant historical models shape Christian constructions of early Christianity. True Christianity (Protestantism) gives way to pagan sacramental mysteries (Catholicism).[35] This is similar to how many Protestants appeal to the Jesus of the canonical Gospels to define the true teaching of the faith before it was corrupted into the male monarchical episcopate of Roman Catholicism. I fear that this is precisely what Gaca and Harper are doing, consciously or not, with sexuality.

Second, Smith shows that Christian comparisons between Christianity and its pagan environment often claim uniqueness for the "Christ event."[36] Such uniqueness requires isolation. But as Smith contends, the moment one compares Christianity to Judaism, or Christian sexual ethics to Greco-Roman ones, all uniqueness is lost. As Smith writes, "The 'unique' is an attribute that must be disposed of, especially when linked to some notion of incomparable value, if progress in thinking through the enterprise of comparison is to be made."[37] For something to be unique, it cannot be comparable to anything else. As Burton Mack explains:

> The fundamental persuasion is that Christianity appeared unexpectedly in human history, that it was (is) at core a brand new vision of human existence, and that, since this is so, only a startling moment could account for its emergence at the beginning. The code word serving as a sign for the novelty that appeared is the term unique (meaning singular, incomparable, without analogue). For the originary event the word is transformation (rupture, breakthrough, inversion, reversal, eschatological). For the cognitive effect of this moment the language of paradox is preferred (irony, parable, enigma, the irrational). It is this startling moment that seems to have mesmerized the discipline and determined the application of its critical methods.[38]

The mere fact, then, that Gaca and Harper see similarities and differences between Greco-Roman sexual ethics and Christian ones means that they're already engaged in the act of comparison, which does away with words like "unique," "unprecedented," and "revolutionary."

Mark C. Taylor demonstrates that all comparative exercises involve the interplay of "sameness and difference."[39] The challenge is "to find a mean between the extremes that allows interpreters to understand differences without erasing them."[40] Though I certainly fall into the interpretive camp Gaca disapproves of, I think we can find things from the ancient world that Christianity modified or reinvented without having to say that what it did was unique. In fact, my goal is to demonstrate that the most important thing Christianity did was to normalize singleness and celibacy over and against an ideology of procreation, which was pervasive throughout the entire Greco-Roman world and parts of Judaism. I'm convinced that this is what Foucault meant when he proposed that "early

Christians introduced important changes, if not in the sexual code itself, at least in the relationships everyone has to his [or her] sexual activity." Regrettably, Gaca and Harper miss this point because they're overly concerned with reducing Christian sexual ethics to being antigay and limiting the term *porneia* to adultery, prostitution, and sex outside of marriage.

Since sex is always mediated by culture, I begin chapter 1 by examining the Augustan marriage legislation, which attempted to regulate gender by linking citizenship to reproduction.[41] In Althusser's terminology, Augustus's marriage legislation is an ideological state apparatus that permeates various sectors of Roman culture. It's an example of an ideology that sought to regulate sexual behavior by codifying it. Since sexual behavior—particularly women's sexual behavior—became a threat to the state, a need arose to impose penalties on bachelors and on those who had fewer than three children.[42] Additionally, Augustus tried to regulate morality by passing laws against adultery. As I demonstrate, citizens resisted Augustus's legislation, since many of them knew that all he really wanted was more soldiers to expand his empire.

But not everyone disagreed with Augustus and his reforms. I continue chapter 1 by detailing how the founding ideology of the emperor's legislation was interpellated and internalized by the philosophical prescriptions of Musonius Rufus and the medical writings of Galen. As I show, their discourses didn't codify sexuality into well-regulated prescriptive acts. Instead, Musonius and Galen codify a regimen that discusses *aphrodisia* and emphasizes, at times, procreation.[43] Musonius and Galen ask questions we in the modern world still ask: "Is sex healthy?" and "When is the best time for sex?"[44] I conclude chapter 1 by attending to a more humane take on sexual ideology in the Roman Empire by exploring Achilles Tatius's romantic novel *Leucippe and Clitophon*. This chapter demonstrates that no single approach to marriage and sexuality existed in the Greco-Roman world.[45] Each discourse, however, does defend an ideology meant to control and manipulate behavior and codify the importance of procreation as the main purpose of the marriage act.

Chapter 2 explores the literature of Second Temple Judaism. This literature is of particular interest to me because modern society in the United States—especially in the realm of conservative politics—is convinced that "Judeo-Christian" ethics guide sexual dos and don'ts.[46] As I establish in this chapter, *some* of the sexual ethics of Second Temple Judaism, especially those discourses composed by elites, look surprisingly similar to the ideological sexual codes of the Roman Empire.[47] An examination of works as diverse as Tobit, the writings of Philo and Josephus, the Dead Sea Scrolls, and many other texts makes it clear that *most* of the ideological discourses of Second Temple Judaism can be found in the laws of Augustus, while a few are at odds with his legislation.[48] As I show, many of the strategies developed in Jewish literature of the Second Temple era privilege the home, marriage, and procreation. In fact, Gaca calls the reigning ideology of extant Second Temple literature "Procreationism." Like its Roman counterpart, much of this literature is committed to heteronormativity, gender hierarchy, and the family. But some of it, likely written by those who were not part of the ruling class, upholds asceticism over and against the dominant ideology of Procreationism.[49] This means, of course, that there is no "normative Jewish sexual ethic" in the Second Temple period, even though many Christians in the United States continue to insist that there is one.[50]

Chapter 3 engages the writings of the New Testament. In this chapter, I argue that the New Testament creates two distinct ideologies that continue battling for superiority well into the patristic age and late antiquity. The first strategy, found in some of the gospels, the authentic letters of Paul, and the book of Revelation, maintains that marriage isn't the norm and instead creates an ideology that I term "antifamily." I point out that this antifamily strategy emphasizes singleness as the distinct Christian way of life and makes no mention of the importance of procreation, which was the dominant ideology of family life throughout the Mediterranean world. The second discourse, found particularly in the deutero-Pauline literature and the Pastoral Epistles, agrees in large part with the Augustan marriage legislation. In these texts, marriage is the norm, as is the rearing of children. I argue that in the New Testament writings, these two powerful ideologies live side by side in competition and tension. Though the *Acts of Paul and Thecla* challenges the profamily discourses of the deutero-Pauline literature and the Pastorals, it takes decades—if not centuries—for one ideology to overtake the other and become the norm.

The development of the antifamily and profamily strategies found in the New Testament is the subject of chapter 4. Here I limit myself to an analysis of Tatian and his encratite argument, Clement's emerging ecclesiastical sexual ethics, and Epiphanes's so-called libertine Christianity, which regarded Platonic and early Stoic sexual principles as the right models for a Christian way of life. Next, I demonstrate how all of these ideas coalesced in the writings of John Cassian, who, according to Foucault, is the quintessence of late antique sexual morality.[51] These texts reveal that throughout Christianity's beginnings, the two strategies created by the New Testament writers competed with each other until the monastic movement declared the celibate life to be superior to the ideas of Jovinian and his followers, who viewed the married life as equal to the ascetic one.[52] This means, of course, that when the fathers of the patristic period and late antiquity confront the value of marriage and childbearing in the Jewish scriptures, they insist on a radical difference between Jewish and Christian sexual ethics. As I contend, they place sexuality on par with Hebrew ritual practices, forcing some Christians to argue that many Jewish rituals were now sub-Christian with the coming of Christ.

Chapter 5 begins by acknowledging that a history of the past is also a history of the present, since the past is not inferior or unenlightened, nor is it superior.[53] The point of history is to diagnose the present.[54] With that in mind, this book concludes by turning to the United States of the twenty-first century and asks which ideology modern American Christians have codified as their dominant strategy of power. In particular, my interest is in Christian groups that want to (re)establish so-called Judeo-Christian values in this country.[55] I argue that without knowingly doing so, many of these Christian groups have codified the imperial discourse of Augustus, with its emphasis on marriage and procreation, instead of the early Christian ideology that won out under the monastics, which emphasized singleness as inferior. My starting point is *The Hyphen* by Jean-François Lyotard. Like all hyphens, Lyotard maintains that the hyphen in "Judeo-Christian" "disunites what it unites."[56] It isn't about continuity, but discontinuity. Indeed, "Judeo-Christian" is a myth. In practical terms, this means that as some people long for the return of so-called Judeo-Christian sexual ethics in this country, they might want to consider that the origins of our sexual ethics go back to Augustus's imperialism, bypassing what they think is "Judeo" and "Christian."

To make my case, I examine the recent Supreme Court decision in *Obergefell v. Hodges*, which, in my estimation, isn't about the ethics of gay marriage but about the meaning and purpose of heteronormative marriages in twenty-first century American society. I also investigate my own tradition, as I explore the ideologies of several Christian documents on marriage and the family written in the past few decades. Furthermore, I investigate writings from members of conservative think tanks, such as the Heritage Foundation, which argue that all societies favor the traditional family because of its emphasis on procreation. I conclude that modern ideologies of marriage—be they Christian or secular—are not "Judeo-Christian" but are narratives fueled by the "false consciousness" known as capitalism, which is particularly evident in the works of conservatives attempting to show the "continuity" between biblical values and American society. Finally, I suggest that we drop our use of "Judeo-Christian" and adopt the term "neo-imperial-capitalist" for our modern belief in the centrality of marriage and the production of children. As I point out, we need to admit, going against much of the conservative talk about marriage and the family, that our society isn't built on the Judeo-Christian ethics of the Bible but on the imperial decrees of Rome.

CHAPTER ONE

AUGUSTUS AND THE ROMAN EMPIRE

The Birth of an Ideology

All this garrulous attention which has us in a stew over sexuality, is it
not motivated by one basic concern: to ensure population, to reproduce
labor capacity, to perpetuate the form of social relations: in short,
to constitute a sexuality that is economically useful and
politically conservative?
—*Michel Foucault*

Politicians are fond of quoting others from the past in order to justify
their actions in the present. Ronald Reagan famously quoted the Puritan
John Winthrop, calling America a "city on a hill" in his 1984 acceptance
speech of the Republican Party nomination. Against the darkness of
Soviet communism, he declared: "Four years ago we raised a banner of
bold colors—no pale pastels. We proclaimed a dream of an America that
would be 'a shining city on a hill.'"[1] Though the original phrase refers to
the salt and light parable of Jesus's Sermon on the Mount (Matt 5:14),
Reagan used it to say to the world that the United States is no sissy.
Its ideology of light would outshine and ultimately crush the godless
ideology of the Soviet Union in a dualistic battle between capitalism

and Marxism, good and evil, theism and atheism, and, ultimately, light and dark.

Similar to Reagan, an *imperator* named Caesar Augustus (63 B.C.E.–14 C.E.) stood on the floor of the Roman Senate desperately trying to win support for his marriage reforms by quoting Metellus Macedonicus (210 B.C.E.–116/115 B.C.E.). Attempting to root his ideology in Rome's glorious past, Augustus read out a speech "written for the hour" in which he bellowed the following notes of misogyny: "If we could survive without a wife, citizens of Rome, all of us would do without that nuisance! But since nature has so decreed that we cannot manage comfortably with them, nor live without them, we must plan for our lasting preservation rather than our temporary pleasure."[2] Apparently, men today aren't as original as they might think, especially when they console one another with sayings such as, "Women . . . Can't live with 'em; can't live without 'em!" The Romans said it before us, as had many other great civilizations before them.[3] Sadly, it seems that our mental evolution hasn't kept up with our technological revolutions.

It's not uncommon to do what Augustus did—codify morality. Christians weren't the first to do it, nor did they perfect it. But what motivates someone like Augustus to say that if it weren't for the survival of the species, Roman men could and would live without women? Is he serious? Is he insane? Was he, as some scholars have suggested, possessed with an overt fear of the vagina?[4]

In this chapter, I focus on the ideology of Augustus with respect to his marriage legislation. Though his basic thinking is that Roman men and women should marry and do their duty for the state by producing children, there's a larger question here regarding motivation—especially regarding the *strategies of power* motivating Augustus's ideological discourse. As we've seen in our own day and age, when empires begin to experience changes, many people long for the old ways, which usually include a return to a fictitious morality believed to have existed in the not-too-distant past.[5] When the Values Voter Summit holds its annual convention, for example, conservative politicians do their best to rally the base by denouncing the depravity of the United States.[6] A clarion call will go out for the country to return to its "Judeo-Christian" roots, while a dire warning with apocalyptic ramifications will be issued if we continue to support gay rights and the legalization of abortion. I argue that something similar occurred in Augustus's Rome that led him to codify morality in an attempt to save the empire. What I wish to unmask, then, is how power operated in the Augustan discourse. What was its ultimate purpose? What did it really want to accomplish? Was it really about morality and making babies, or something else?

I also insert contemporary voices into dialogue with Augustus that address the same topics found in the Augustan legislation. I'm particularly interested in the philosophical discourses of Musonius Rufus, since Augustus's legislation can be read with him and vice versa. I not only explore how Musonius turns Augustus's moral prescriptions into a patriotic duty, but also how the "radical" ideas of this philosopher have led many modern interpreters down the wrong ideological path, proclaiming him an ally of modern feminism. As I demonstrate, Musonius was anything but a feminist since he's responsible for creating what Paul Veyne calls "the myth of the couple."[7] Like many other moral philosophers, Musonius codified a regimen that analyzes *aphrodisia* and emphasizes procreation. The liberation of the feminine was not his concern, but the place of women in society was foremost in his mind.

Since Augustus's legislation and Musonius's philosophy emphasize the importance of procreation, I examine the contrary advice of medical writers who around the same time period asked whether or not sex was even healthy. The main concern of medical writers such as Galen was to uncover the acceptable time for sex and the best methods for ensuring pregnancy. Finally, I explore legal, philosophical, and medical contributions reconstructed in the romantic novel *Leucippe and Clitophon*. The author of this erotic tale, Achilles Tatius, shows us how pleasure can serve the purposes of empire.

Throughout this chapter, I don't expect to find a unified voice. As I stated in the introduction, my concern is the struggles and contradictions of unmerged ideologies. But before I get ahead of myself, it's best to begin by turning to Augustus and his legislation, since they provide a starting point for everything else I explore in this book. In fact, as we'll see in the last chapter, Augustus and his legislation are still with us in spirit, as is the illusion of the crisis he created.

Augustus and the "Family Values Movement" of the Ancient World

Against the advice of many of his officials, Augustus decided to codify his ideology into what is now known as the *lex Iulia de maritandis ordinibus* (Julian law on the marriages of the social orders) of 18 B.C.E.; the *lex Iulia de adulteriis* (Julian law on adultery), also composed around 18 B.C.E.; and the *lex Papia Poppaea* (Papian-Poppaean law) of 9 C.E.[8] We might think of these laws as the "family values movement" of the ancient world.[9] The official reason for these laws was to stimulate the birthrate and secure the state's military manpower.[10] The legislation arose out of a need to "encourage nuptiality and reproductivity in order to supply Rome with soldiers and administrators, making Augustus' moral reform program a type of 'eugenics program.'"[11] Of course, we might wonder what is "moral" or "familial" about a eugenics program.

Moral or not, it was common in the ancient world for philosophers, such as Plato, to argue that the reason the state was in decline was because men and women weren't producing enough children.[12] In the *Republic*, for example, Plato declares, "But the number of the marriages (*gamois*) we will leave to the discretion of the rulers, that they may keep the number of citizens as nearly as may be the same, taking into account wars and diseases and all such consideration, and that, so far as possible, our city (*polis*) may not grow too great or too small" (5.460A). Plato's remedy is simple: Men and women should copulate in order to produce children for the state (5.460E). Women should engage in this patriotic duty starting at the age of twenty until they turn forty, while men should produce children for the state as soon as they're capable and until they turn fifty-five (5.460E). Women and children are necessary because they help to stabilize the state. They serve a needed purpose because men can't survive without them. This kind of thinking, however, has nothing to do with our modern notions of egalitarianism and partnership.

In typical patriarchal fashion, Plato asserts that sons are more important than daughters (5.461B). He also concludes that any children born with defects should be disposed of in secret so that the purity of the state is protected even at the cost of killing children who don't make the grade (5.460C). Protecting the purity of the state is such a priority for Plato that part of his strategy has to do with pairing the right men with the right women in order to produce the best possible offspring. As he relates, sounding as if he's conjuring up the terrifying utopian ideals from Margaret Atwood's *The Handmaid's Tale*, "The flock is to be as perfect as possible" (5.459E).[13]

There was nothing wrong, then, with creating class conflict between the elites of the state and second-rate citizens. Plato maintains that the best men must cohabit with the best women so that they may form a more perfect union (5.459D). Elite citizens would be fused together into a kind of master race, as certain groups are excised from the gene pool of the *polis*. It's from the wells of Plato that Augustus will draw his water, creating a similarly repressive society.

In his autobiography, the *Res Gestae*, Augustus declares that he's doing nothing but upholding ancestral law when he promotes his marriage legislation.[14] Prior to Augustus, two censors periodically assessed the moral conduct of all Roman citizens, especially during a census.[15] If a male Roman citizen was found guilty of an infraction against the laws of Rome, he would be removed from his voting tribe. If he was a senator or an equestrian, he would be demoted. What made Augustus's moral legislation different is that he figured out a way to infuse it with the mythology of Rome's past.[16] It played directly into the ideology of the return of the Golden Age.[17]

In his *Epodes*, Horace describes the time of the civil wars as dark days of tumult (16). In what can only be described as apocalyptic longing for a better future, he proclaims Jupiter's election of the Roman people, who are a "righteous people." Next he praises the return of the *tempus aureum*, or Golden Age, which is ushered in by Augustus. The poet Virgil follows Horace: "No more will wool be taught to put on varied hues, but of himself the ram in the meadows will change his fleece, now to sweetly blushing purple, now to a saffron yellow; and scarlet shall clothe the grazing lambs at will" (*Ecologues* 4.42–45). The apocalyptic imagery suggests that something new is about to happen—something wonderful that will change the future course of the empire.

Driving Augustus's reforms is the devastation of the civil wars, which had disastrous effects on the Roman family, as war so often does.[18] After the battle of Actium in 31 B.C.E., the belief spread throughout Rome

5

that the abandonment of morality had precipitated the civil wars.[19] As Veyne notes, this was all an illusion exploited by Augustus.[20] People had thought this kind of thing before, especially in the days of Julius Caesar. Cicero, for example, once argued that the censors should register the children of citizens, prevent celibacy, and control morals (*De legibus* 3.7). He went so far as to link the origin of the family to the ideals of unity and justice:

> In the whole area of what is morally right of which we are speaking, there is nothing so glorious or wide-ranging as the unity of human beings (*homines hominum*) with each other and the partnership and sharing in advantages and love of the human race, which springs from our first begetting, since children are loved by their parents and the whole household is joined together by marriage and offspring. Then it gradually spreads outside the house, first to blood-relatives, then to relatives by marriage, then to friends, neighbors, fellow citizens, and the allies of the state, and eventually embraces the whole human race. This attitude of mind, which gives each his own and which generously and fairly protects that partnership of human unity, is called justice (*iustitia*). To it are linked dutifulness, goodness, liberality, kindness, courtesy, and similar virtues. (*De finibus* 5.65)

The Romans longed for *harmonia*, or unity. To drive this point home, Sallust speaks of Rome's mythical past as a time when the country had grown great and people practiced justice (*Bellum catilinae* 10). Next he mourns the present when fortune (*fortuna*) grew cruel and the Romans began to lust after money and power. Further demands for the good old days can be seen as early as 46 B.C.E., when Cicero calls upon Julius Caesar to remedy the ills of the day: "It is for you alone, Gaius Caesar, to reanimate all that you see lying shattered, as was inevitable by war itself" (*Pro Marcello* 8.23). For Cicero, Caesar needed to fix the courts and put an end to the licentiousness of the Roman people; Caesar needed to step up and be a hero. It would be "morning in Rome" once again.

The mythology Augustus concocted insists that the way back to the Golden Age is through legislation. In Horace's *Carmen Saeculare*, for example, the *tempus aureum* is preceded by the "yoking together of men and women and on the marriage law (*lege marita*) for raising a new crop of children" (4.5.21–24).[21] The poem, written around 17 B.C.E., envisions a situation in which Rome's handsome youth triumphantly sing this hymn as the people of Rome wish for a future *saeculum* in which there will again be many Roman children. This celebration of peace is directly connected to Augustus's legislation. We might even imagine that the sticker on chariots accompanying the legislation would have read, "Want peace? Make babies!"

Horace is saying that with Augustus's moral code, Rome can return to its glorious past. Later on in the *Carmen Saeculare,* Horace will burst forth with the mellifluous utterance, "Now Good Faith, Peace, and Honor, along with old-fashioned Modesty (*pudor*) and Virtue (*virtus*), who has been so long neglected, venture to return, and blessed Plenty with her full horn is seen by all." Old-fashioned *pudor* and *virtus* have disappeared because the Romans have fallen into moral degradation. With Augustus, the moral decline could be remedied and better times could be hoped for. This is why Horace speaks not only of the redemption of nature (4.5.29–32), but also of the "regeneration of humanity." In short, a true champion of morals, a true savior, is what the Roman people needed.

Three years after he composed the *Carmen Saeculare,* Horace broadened his utopian hopes for Augustus's moral reforms:

> For then the ox ambles over the pastures in safety; Ceres and kindly Prosperity give increase to the crops, sailors wing their way across a sea clear of lawlessness, fidelity takes care not to incur blame, the home is pure, unstained by any lewdness, custom and law have gained control over the plague of vice, mothers are praised for having children, punishment follows hard on the heels of guilt. (*Odes and Epodes* 235)[22]

He honors his newfound savior in his *Epistles.* Here he commends Augustus for "carrying the weight of so many great changes" and for "guarding our Italian state with arms, gracing her with morals, and reforming her with laws" (2.1.1–4). The remark is of particular interest because it combines Augustus's moral reforms with the act of war itself.

Whatever we make of Horace's flattery, he was full of contradictions, as are most human beings. The great irony of Horace is that while he lauded the spirit of Augustus's reforms, he himself remained unmarried and engaged in questionable sexual behavior.[23] Still, Horace's imagination construed a new world order ruled by Augustus. As Ronald Syme puts it, "The New State of Augustus glorified the strong and stubborn peasant of Italy, laboriously winning from the cultivation of cereals a meagre subsistence for himself and for a numerous virile offspring."[24] Finally, the myth was set.

The basic premise of the *lex Iulia et Papia Poppaea*, as the laws came to be known, was simply that marriage was a duty incumbent on all Roman men between twenty-five and sixty years of age and on all Roman women between twenty and fifty. This should sound familiar, since Augustus's legislation was a reification of Plato's ideology. Perhaps the *chose de nouveau* in Augustus's laws is that he ordered widows and divorced people between ages twenty and sixty to remarry, which he would later regret. The only exemptions seem to have been for freeborn people who had produced at least three children, and freed people who had produced four. Failure to procreate was a punishable offense that affected a person's right to inherit from anyone except cognates to the seventh degree. *Caelibes* or bachelors could inherit nothing, because singleness created the empire's crisis.[25] People who were married but childless could inherit only one-half.[26] Additionally, something that had previously been a private matter in Rome now became a matter of the state.[27] It must have seemed like everyone was involved in everyone else's business. As Veyne observes, "The new moral code said: 'here are the duties of the married man' . . . one must marry out of civic duty."[28]

Augustus's strategy codified the link between marriage, rank, and status. Because of his legislation, the state's power could now be used to penalize marriage between citizens and noncitizens, as well as marriages between senators and freed people and marriages between slaves and freed people. The state now regulated everything, designating illicit unions as *matrimonia iniusta*, declaring children from such marriages illegitimate, which means they didn't count toward earning inheritance rights. In fact, such children couldn't inherit at all. They couldn't even be issued an official birth certificate or be entered into a town's list of inhabitants (*album*).[29] But before we judge Augustus as an out-of-control, maniacal ruler who made impossible demands of his subjects, we should note that he did handsomely reward those who agreed to go along with the socialization of his procreative ideology.

The *Institutes* of Gaius tell us, for example, that women were required to have guardians (*tutores*). The law, officially called the *tutela mulierum*, said that parents were permitted to give guardians (*tutores*) to their children. Specifically, it required guardians to be given to male children younger than the age of puberty and to female children both younger than and older than the age of puberty. Why? Because "the ancients wanted women, even if they are of full age, to be in guardianship (*tutela*) on account of their lightmindedness (*animi levitas*)" (1.144). For married women, this meant they were subject to a male guardian (*tutor*), under *tutela mulierum perpetua*, unlike men, who had a *tutor* only until they became adults. As Miriam J. Groen-Vallinga informs us, "The institution remained in place, though it gradually became eroded under the emperors Claudius, Hadrian and Marcus Aurelius and finally disappeared in the 3rd century AD, its practical implications having become negligible long since."[30] The continued existence of *tutela* as an inane institution, however, suggests that it had become a major part of the social discourse. Its purpose was to keep women in their place.

As time went on, many Romans found creative ways to subvert Augustus's policies. One way for a woman to rid herself of the *tutela* was to have at least three children (*ius liberorum* or "right of children"):

> And so if anyone has given a tutor to his son and daughter in his will and they have both arrived at puberty, the son of course stops having a tutor, but the daughter remains nevertheless in *tutela*: only according to the Julian and Papian-Poppaen law are women freed from *tutela* by means of the *ius liberorum*. We are speaking, however, of women other than the Vestal Virgins, whom indeed the ancients wished to be free out of honor for their priesthood: thus it was decreed even by a law of the Twelve Tables. (*Institutes* 1.145)

But while freeborn women are relieved from *tutela* by the right of three children (*ius trium liberorum*), freedwomen must have four children, which ultimately led to class stratification.[31]

What Augustus accomplished by setting up the *ius liberorum* was the creation of a Pavlovian system of rewards and punishments that could accompany his codification of morality.[32] Not only were women freed from *tutela* by having three or four children, but certain privileges were granted to fathers, especially when running for public office. Not unlike the case in modern, twenty-first century politics, richer and more influential Romans could obtain a dispensation without having three children, which meant that lower-class Romans couldn't obtain one. In other words, the system was rigged from the start.[33] As Beryl Rawson declares, "Poverty must also have been a disincentive sometimes [to having children], but there is little explicit evidence that in wealthier circles the number of children was limited to prevent fragmentation of estates."[34] The *ius liberorum* demonstrates, then, that Augustus's codification of morality in ancient Rome made the entire process of coitus, through pregnancy and childbirth, a public event.[35] Furthermore, these rewards and punishments enabled the state to control women. As Michel Foucault reminds us, sex, power, and control are always related, even if these relationships are murky and complex.[36]

Going back to Cicero, Roman women were stereotyped in Roman literature and Roman legal codes.[37] The Augustan laws were no different. As Susan Dixon points out, "Clichés were applied particularly to women perceived as intruding illegitimately in masculine domains or when the author/speaker wished to attack a man for failing to prevent such intrusion by his female connections, whether wives or sisters."[38] As a consequence, there was an "overt fear of the vagina" in the ancient world which led to a belief that women were more sexually charged than men.[39] This irrational fear produced a "difference in hierarchy" between Roman women and men. "Although some women in the Roman world had more power than some men, there is no question that, structurally, Roman society evolved in such a way as to enable elite men to establish and maintain power over everyone else."[40] A rather consistent belief pervaded Roman society: A woman was always *less than perfect* when compared with a man; her money and prestige were of no consequence.

In Augustus's own family, womanly virtues were carefully codified in the mythology of his wife Livia. She was praised for weaving cloth (*lanificium*), an activity symbolically understood to mean that Livia was a "good wife." Indeed, Augustus is said to have worn clothes made by his sister, wife, daughter, and granddaughters.[41] Most historians believe the story is more fiction than fact. Like many politicians today, Augustus had mastered the art of propaganda.

Cracks in Augustus's ideology began to show when it came to the application of his laws to widows. We've already seen that the ideal woman in Roman society was chaste, unless she was married—or so the literature would have us believe.[42] It was also assumed that widows upheld this ideal. As Dixon explains: "It is notable that many of the mothers cited for their great qualities were widowed while their children were young. Given the age differential between Roman marriage partners, women who survived the dangers of reproduction were likely to outlive their husbands."[43] Inscriptions on epitaphs often praise a woman who had had only one husband throughout her life—or married only once (*univira*). Some inscriptions use the phrase *solo contenta marito vel sim* (content with her husband alone; *CIL* 3.1537 = *CE* 597), while others employ the phrase *uno contenta marito* (content with her one husband) to make a similar point (*CIL* 3.2667 = *CE* 643). The language of these epitaphs is also found in the poems of Catullus, who borrows the phrases to point out the failure of his mistress, Lesbia, to remain chaste:

> Even so kind, or but little less, was she, my bright one, who came into my arms; and often around her flitting hither and thither Cupid shone fair in vest of saffron hue. And though she is not content with Catullus alone, I will bear the faults, for few they are, of my modest mistress, lest we become tiresome as jealous fools. Juno, too, greatest of the heavenly ones, has often beaten down her anger for her husband's fault, as she learns the many loves of all amorous Jove. Yet it is not reasonable that men should be compared with gods. (68.131–135)

The Roman mythical ideal of the *univira* and lifelong monogamy was so popular that the church father Tertullian later endorsed it.[44] Despite all kinds of praise for the *univira* by the Roman people, Augustus decided to break with this ancient tradition. The results were catastrophic.

In his attempt to codify morality by rooting it in Rome's past, Augustus, like any politician, flip-flopped on the importance of tradition. According to his reforms, a widow had to remarry within two (or three) years of her husband's death.[45] If she failed to remarry, she wouldn't be able to inherit from people who weren't related to her in the sixth degree.[46] Because Augustus didn't respect the ancient tradition of the *univira*, he was forced to introduce other provisions that somewhat mitigated the rigorous demands of his earlier legislation.[47] Ulpian's *Rules*, for example, suggest, "The *lex Iulia* granted exemption from its penalties to women for a year after the death of their husbands, and for six months after a divorce had taken place; the *lex Papia* granted them two more years from the death of their husbands, and a year and six months after a divorce" (14.1). Of course, this wasn't the only issue facing Augustus and his legislation.

The Golden Age of Augustus may not have been so golden, just as President John F. Kennedy's Camelot wasn't exactly chivalrous. Whenever a government or a ruling party tries to dictate what goes on in a bedroom, things get complicated. Depending on which literature we read, Augustus was either ushering in a new Golden Age, or he was making a huge mistake. Ovid briefly mentions the Augustan laws in his *Fasti: florent sub Caesare leges* ("prosper under Caesar's laws"; 2.139). This remark should be read in light of Ovid's other works, especially his *Ars amatoria*, which demonstrate that he was out of step with the official Augustan moral reform program and that he had no reservations saying so in his works. In other words, there was an internal critique of Augustus that extended from the historians to the poets, who wished to unmask the hypocrisy and political violence of Augustus.[48]

One of the main things we learn from Ovid is that some Romans believed love and sex should remain a private mater.[49] Additionally, Ovid is one of several writers who alert us to the many double standards prevalent in Augustan Rome. His calendar, for example, demonstrates how the Augustan laws punished only women caught in adultery and not men.[50] And Ovid points out that, like modern politicians who condemn gay marriage but find themselves caught in bathroom scandals, Augustus had no problem attending erotic theater shows, which flouted the very adultery he was so adamantly against.[51]

Another example is Cassius Dio. He too is well aware of Augustus's moral hypocrisy. In his extant writings, he presents a straightforward narrative about how Augustus imposed penalties on unmarried women and men who failed to produce children for the state (54.16). He even mentions how the Senate condemned the loose morals of women and young men in Rome: "This conduct was cited as a reason for their unwillingness to accept the marriage bond." In fact, he tells us that the Senate had no problem catching Augustus in a lie: "When the senators urged Augustus to correct this abuse too, and hinted mockingly at his own relations with a large number of women, he began by replying that the essential prohibitions had already been laid down, and that it was impossible to regulate people's conduct further by bringing in more legislation of this kind." Forced to answer for his behavior, Augustus reportedly told the Senate, "You yourselves should guide and command your wives as you see fit; that is what I do with mine!" Like Louis XIV, Augustus might as well have said, "L'État, c'est moi!"

Eventually, the Senate's interrogation turned personal as they questioned Augustus about his wife. "When they heard this, they pressed Augustus still more eagerly, since they desired to learn what guidance he professed to give to Livia" (54.16). After stalling for an answer, Dio records that Augustus murmured something about women's clothing, ornaments, and modesty in general. The entire spectacle ended with Augustus declaring, "The feuds which have divided us have brought terrible consequences; let us forget these and turn our minds to the future, so that nothing of this kind may occur again!" (54.16). It seems, then, that Augustus's "unofficial" policy was to sweep certain things under the rug—especially those things he didn't want to admit as factual.

As his work comes to a close, Dio explains that many Romans discovered a way of protesting against Augustus's reforms by finding loopholes in the legislation (54), just as billionaires today discover loopholes in the tax code. Some men, for example, were getting engaged to infant girls yet never going through with the marriage ceremony. These men figured out a way to enjoy the privileges of a married life (i.e., the rewards Dio mentions at the beginning of section 16) without ever having to get married. There's even some indication that women got around the requirements of the legislation by registering themselves as prostitutes.[52] As Jane Gardner relates: "From this it appears that some people had actually deliberately contrived to incur *infamia*, either from a criminal conviction or in some other way, so as to forfeit the status of their rank and be able to pursue their passion. (One is reminded of the women who registered as prostitutes in an attempt to evade the adultery law)."[53] In other words, the deed doesn't count as adultery if it's committed with a state-registered prostitute. Of course, Augustus was none too thrilled by these creative attempts to subvert his laws, probably because such subversion pointed out the illusory nature of the laws.

The laws were illusory because Augustus's moral code was really all about eugenics. As J. P. V. D. Balsdon perceptively notes, "Romans were obsessed from the second century B.C. onwards with the problem of a falling birth-rate, a problem all the more serious on account of the high rate of infant mortality and, indeed, of deaths in childbirth."⁵⁴ The situation was so dire that some studies suggest that Roman women who lived to the age of fifty would have needed to produce 5.1 children for the state in order to sustain the Roman population.⁵⁵ In other words, like Plato's ideal *polis*, Roman women were necessary for the survival of the state. This is why Augustus was so quick to say to the Senate, "If we could . . . we would live without them . . . but we can't."

In Livy's *History,* there's an interesting quotation which suggests that all this talk about legislating morality was subterfuge meant to persuade men and women to produce sons so they would grow up to become good citizen soldiers:

> I hope everyone will pay keen attention to the moral life of earlier times, to the personalities and principles of the men responsible at home and in the field for the foundation and growth of the empire, and will appreciate the subsequent decline in discipline and in moral standards, the collapse and disintegration of morality down to the present day. For we have now reached a point where our degeneracy is intolerable—and so are the measures by which it can be reformed. (Para. 9)

It's left to Propertius to unmask and parse the true nature of Augustus's strategy of power. He'll ask the question that others aren't asking: "Is it for me to supply sons for our country's triumphs?" He'll respond with the declaration, "There'll be no soldiers from my line!" (*Elegies* 2.7). Augustus's reforms have now been shown for what they really are. They're not about "family values," nor are they about a return to the glorious past. Instead, they're about imperial expansion at the cost of Roman sons. The basic purpose, then, is economic and political: It's to ensure population growth for the expansion of the empire.

Musonius Rufus: Internalizing Augustus's Marriage Reforms

But not everyone was ready to show that the emperor had no clothes. In fact, many moral philosophers agreed with Augustus that *marriage is good for the state.* What's important is sexual regulation, which should ultimately lead to *harmonia,* or unity. As Foucault explains, "The diverse schools of philosophy of the Hellenistic period proposed different solutions to the difficulties of traditional sexual ethics."[56] In particular, both Greek and Roman moral philosophers were concerned with moderation and self-control (*sōphrosynē*). Indeed, if one could learn self-control, one could gain freedom from enslavement to pleasures and win independence from the uncertainties of fate. To achieve self-mastery of the passions, moral philosophers prescribed a remedy of contemplating the soul of divine truth, which was also an act of union with the divine.

When scholars address topics in Greco-Roman moral philosophy, they more often than not focus on the Stoics of the early imperial period, giving pride of place to the first-century Stoic Musonius Rufus. This is a procedure found mostly among scholars of the New Testament and early Christianity. As Kyle Harper points out, "Christianity did not so much unconsciously absorb Stoicism as provide radically new answers to some of its most difficult questions."[57] Since I'm a scholar and interpreter of the New Testament and early Christianity, I'll follow the procedure set by others in my field and explore the teachings of Musonius. But I hasten to add that Musonius is particularly important for my purposes because he directly refers to Augustus's laws—something far too many scholars overlook when analyzing his teachings.

Gaius Musonius Rufus (25–95 C.E.) flourished under Nero and the Flavians during an era when men of the upper class began to devote increased attention to the preventative maintenance of their bodies and the care of their souls. A native of Etruria, Musonius was a member of the equestrian order and lived in Rome (Tacitus, *Annales* 62.27.4.4). He dedicated his life to the teachings of Stoicism and gave his moral lectures in Greek throughout the empire. He was also the tutor of Epictetus, whom Marcus Aurelius admired. Nero and Vespasian exiled him for, among other things, teaching that it was right to disobey an immoral command from a superior. Foucault maintains that Musonius took up the classical theme of marriage as a twofold contribution to procreation and community life and transformed it in a radical way. He refers to Musonius's emphasis on companionate marriage and the privileging of spousal affection. He argues that Musonius's teachings on marriage are exceptional for the first century.[58] He's right that for Musonius human nature is communal. What Foucault fails to recognize, however, is that Musonius isn't really doing anything all that new. On the contrary, he's providing a philosophical framework for the internalization of Augustus's marriage reforms. In other words, he's helping further entrench a strategy of power already present in Roman society. His is a philosophy, then, in service of the fatherland.[59] We see this most prominently in his discourses.

In a lecture titled "Should Every Child That Is Born Be Raised?," Musonius declares that his philosophical musings on the subject of marriage are rooted in the ideology of Augustus's legislation.[60] In particular, he's concerned about the decline in Rome's population. What he has to say about this matter is so important it's worth quoting in full:

> Is it not true that the lawgivers, whose special function it was by careful search to discern what is good for the state and what is bad, what promotes and what is detrimental to the common good, all considered the increase of the homes of the citizens the most fortunate thing for the cities and the decrease of them the most shameful thing? And when citizens had few or no children did they not regard it as a loss, but when they had children, yes, plenty of them, did they not regard it as gain? So it was for this reason that they forbade women to suffer abortions and imposed a penalty upon those who disobeyed; for this reason they discouraged them from choosing childlessness and avoiding parenthood, and for this reason they gave to both husband and wife a reward for large families and set a penalty upon childlessness. (XV)

Indeed, Musonius upholds the Augustan ideal that children are essential to the survival of the empire. More importantly, he declares that the more children a man produces, the more powerful he'll be. The *telos* or goal of marriage is community (*koinōnia*). The community formed by the husband and wife should naturally lead to the procreation of children (*geneseōs paidōn*).[61] As he reasons, "The husband and wife . . . should come together for the purpose of making a life in common and procreating children, and furthermore of regarding all things in common between them" (XIIIA). This means marriages should include perfect companionship (*pantōs symbiōsin*) and mutual care between husband and wife (*kēdemonian*). Such reasoning asserts that the single life (*ho monērē bion*) is inferior to the married one. In fact, the man who chooses the single life is far less patriotic than the one who gets married and rears children, since children contribute to the welfare of the state: "Can it be that the man who chooses the single life is more patriotic, more a friend and partner of his fellow man, than the man who maintains a home and rears children and contributes to the growth of his city, which is exactly what the married man does?" (XIV).

Though we may find Musonius's love of country romantic and admirable, he holds some rather puzzling ideas about sex and marriage, especially for us moderns. For one thing, he believes, as some people do today, that sex is justified only if it occurs within the context of marriage.[62] But unlike some people in the modern world, he declares that even when a husband and wife have sex, it's unjust and unlawful if they do it for pleasure: "Men who are not wantons or immoral are bound to consider sexual intercourse justified only when it occurs in marriage and is indulged in for the purpose of begetting children, since this is lawful, but unjust and unlawful when it is mere pleasure-seeking, even in marriage" (XII). For Musonius, lawful sex is about self-restraint, and certainly no man with any kind of character would think of sleeping with a courtesan, a free woman, or his maidservant apart from marriage.

Since Musonius says marriage is about procreation (*geneseōs paidōn*) and companionship (*koinōnia*), many scholars conclude that he must have been a feminist and believed in the equality of the sexes.[63] In two separate discourses, Musonius makes a number of claims that sound as if he's declaring men and women equals. In a discourse titled *That Women Too Should Study Philosophy*, for example, he contends that women have the same *logos* as men, especially when it comes to general interactions and judging the ethics of individual actions (III). Observing that men and women have the same sense organs and the same number of body parts, he concludes that they both possess an innate desire for virtue.

On the surface, it sounds like he's saying that men and women are equal, but probing a bit further into his thought, we discover something else. Instead of focusing his attention on equality, Musonius focuses it on the practical implications of Stoic ethics in the imperial period. In other words, most of his attention centers on why it's important for women to learn philosophy. As one might guess, it has something to do with preserving the empire.

Musonius argues that women should study philosophy in order to become better servants. He surmises, "So it is that such a woman is likely to be energetic, strong, to endure pain, prepared to nourish her children at her own breast, and to serve her husband with her own hands, and willing to do things which some would consider no better than slaves' work" (III). By making her docile, philosophy helps a woman attend to her husband's needs. Studying makes a wife a better housekeeper, a better accountant, and a better slave owner. It creates better *harmonia*. Nothing Musonius says here is surprising since the ancient world consistently viewed women as flawed creatures capable of all sorts of immoral acts.[64] All Musonius is saying, then, is that the antidote to a woman's uncontrollable desire is the study of philosophy. "But above all a woman must be chaste and self-controlled; she must, I mean, be pure in respect of unlawful love, exercise restraint in other pleasures, not be contentious, not lavish in expense, nor extravagant in dress" (III).

Musonius draws for us a picture of his idealized female companion. She's free of greed and will defend her husband and children no matter the cost to herself. Indeed, the woman who studies philosophy is a woman who knows her place in the home and in society. Like Augustus's ideal woman, Musonius's ideal woman stays at home and spins wool (*lanificium*), because that's what good Roman wives do.

In a second discourse, *Should Daughters Receive the Same Education as Sons?*, Musonius adopts a famous argument found in Plato's *Republic* (455d). After observing the training of horses and dogs, Musonius notes that whether the animals are male or female is irrelevant to the kind of training they receive (IV). People treat female horses and female dogs the same way they treat male horses and male dogs. Through a simple act of deduction, he concludes that a man's and woman's virtues (e.g., sagacious intelligence, fairness, and courage) are the same. The most important thing is for men and women to learn self-control. When asked whether or not a man should learn spinning, however, Musonius responds, "No, that I should not demand [of him]" (IV). There are things that only women do and things that only men do.

Even though their virtues may be the same, men and women aren't equal. Musonius declares that men's constitutions are stronger and women's are weaker. Men can easily engage in heavier tasks because they're physically more muscular, while women are suited for lighter jobs since they're timid and weak by nature. A woman's weakness is also evident by her lasciviousness. In *On Sexual Indulgence,* for example, Musonius ponders whether it would be appropriate for a woman to have sex with one of her slaves. For him this is something a man would never do, but for a weak woman, it's a real possibility. "And yet surely one will not expect men to be less moral than women, nor less capable of disciplining their desires (*epithumias*), thereby revealing the stronger in judgment inferior to the weaker, the rulers to the ruled" (XII). One wonders whether Musonius wouldn't have agreed with Augustus: "Women . . . if we could . . . we'd live without them."

Unquestionably, Musonius isn't interested in feminism. He might believe in companionate marriage, but nothing in his extant writings suggests that he believes in the equality of the sexes. For him, ancient gender binaries must be maintained because women are naturally weak. Culture and nature have dictated this fact for centuries.

What many scholars fail to notice is that Stoics like Musonius aren't discussing gender equality but utility. The most utilitarian thing Musonius writes is that women should study philosophy in order to become better housekeepers. He's not suggesting that a woman learn philosophy like a man because the two are equal. He's not even suggesting that women are capable of doing what men do. Instead, he maintains that a wife should learn philosophy because that's how she'll better learn to serve her husband. As David Engel observes: "It is one thing to say that a man should know something of cooking and cleaning and that a woman should know something of politics and warfare. It is quite another to say that women should participate in politics. And it is quite clear . . . that the portion of men's activities that women should know is not politics but field work."[65]

It's not difficult to uncover what Musonius thinks of marriage. Like Augustus's legislation, marriage is one part of a larger system of morality, connected to the immediate needs of the household and the larger needs of the state. Indeed, he was able to fine-tune preexisting concerns about sexuality and morality into the notion of "companionate marriage," because the necessary pieces for his philosophical musings had already been articulated by others in the classical and Hellenistic periods. As Paul Veyne insists, "The household is the household, and husband and wife each have their respective duties to perform."[66] Their ultimate purpose is to keep the empire going.

According to one of Musonius's colleagues, Antipater of Tarsus, one must marry "in order to provide one's country with new citizens because the divine plan of the universe requires propagation of the human race."[67] The best way to ensure the survival of the empire is to argue that, unlike the old days, marriage is now about unity and friendship. As Veyne puts it, "Because marriage was friendship, husband and wife could make love only in order to have children, and even then with care not to indulge in too many caresses."[68] As we'll see in later chapters, it will take Christianity to blur the outlines of this system.

Galen: Medicine and the Social Order

Medicine, a philosophical discipline in the ancient world, agreed and disagreed. Under the Roman Empire, the one-sex model prevailed.[69] Soranus (first/second century C.E.), for example, affirmed that the uterus was substantially the same as other organs and denied the existence of conditions specific to women other than those directly related to reproduction: "Thus they say that females have no conditions peculiarly their own, since the physiology, etiology, and therapy is a general one" (*Gynecology* 3.3). The only real difference in the reproductive organs was their internal or external positioning.[70]

Galen (130–210 C.E.) asks his readers to imagine the male parts turned inside out and placed inside the body, and the converse for the female parts. The scrotum takes the place of the uterus, while the penis replaces the vagina:

> Consider first whichever ones you please, turn outward the woman's, turn inward, so to speak, and fold double the man's, and you will find them the same in both in every respect. Then think first, please, of the man's turned in and extending inward between the rectum and the bladder. If this should happen, the scrotum would necessarily take the place of the uteri, with the testes lying outside, next to it on either side; the penis of the male would become the neck of the cavity that had been formed; and the skin at the end of the penis, now called the prepuce, would become the female pudendum [the vagina] itself. Think too, please, of the converse, the uterus turned outward and projecting. Would not the testes [the ovaries] then necessarily be inside it? Would it not contain them like a scrotum?

Would not the neck [the cervix], hitherto concealed inside the perineum but now pendent, be made into the male member? And would not the female pudendum, being a skinlike growth upon this neck, be changed into the part called the prepuce? It is also clear that in consequence the position of the arteries, veins, and spermatic vessels [the ductus deferens and Fallopian tubes] would be changed too. (*On the Usefulness of the Parts* 14.6)

The one-sex model, designed to explain gender and sexuality, is, like all things, about politics and social order.[71] To be "one flesh" is a reinforcement of patriarchy, since it's a return to the norm. And, of course, that norm is male, considered the "standard," or, more precisely, the perfect human being.

No one doubts that Galen viewed a woman as an imperfect man. But from such an assertion he concludes that a woman's imperfection is perfect for human reproduction, since it provides a safe place for gestation. As Rebecca Flemming reminds us, "Galen has good reason for taking this approach, for without female imperfection reproduction would not be possible."[72] Though this kind of reasoning surprises modern sensibilities, it's important to remember that well into the eighteenth century Galen's anatomical model remained the standard paradigm for Western medicine.[73] It wasn't only consulted for diagnosis and treatment; it also controlled cultural assumptions about gender.[74]

Galen was born into an upper-class family in the thriving city of Pergamum in Asia Minor. Nicon, his father, worked as an architect and ensured that his son received the best possible liberal arts education. According to Galen, his father was the example par excellence of the life well-lived, both morally and intellectually: "As for myself, I cannot tell with what qualities I was endowed by Nature . . . I did have the great good fortune to have a father who was extremely slow to anger, as well as extremely just, decent, and generous" (*The Affections and Errors of the Soul* 5.40). By contrast, his mother, at least according to Galen, was crass, with a very bad temper: "My mother, on the other hand, was so bad-tempered that she would sometimes bite her maids; she was perpetually shouting and fighting with my father, treating him worse than Xanthippē did Socrates" (5.40–41). One might wonder whether his mother's behavior is why Galen never married.

Despite his parents' violent marriage, Galen treated female patients and listened to advice from midwives.[75] But that's rare. As R. J. Hankinson points out, Galen's world was an "exclusively masculine one" in which female company was considered more of a nuisance than something to be praised.[76] When the wife of Boethus fainted during a bath, for example, Galen excoriated her maidservants for standing around and doing nothing (*On Prognosis* 14.643–644).[77] The only exception seems to be his attitude toward the female Platonist Arria, whom, at the very end of his life, he describes as "dearest of all to me, and most highly praised by all on account of her rigorous philosophizing and her great appreciation for Plato's writings" (*On Theriac to Piso* 14.218).[78] But this kind of praise is exceptional for Galen.

Like most Roman men, Galen maintained that women were markedly inferior to men. They may be rational animals capable of acquiring knowledge, but since they're adapted for childbearing, they're in no way equal to men (*UP* 4.145–158).[79] To make his case, he begins with a concept Aristotle knew but didn't fully develop: "The female is less perfect than the male" (*UP* 14.6). In Galen's mind, a woman's defective state is based on two things: (1) a woman is colder than a man, and colder animals are inferior to warmer ones, and (2) though a woman has all the same parts as a man, hers are inside her body and his are outside. Obviously, the outside is better. The reason why a woman's "generative parts" didn't emerge externally is due to the fact that she lacks sufficient heat, "For the parts were formed within her when she was still a fetus, but could not because of the defect in the heat emerge and project on the outside" (*UP* 14.6). Yet like Augustus, Galen recognizes that women are necessary because without them men couldn't reproduce: "Indeed, you ought not to think that our Creator would purposely make half the whole race imperfect and, as it were, mutilated, unless there was to be some great advantage in such a mutilation" (*UP* 14.6). Moreover, he indicates a marked ascetic dislike for sexual excess and same-sex relations: "So it is not at all surprising that those who are less moderate sexually turn out to be weaker, since the whole body loses the purest part of both substances; and there is besides an accession of pleasure, which by itself is enough to dissolve the vital tone, so that before now some persons have died from excess of pleasure" (*On Semen* 1.16.31–32). In another work, Galen derides men who have slept with other men as "woolworkers," an epithet, as we've seen, reserved for a loyal Roman wife (*On the Therapeutic Method*

10.10–11). It should come as no surprise, then, that he has a negative attitude toward such practices as fellatio and cunnilingus (*On the Powers [and
Mixtures] of Simple Drugs* 11.248–250). But despite disliking these things, he
understands quite well that sex and pleasure go hand in hand.

In the Galenic system, "Nature" is responsible for the pleasures of sexual intercourse. The reason why Nature made the sex act so extremely
gratifying is to ensure the continuation of the species (*UP* 4.144, 181–182).
In fact, Galen marvels at the immense skill of the Creator, who constructed the functional architecture of the penis (*UP* 4.211–219). Still, he
contends that a mind that is overly preoccupied with sex is bestial and in-
compatible with the highest human ideals (*The Best Doctor Is Also a
Philosopher* 1.59). In his treatise *On Moral Character*, for example, he surmises
that most people satisfy their sexual appetites in private as a sign of their
shame. As he relates, "The rational soul behaves like this when the appetitive soul attempts to win it over to desiring sexual intercourse, since it
sees this is harmful both to the body and to the soul" (2.245–246). This
means that pleasure isn't the goal of the "appetitive soul." Instead, the goal
is "the [preservation of the] life of the body, and the pleasures of food
and sexual intercourse are like the bit that is placed in the trap in order to
snare the animal" (2.249).[80] Finally, in *On Affected Parts*, he contends that,
even though the retention of semen and menstrual fluid, even in minute
amounts, can have serious pathological effects, one should not have sex
just for fun (8.417–421). It comes as no surprise, then, that Galen praises
the example of Diogenes the Cynic for relying on masturbation rather
than loose women for such purposes, "as all moderate men should."[81]
What Galen is concerned with here is hysteria. For him and other ancient
medical practitioners, retention of fluids (cf. Paul 3.71), primarily semen
(both female and male) and menstrual flow, leads to madness.
Interestingly, the principal cause of hysteria is lack of sexual intercourse.
This means that widows are especially prone to madness, "when they
previously had healthy menstruation, got pregnant, and had sex with
their husbands but now are deprived of these things."[82] As verification,
Galen cites a case in which a widow, suffering from hysteria, is treated
with warming remedies, presumably in the form of wool tampons.
According to her, she feels "pleasure similar to that in intercourse," has
an orgasm (*synolkai, taseis*), secretes a great deal of thick, retained female

semen, and is cured (*Loc. Aff.* 6.5 = 8.420 K). As Holt Parker notes, Galen's cure for hysteria is "intercourse followed by pregnancy," a leitmotif running through many of the medical texts (e.g., Hp. *Mum.* 1–7, 199, 121, 127, 137, *Nat. Mul.* 2, 3; Aristotle, *HA* 582b23–25; Galen 13.319–320; Aet. 16.87).[83]

Since Galen has had such an influence on Western medicine, it's worth probing his thought a bit more deeply. To be female means to have weaker seed, or as Thomas Laqueur terms it, "Seed incapable of engendering, not as an empirical but as a logical matter."[84] For Galen, female seed is smaller and less powerful because a woman's testes are less than perfect—Nature made them that way (*UP* 14.6). The seed, or *semen*, generated by these imperfect testes is "scantier, colder, and wetter," because women produce less heat than men.

In the Galenic lexicon, there's no word for ovaries. A woman's ovaries are equivalent to a man's testes (*orcheis*). As evidence, Galen cites the dissections of the third-century B.C.E. Alexandrian anatomist Herophilus, who contends that women have testes with accompanying seminal ducts like a man's.[85] With one testicle on each side of her uterus, the woman is the same as a man except for the fact that the male's testes are in the scrotum and the female's are not: "For even if the female most certainly produces semen, and generative semen at that, yet it is by no means more abundant or more generative than the male semen" (*On Semen* 2.2.2). Galen is constructing a medical hierarchy based on heat and imperfection, which is the goal of the one-sex model.

In order to stabilize his world order, Galen relies on an elaborate simile between the eyes of the mole and the genitals of women that harkens back to an idea already popularized by Aristotle (*HA* 1.9.491b26 and 4.8.533a1–13). For Galen, the eyes of the mole have the same structures as the eyes of other animals except that they don't allow the mole to see, since moles are, by nature, blind. Since their eyes don't open, nor project, they're *imperfect*. Like the mole's eyes, female genitalia do not open but remain an imperfect version of what they would be if thrust outward. The mole's eyes "remain like the eyes of other animals when these are still in the uterus." Thus the womb, vagina, ovaries, and external pudenda remain entrapped inside the womb. Stuck in stasis, the vagina remains an unborn penis, while the womb is a stunted scrotum (*UP* 14.6).

This curious state of affairs becomes what Laqueur terms "the pur-ported telos of perfection."[86] As Galen maintains, "Now just as mankind is the most perfect of all animals, so within mankind the man is more perfect than the woman, and the reason for his perfection is his excess of heat, for heat is Nature's primary instrument" (*UP* 14.6). Returning to the simile of the mole's eyes and female genitalia, he further observes that though the mole is a more perfect animal than animals without eyes, and women are more perfect than other creatures, they're both substandard. In a woman's case, her lack of bulging sexual organs marks an absence of heat and consequently perfection. It becomes possible, then, for Galen to interpret the "interiority" of the female reproductive system as "the material correlative of a higher truth without its mattering a great deal whether any particular spatial transformation could be performed."[87]

Strange as all of this may sound to us, Galen took these truths to be self-evident. What we take as basic facts of sexual difference—males have a pe-nis and females a vagina; males have testicles and females ovaries—Galen would dispute. For him, the empirical data suggest otherwise. Observation led him to conclude that men and women both produce seed, that they both have the same sexual organs, and that they are essentially one sex, though one is, of course, superior to the other.

Galen sees the superiority of the male over the female most clearly in the differences between their semen. In the one-sex model, each parent con-tributes fluid to the production of a child. But not all seed is equal. Going back to the Hippocratic texts, the more potent seed by definition is always the male seed. As a student of these writings, Galen went even further, ar-guing that the female parent's seed is less powerful, less "informing," than the male parent's; "therefore the female semen should always be ruled and indeed defeated, and the male should prevail over it, so as to exercise by it-self control of both kind and similarity" (*On Semen* 2.2.3). In contrast, the Hippocratic texts resolutely resist correlating the gender of the seed, its strength or weakness, with the sex of the person who produced it. Instead, their version of things maintains that the more potent seed is by definition the "more male," whether produced in a male or female body.

Semen, which is "power and matter" for Galen, is what excites a woman to sexual desire. As he posits, "The excitement of the female to sexual desire (*aphrodisia*) is most especially in the power of the female semen" (*On Semen* 2.1.32). A female's semen is necessary because it isn't possible for the male semen to coat all of the necessary parts of the uterus (2.2.18). The female's semen, then, provides a necessary service to the coming fetus, and it also functions as a "kind of congenial nutriment for the male semen, being moister and colder, whereas that of the male is thicker and hotter" (2.2.19). So, echoing Augustus and Musonius, women are necessary for the survival of the human race as long as they stay in their preordained place.

Given that Galen lives within the Roman Empire, we expect to find some sort of justification in his writings for the production of children. But he parts company with Hippocrates, who articulated the direct relationship between reproductive functioning and female health. In fact, Galen asserts that childbearing is systematically dangerous to women, even though it's necessary for the survival of the species. In the *Epidemics*, for example, he notes that pregnancy, miscarriage, parturition, the failure of lochial purging, and nursing are all harmful to a woman. In a discussion of a Thasian woman whose lochial purges failed to arrive after the birth of a daughter, Galen declares that pregnancy is the problem:

> For it seems that the disease was engendered in the woman by the retention of the postpartum purge. For the retention of the menses tends to produce disease, but is not as damaging to the woman as [retention] after birth, since not only is [this retention] itself an excess, but it also produces considerable cacohymy (i.e. evil humours). For the embryo attracts the most useful blood to itself, as nourishment, and the poorer remainder becomes the cause of cacochymy in the pregnant, which *physis* evacuates after birth. (*Hipp. Epid.* 3.77)

And though he acknowledges that procreation is necessary for survival, he points out that it's "foolish" and "altogether without reason" (*UP* 14.2). Then again, we must hold his thinking here in tension with his belief that too much retention of fluid causes madness.

Like any Roman male of his day, Galen isn't immune to stereotyping women. Part of acknowledging that women are weaker and men are stronger means adapting *pharmaka* to different kinds of bodies. In his introduction to the book on "green plasters" in the *Compound Pharmaka According to Kind*, he asserts that the compounding of remedies must take into account the differences that exist between stronger and weaker bodies: "I say stronger bodies are those that are drier in their *kraseis,* as those of farmers, sailors, and hunters are. The weaker are the softer according to nature or habit, such as [the bodies] of women, eunuchs, and children who are wet in their *kraseis* by nature and have a white and soft body" (2.1). As Flemming points out, there's a fairly consistent message in Galen's writings: "Women, eunuchs, children, and anyone else with a soft, delicate, white body require especially gentle treatment, while the most hardened men of soil and sea require especially bought treatment otherwise being automatically geared to the moderate man."[88] But we would be remiss if we concluded that Galen saw women as mere "baby factories."[89] As Parker declares, "There is considerable concern for women in pain, even though diseases in women seem often to be equated with women's diseases."[90] Additionally, there's no evidence that doctors considered women "less worthy" of being treated or that they received inferior care. But it will take the writers of romance literature to figure out how *pleasure* can be used in the service of empire.

Achilles Tatius: Pleasure in the Service of Empire

Achilles Tatius's *Leucippe and Clitophon* revamps Plato's *Symposium* in what Kate Cooper dubs "a fondly ridiculous version."[91] At the start of the novel, the unnamed narrator is approached by a young man, Clitophon, who is cajoled into speaking of his adventures. Clitophon tells this narrator how Leucippe, his cousin, traveled to his home in Tyre, where he fell in love with her. Adding tension to the drama is the fact that Clitophon has already been promised in marriage to his half-sister Kalligone. With little choice, he seeks out the advice of his cousin Cleinias, a man experienced in love, who will soon lose his young male lover to the arms of death. After several attempts to woo Leucippe, Clitophon wins her affection, even though his marriage to Kalligone is fast approaching. The marriage is thwarted, however, when Kallisthenes, a young man from Byzantium who's heard of Leucippe's beauty, comes to Tyre to kidnap her. By mistake, he kidnaps Kalligone.

The story ends in momentous fashion with Clitophon's innocence proved in court. Leucippe proves her virginity by entering the magic temple of Artemis where she passes numerous tests. Her father, Sostratos, journeys to Ephesus and reveals that Clitophon's father gives his blessing to the two young lovers. As a side note, Kallisthenes, Kalligone's kidnapper, is shown to have become a true and honest husband. The novel ends with the marriage of Clitophon and Leucippe in Byzantium, Leucippe's hometown. In a sense, everyone lives happily ever after. Or do they?

Achilles Tatius (early second century C.E.) wrote during "the Second Sophistic," which is the modern term for the cultural characteristics of the first three centuries C.E. Though the term is erroneously used by modern scholarship to denote this historical period, it was first coined by Philostratus in the third century C.E. He uses it to refer to a style of oratory known as *in persona*—improvisations based on historical figures (*Lives of the Sophists* 481). Modern scholars have increasingly used the term to refer to the resurgence of interest in Greek education and values under the Roman Empire.[92] During this period, there was an increased economic prosperity as a result of the *Pax Augusta* and the enthusiasm of Hellenophile emperors such as Hadrian.

In the modern era, *Leucippe and Clitophon* remains the least studied of the five major Greek novels (i.e., Chariton, Xenophon of Ephesus, Longus, Achilles Tatius, and Helidorus). Helen Morales suggests that the reason for this lack of interest is that no one knows what to make of Tatius's work; she asks, is it "Parody? Pastiche? Pornography?"[93] On the basis of evidence in the story, Simon Goldhill classifies it as a kind of ancient porn, or *erotikoi logoi*.[94] His classification tends to be the most accurate and is the one I use here.

When Leucippe arrives at the house of her uncle, she meets Clitophon for the first time, who, as I noted above, is engaged to his half-sister Kalligone. As soon as Clitophon sees Leucippe, he falls into the passionate arms of *erōs*:

> As soon as I had seen her, I was lost. For Beauty's wound is sharper than any weapon's, and it runs through the eyes down to the soul. It is through the eye that love's wound passes, and I now became a prey to a host of emotions: admiration, amazement, trembling, shame, shamelessness. I admired her generous stature, marveled at her beauty, trembled in my heart, stared shamelessly, ashamed I might be caught. My eyes defied me. I tried

to force them away from the girl, but they swung back to her, drawn by allure of her beauty, and finally they were victorious. (1.4)

This is the classic "fall into passion at first sight" encounter.[95] Later at a
dinner party, Clitophon is placed precisely where he can gaze upon the
object of his desire—Leucippe. A slave enters with a lyre and sings of how
Apollo loved and pursued Daphne, who was turned into the laurel tree,
destined to provide Apollo with his garlands. In response, Clitophon says:

> This lyrical interlude fanned higher the fire in my soul, for stories of love
> stir feelings of lust. In spite of all our admonitions to moderation, models
> excite us to imitation, particularly a pattern set by our betters. And more,
> the shame we feel at wrongful deeds is changed by the good repute of su-
> perior people to saucy freedom of speech. So I said to myself: "Look here,
> Apollo himself loves a maiden; unashamed of his love, he pursues her—
> while you hesitate and blush: untimely self-control! Are you better than a
> god?" (1.5)

Here we have erotic literature at its finest. It is the "fuel of passion" even
if a man has schooled himself in *sōphrosynē* (self-control), striving in vain
to resist its allure.

There are some general things to note about *erotikoi logoi*.[96] First, ancient
erotic literature is a stimulant (i.e., the "fuel of passion"). One ancient
doctor, Theodorus Priscianus, even recommends reading erotic novels as
a cure for impotence (if a lover isn't obtainable).[97] We see erotic stimula-
tion when Clitophon woos Leucippe, telling her a set of stories designed
to make her think erotically: "To lay the ground for Leukippe's more am-
orous inclination, I began speaking to Satyros, taking as my text the
timely presence of the bird, the peacock, who at the very moment (as
luck would have it) spread his beautiful tail and showed the amphitheater
of his feathers" (1.16). Second, Clitophon tells the fable of the palm,
which withers away if the male tree is separated too far from the female
tree. Third, he describes the flowing together of the river, Alpheus, and
the spring, Arethusa, as a "marriage" (*gamos*). The watercourse that links
them is the "marriage-broker." Finally, Clitophon tells a lengthy story
about a viper, a land-snake, and his passion for the eel, or water-snake.
When the snake and the eel wish to get married, the land-snake hisses
a welcome to the eel, who slithers onto the shore in a kind of premating

ritual. As a sign of affection, the viper vomits "the poison that frightens his bride, and she sees the deadly serum spilled onto the sand" (1.18). Descending from the rock, she swims to the mainland and "coils around her lover, no longer afraid of his kisses." As Goldhill notes, "The poison of love, a common image of the sickness of desire—transmitted by the bite of the mouth, the kiss—is here both liberalized and played with, as the two lovers, alone on the liminal space of the shore, stare at one another and finally embrace in a fearless kiss."[98] At this point, Achilles Tatius is playing with the tradition of the connection between desire in nature and the natural desire in human beings. The natural world is playfully eroticized as a model for human intercourse. Apparently, Clitophon's "moves" worked, since Leucippe wasn't displeased:

> I was looking at the young lady to see how she reacted to my erotic lesson. She discreetly indicated that she had not been displeased (*ouk aēdōs*) by my discourse. The radiant beauty of the peacock struck me less forcefully than that glance from Leukippe. The beauty of her body challenged the flowers of the field: her face was the essence of pale jonquil; roses arose on her cheeks; her glance was a revelation of violet; her hair had more natural curls than spiral ivy. Such was the meadow of Leukippe's face. (1.19)

There's an additional set of erotic stimulants with a series of set-piece descriptions known as *ekphrases*. Throughout the novel, works of art often call for further analysis and comment from the narrator or other characters.[99] They also turn out to be programmatic in a variety of ways for the erotic narrative of the story. Beginning with the prologue's lengthy description of the picture of the rape of Europa, the reader is led into a hermeneutic game that "matches the play of chance, foreknowledge, control, and disaster in the narrative."[100] Both the reader of the text and the characters within the story become complicit in a kind of erotic voyeurism.[101]

Like Clitophon, we also gaze at the heroine. She is on display involuntarily throughout the novel as the object of the hero's desire and perhaps ours as well. David Konstan points out that there's an "element of aggression and control" created by the "unseen observation of another, who is thereby reduced to the condition of an unwitting performer."[102] To gaze upon a woman like this—whether one is the reader or the hero of the tale—is a form of masculine domination. As Luce Irigaray reminds us: "Investment in the look is not privileged in women as in men. More than the other senses, the eye objectifies and masters. It sets at a distance [and] maintains the distance."[103] As in our own day and age, sexual longing in *Leucippe and Clitophon* is largely visual; then, as now, sexual desire in the ancient world was primarily a visual impulse. "*Horan* (to see) and *eran* (to desire) were closely associated, both linguistically and conceptually."[104] Furthermore, in Greek and Roman art, the eye was usually associated with the phallus.[105] Like penises, eyes penetrate. And we must remember that a penis also has an eye.

Kyle Harper suggests that *Leucippe and Clitophon* is a novel with a moral: "Honorable matrimony is the final destiny of the erotic tale."[106] For him, all the Greek novels are "stories of adventure, trial, and intrigue that end happily in marriage."[107] Though it's true that most of the Greek novels uphold the value of matrimony, *Leucippe and Clitophon* is much more complex than Harper's simple explanation. In fact, sixteenth-century translations of Tatius's tale expurgated and altered the text so that the novel could be read as a story that "promotes good, honest values."[108] The point is this: *Leucippe and Clitophon* fits Harper's pattern if and only if various episodes are excised. Thus we must penetrate deeper into the story in order to understand its convoluted message.

On page after page, Tatius develops a "new erotics."[109] What scholars often overlook is the exchange between Clitophon and Menelaos, where we find a "heteronormative" relationship, marked by a "male-female polarity," insistent on an "abstention that is modeled much more on virginal integrity than on the political and virile domination of desires; and finally, the fulfillment and reward of this purity in a union that has the form and value of a spiritual marriage."[110] In other words, what might seem on the surface like a story of valor and honor, still entices readers with the love of boys.

Toward the end of Book 2, Clitophon and Menelaos meet over breakfast on the ship that will soon meet its demise. Clitophon speaks first: "Where do you come from, my young friend, and what is your name?" (2.33). Menelaos tells him that he's an Egyptian. Pleasantries are exchanged, with Clitophon introducing Cleinias to Menelaos.

After some brief banter, Clitophon and Cleinias persuade Menelaos to tell them his story. He informs them that the principal reason for his travels has to do with the "jealousy of Eros" and a "fateful safari" (2.34). We discover that while on safari, he accidentally killed his male companion while trying to protect him from a wild boar:

> The boar was moving fast, covering ground by leaps and bounds, making straight for my lover. They were on a collision course, and I was shaking with fright as I watched. Afraid that the boar would strike first and gore the horse, I wound the thongs of my javelin and hurled it at the target without taking careful aim. My lover veered straight into its trajectory and intercepted the weapon. (2.34)

Upon hearing the story, Cleinias begins to weep. He is weeping "outwardly for Patroklos" and "remembering Charikles," his lost friends. Wondering what is going on, Menelaos asks Cleinias to tell his story, which he does, followed by a story from the lips of Clitophon.

Noticing that Cleinias is weeping and Menelaos is visibly distraught, Clitophon engages the men in a famous reenactment of a Socratic dialogue on women and young boys: "Cleinias always comes out ahead of me. I know he was looking for an opportunity to deliver his diatribe against women as usual, which he could easily do now that he has found a companion who shares his view of love" (2.35). The debate centers around whether or not "male-directed love" is now the norm.

Without missing a beat, Menelaos declares that the love of men is better than the love of women: "Surely it is much preferable to the alternative" (2.35). For him, young men are more open and forthcoming than women, and their hairless bodies cause more arousal. But how can this be? For Clitophon, the beauty of young men doesn't last long. It vanishes within a few short years, whereas the beauty of a woman can be savored over a great length of time. In fact, for him, young men always leave a man unfulfilled and wanting more: "A lover cannot come to the end of an affair with a boyfriend feeling unqualified gratification, for he is invariably left thirsty for something more" (2.35).

For Menelaos, being "left thirsty for something more" is precisely the point. To be unsatisfied is the optimal state, since a lack of satisfaction and fulfillment brings about the most pleasure. Desire is the key: "Constant recourse to anything makes satisfaction shrivel into satiation. What can only be snatched is always fresh and blooming—its pleasure never grows old ... The rose for this reason is lovelier than other plants: its beauty soon is gone" (2.36).

Menelaos continues by noting that there are two kinds of beauty among mortals. One type is heavenly, while the other type is vulgar. But he also surmises that no woman has ever ascended to the heavens because of her beauty—even though Zeus has been known to resort to women: "Alkmene became a tearful fugitive; Danae was consigned to the sea in a chest; Semele fed the fire. But when Zeus desired a Phrygian youth, he gave him the sky, that Ganymede might live with him and serve his nectar" (2.36). In other words, even Zeus knows that women are inferior to young men.

But Clitophon will have none of Menelaos's argument. For him, the timeless beauty of a woman is "next to godliness" (2.37). Yes, Zeus indeed lusted after a Phrygian youth and brought the youth to heaven; but as he reminds Menelaos, "The loveliness of women brought Zeus himself down to earth" (2.37). So women must be better than young men, since they're capable of getting gods off their thrones.

Clitophon continues by telling Menelaos that he has very little experience with women, except with women of the street:

> If we might pass from this heroic casuistry to speak of the real pleasures involved, though I am only a novice in my experience of women, and that has been restricted to commercial transactions with women of the street, and though another more deeply initiated into their secrets might well have more to say, yet I will speak in their behalf, even though I have no very wide experience. (2.37)

Scholars have struggled with what Clitophon means by "a novice in my experience of women." Clearly, he isn't claiming to be a complete neophyte or a virgin. In fact, other portions of the novel query whether there's such a thing as a male virgin, as when Clitophon explains to his father that he and Leucippe "have acted like sage philosophers ... while we have been away from home. Passion was hot on our trail; we fled as lover and beloved, but in our exile we were like brother and sister. If one can speak of such a thing as male virginity, this is my relationship to Leukippe up to now" (8.5). So what does Clitophon mean?

Goldhill maintains that there's "no fetish of sexual innocence here, merely a rhetorical disclaimer of not being quite an intimate *memuemenos.*

('Initiation' here implies more than a first act of sexual intercourse, as in so many modern romances. Nor is there any talk or implication of 'love' as opposed to 'sex,' that other favourite of the modern romance)."[111] Although Clitophon has consorted with only prostitutes, he doesn't regard himself as having "gone all the way." Obviously, he knows something about sex, since he gives quite a descriptive speech of "pleasure in the thing itself":

> A woman's body is well lubricated in the clinch, and her lips are tender and soft for kissing. Therefore she holds a man's body wholly and congenially wedged into her embraces, into her very flesh; and her partner is totally encompassed with pleasure. She plants kisses on your lips like a seal touching warm wax; and if she knows what she is doing, she can sweeten her kisses, employing not only the lips but the teeth, grazing all around the mouth with gentle nips. The fondled breast, too, is not without its special pleasure. (2.37)

What happens next is a detailed description of a female orgasm, and what we fondly refer to as "French kisses":

> When the sensations named for Aphrodite are mounting to their peak, a woman goes frantic with pleasure; she kisses with mouth wide open and prances about like a mad woman. Tongues all the while overlap and caress, their touch like passionate kisses within kisses. Your part in heightening the pleasure is simply to open your mouth. When a woman reaches the very goal of Aphrodite's action, she instinctively gasps with that burning delight, and her gasp rises quickly to the lips with a love breath, and there it meets a lost kiss, wandering about and looking for a way down: this kiss mingles with the love breath and returns with it to strike the heart. The heart then is kissed, confused, throbbing. If it were not firmly fastened in the chest, it would follow along, drawing itself upwards to the place of kisses. Schoolboys are hardly so well educated in kissing; their embraces are awkward; their lovemaking is lazy and devoid of pleasure. (2.37)

As Goldhill explains, "Even for an admittedly (or inevitably) male version of female pleasure, this frankly eroticized account is hard to parallel in the ancient Greek world at least."[112]

Foucault is right to suggest that the love of a boy is only "episodic" and "marginal" in *Leucippe and Clitophon*.[113] It's true that Menelaos, for his part, rambles on about a boy's kiss, while Cleinias, who tries to dissuade his own male lover from marriage, provides Clitophon with some much needed advice on how to woo and seduce a woman. But the major focus of attention in the novel centers on the relationship between a boy and a girl. Despite this fact, I'm left to wonder whether Clitophon has no experience with boys. In his defense of women, he never denies having had any sexual experiences with young men. In fact, he seems to indicate some experience with the kisses of "schoolboys," along with their "awkward" embraces and "lazy" lovemaking. His argument is one of comparison. After experiencing the love of both women and young boys, he prefers women. But nothing in the novel suggests that he has never experienced sex with a young man. In fact, Menelaos is well aware of Clitophon's experience: "You seem less like a novice and more like an old, a very old pro at Aphrodite's business, bombarding us with all these fancy refinements devised by women" (2.38). I would also add that even though he may not be a "pro" when it comes to young boys, Clitophon hardly lacks knowledge of them.

In response to Clitophon's apologia, Menelaos defends young men. Women are evil and boys are better: "Women are false in every particular, from coquettish remarks to coy posturing" (2.38). His thoughts are not different from Augustus's speech to the Senate, and his critique is the standard critique of the Greco-Roman world. Men—or youths in this case—are superior in every way: "The softer sex are flabby opponents in Aphrodite's ring, but boys' bodies compete on equal terms, striving like athletes whose mutual goal is pleasure" (2.38).

One of the major problems with an erotic tale such as *Leucippe and Clitophon* is situating it in its historical setting. What is its historical moment? Given all I've discussed to this point, Harper is surely wrong when he suggests that "honorable matrimony is the final destiny of the erotic tale," that is, it has a moral. True, the tale ends in matrimony, but it takes more than its fair share of twists and turns to get there.

Conclusion

Since I began this chapter with Augustus and his laws, it's fitting to end with them. There are two basic approaches to the historical moment of the romantic novels. One maintains that the romances are anti-empire and thus anti-Augustus and his reforms, while the other declares that they actually uphold the tenets of Augustus's moral program.

David Konstan backs the first approach, arguing that "sexual symmetry" of the Greek romances stresses the reciprocal passion of their young heroes and heroines. "In celebrating the celebration of *erōs* or personal romance as the grounds of marriage," he says, "the Greek novelist sublimated the public function of marriage, which was bound up with the traditions of the city-state as a discrete social and political entity."[114] The erotic novels, then, provide us with literary insights into the transition between the Hellenistic era and Roman Empire. In other words, the stories are all about the erosion of the old way of life. Marriage is recast as the end result of a long quest by both male and female protagonists. But as Cooper points out, Konstan's reading paints the romance novels as documents of "social devolution," or "an articulation of the changing place of the individual as the close-knit communities of the classical and Hellenistic period give way to the more impersonal social matrix of empire."[115] What he has in mind, then, are literary works that describe the "cost of empire."

Konstan's argument is valuable for its attempt to reconstruct the social imagination of the erotic novels. But his is only one option. As Cooper declares, "We should not feel obliged to dismiss the possibility that the impulse of the texts is deeply-conservative."[116] If we set a novel like *Leucippe and Clitophon* in the midst of the Roman Empire during the Second Sophistic, marriage based on romantic love would hardly be deemed mutually beneficial as Konstan proposes. On the contrary, having erotic literature with all its twists and turns ending with marriage might have been perceived by its original readers as an attempt to fortify Augustus's reforms. "The romantic celebration of desire in all its forms may be no less and no more than an attempt to remind the citizens of the Roman Empire that while marriage and procreation were a public duty, the fulfillment of duty was not always unpleasant."[117] Much like Musonius, then, Achilles Tatius writes about fulfillment of the common good through marriage. The key is pleasure, which is celebrated in *Leucippe and Clitophon*, whether it's male-male or male-female. "Pleasure, well-measured and harnessed to the common good, was understood by the ancient not to contradict but to ratify the actions of honorable men and women."[118] Thus *Leucippe and Clitophon,* with all its eroticism, supports empire and celebrates it and all its "costs."

Moral codes are more than just collections of precepts. At some stage in the development of those codes, people begin to *internalize* their ideologies and make them their own.[119] Aside from Galen, the majority of discourses in the early Roman Empire preached the importance of marriage and monogamy. As Paul Veyne points out: "The older moral code said: 'To marry is one duty of the citizen.' The newer said: 'To be a good man, one must make love only in order to have children.'"[120] The byproduct of the newer code was "the myth of the couple," seen particularly among the Roman Stoics. The mixture of good intentions and conformity gave rise to this ideology of the family. And the best way to perpetuate the myth was to do what Augustus did: create an illusion of a marriage crisis spread by celibacy and singleness. "The Romans suffered from this illusion before their historians took it up, and the emperor Augustus promulgated special laws to encourage citizens to marry."[121]

Most of the discourses I've examined from the early imperial period declare that marriage and sex have nothing to do with pleasure. Instead, they're vehicles that foster procreation. Of course, we've also seen that Achilles Tatius knows how to make pleasure serve the purposes of empire. It's not clear where this new morality came from. It could have come from the Stoics as easily as from anyone else. Though the origins aren't clear, the purpose of this new morality is *harmonia,* its ultimate goal. It was a symbol not so much of marriage, but of concord. It was also pure and simple ideology.

The illusion of a marriage crisis prompted Stoics such as Musonius to discuss the patriotic nature of procreation. People reproduce because that's what the state needs. Women are important because men can't reproduce without them. And if pleasure is what it takes to entice people to perform their duty for the empire, then so be it. Except for Galen, many people seem to have internalized this ideological myth. There really was a crisis that needed to be fixed. But as Veyne notes, people become victims of their own ideologies and their own success. Ultimately, "a clique of rich and powerful men of letters . . . was reduced to little more than a sophisticated version of prevailing morality: a man's duties to himself and others were identified with institutions, which this bastard doctrine ingeniously sought to internalize as moral precepts."[122]

If any of this sounds familiar, it is because these views are closer to our own time than some of the discourses I explore in the following pages. As I said in the introduction, as much as we try to persuade ourselves that our values are Judeo-Christian, that hyphen is suspect for all kinds of reasons. We, too, have internalized an ideology of the family, but it's not the one many of us think we've internalized.

CHAPTER TWO

JUDAISM

An Ideology of Procreationism

The duty to procreate is central in traditional Jewish and Christian life. It is true that Christianity in principle prefers celibacy. But if you are not up to it—and the vast majority of humans are not—the proper path to take is the Jewish one: marriage with a view to having children. The dutiful seeking of children will justify the non-celibate, second-best course.

—*David Daube*

Before the rise of rabbinic Judaism and the destruction of the Jewish temple in 70 C.E., a variety of perspectives persisted among Jews regarding marriage, sex, and the family.[1] What each view held in common was the authority of the Torah, though there was no uniform way of interpreting it. Central to Second Temple Judaism (515 B.C.E.–70 C.E.) was the reinterpretation of the blessing "be fruitful and multiply" as a commandment (Gen 1:28).[2] Though anyone reading this text can see that it's a positive evaluation of human sexuality, not all Jews agreed on how to interpret it and apply it in everyday life.[3] As I establish in this chapter, *most* of the sexual ethics of Second Temple Judaism look surprisingly like the ideological sexual codes of the Roman Empire. An examination of works as diverse as Tobit, the writings of Philo and Josephus, the Dead Sea Scrolls, and many other texts makes it clear that there's little in the ideological discourses of the Second Temple era that can't be found in the marriage laws of Augustus. The strategies developed in most of the Jewish literature of the Second Temple period privilege the home, marriage, and procreation. In fact, we might call the majority ideology of Second Temple Judaism "Procreationism."[4] A procreationist sexual ethic is "'for reproduction' and not 'for pleasure.'"[5] Augustus would surely approve of this ideology of the family since, like its Roman counterpart, it was committed to heteronormativity and the family, with only a minority of Second Temple Jewish voices objecting. This means that most of the Jewish literature of this period upholds the same hegemonic ideology of empire, reducing a woman's body to the reproductive act. It also means that the Greco-Roman ideologies I discussed in chapter 1 are part of a broader cultural pattern found throughout the ancient Mediterranean world. The one major difference between Second Temple Jewish ideologies of the family and Greco-Roman ideologies is that Jews of the Second Temple era harness their sexual desire in strict devotion to their God, which prevents them from committing idolatry. In fact, according to one text, Jews differ from gentiles to such a degree that even their men enter marriages as virgins (*On the Life of Joseph* 43).

Tobit: A Template for Marriage

The book of Tobit outlines the basic steps that lead to marriage among Second Temple Jews. Though an ancient fairytale, Tobit, set in the eighth century B.C.E., reflects Jewish life in the diaspora between 225 and 175 B.C.E.[6] The book tells the story of a righteous Israelite of the tribe of Naphtali named Tobit, who lives in Nineveh after the deportation of the northern tribes of Israel to Assyria in 721 B.C.E. under Sargon II. Deborah, Tobit's paternal grandmother, raises him in the ways of his ancestors. As a result, Tobit's loyalty is to Yahweh, whom he worships at the temple in Jerusalem, instead of joining the cult of the golden calf at Dan. As a devout follower of Yahweh, he provides proper burials for Israelites who have been slain by Sennacherib. His loyalty costs him everything since Sennacherib seizes all of his property and sends him into exile.

After Sennacherib's death, Tobit returns to Nineveh and buries a man who was murdered on the street. That night, as he sleeps in the open, bird droppings fall into his eyes, blinding him. Because he is blind, his wife must work to support them, leading to strife between them. In his anguish, he prays for death (2:7–3:6).[7]

Faraway in Media is a young woman named Sarah. She, too, prays for death, since she has lost seven husbands to the demon Asmodeus. He abducts and kills every man she marries before the marriage can be consummated. God sends the angel Raphael, disguised as a human, to heal Tobit and to free Sarah from the demon:

> At that very moment the prayers of both of them were heard in the glorious presence of God. So Raphael was sent to heal both of them: Tobit, by removing the white films from his eyes, so that he might see God's light with his eyes; and Sarah, daughter of Raguel, by giving her in marriage to Tobias son of Tobit, and by setting her free from the wicked demon Asmodeus. For Tobias was entitled to have her before all others who had desired to marry her. (3:16–17)

When Tobias, Tobit's son, arrives in Media, Raphael tells him about the beautiful Sarah, whom he has the right to marry because he's her cousin and close relative. So Raphael instructs Tobias to burn a fish's liver and heart to exorcise the demon, who was planning to attack on Tobias's wedding night. He does exactly what Raphael instructs him to do, and Sarah and Tobias marry without interference from Asmodeus.

The story of Tobit, Tobias, and Sarah contains the basic steps of a Jewish marriage in the Second Temple era: (1) A negotiation takes place between the groom's father and the father of the bride, either directly or through the former's representative. In Tobit's case, the angel Raphael acts as Sarah's representative (5:4–8).[8] (2) The father places the daughter into her future husband's hands, reflecting the norm that the woman passes from one man to another. (3) A contract is then signed according to the law of Moses, and a celebration begins (8:1–9).[9] (4) Finally, a feast follows, together with the payment of a dowry (8:21, 10:10; cf. 2 Macc 1:14). In the Tobit narrative, everything from the meeting to the marriage happens overnight, which is somewhat unrealistic. In most cases, an extended period of time would elapse between the agreement among the fathers and the wedding. This interim period is known as the "betrothal" period, though its legal standing is unclear. The agreement, however, would need to be secure in order to proceed with all of the arrangements. In the case of Mary and Joseph, for example, the time of betrothal is assumed to be several months (Matt 1:18).

We also learn from the book of Tobit that taking a non-Jewish wife is tantamount to illicit sex (*porneia*). During a touching scene in which Tobit instructs Tobias on how to live a righteous life, he tells him: "Beware, my son, of every kind of illicit sexual act. First of all, marry a woman from among the descendants of your ancestors; do not marry a foreign woman, who is not of your father's tribe; for we are the descendants of the prophets" (4:12). Furthermore, before Sarah and Tobias consummate their marriage, Tobias blesses God and promises that he isn't taking Sarah as a wife because of lust (*porneia*) but out of sincere motives (8:4–7).[10] This statement likely means that Tobias isn't marrying Sarah out of sexual desire, but out of duty to his father and to his God. Part of that duty includes procreation.[11] As David Daube maintains, "Almost certainly, he means that he is acting from allegiance to his family and people: that sets him apart from his predecessors."[12] Even though the book of Tobit never mentions Tobias and Sarah having sex, it, like the rest of the Hebrew Bible, places the highest value on children: They are a blessing (Tob 2:1, 5:16, 8:17, 10:4–11, 11:14).[13]

The Purpose and Meaning of Sex in Second Temple Judaism

By and large, Jewish texts of the Second Temple era view marriage positively, but as we'll see, debates center on the purpose of sex. The *Damascus Document*, for example, clearly affirms marriage as something positive and divorce as something negative. In fact, divorce is a sin: "The Inspector of the camp shall proceed in consultation lest they err. And likewise with regard to anyone who marries a woman and in consultation. And likewise, with regard to anyone who divorces; he shall instruct their children and their small children with a spirit of modesty and with compassionate love. He should not bear resentment against them in anger and rage because of their sins" (*CD* XIII 17b–19a). Additionally, Pseudo-Phocylides (first century B.C.E.–first century C.E.) cites Homer's homage to marital bliss with approval: "Love your own wife, for what is sweeter and better than whenever a wife is kindly disposed toward her husband and a husband toward his wife till old age, without strife divisively interfering?" (195–197).[14] Philo (25 B.C.E.–50 C.E.) affirms the importance of sexual pleasure in a rereading of Adam and Eve's first encounter in the book of Genesis, despite his persistent concerns about pleasure's dangers elsewhere: "And this desire begat likewise bodily pleasure (*sōmatōn hēdonēn*)" (*On the Creation of the World* 152).

Getting married, then, is a good thing. In fact, we find numerous examples of married Jews advising single Jews to get married. Nicanor, for example, encourages Judas Maccabaeus to settle down and marry: "Nicanor stayed on in Jerusalem and did nothing out of the way, but dismissed the flocks of people that had gathered. And he kept Judas always in his presence; he was warmly attached to the man. He urged him to marry and have children; so Judas married, settled down, and shared the common life" (2 Macc 14:23–24). If no spouses are available, people take measures to find them. Pseudo-Philo, for example, reports on initiatives to find husbands for Kenaz's daughters and for having the Danites find themselves wives:

> Now Kenaz had three daughters, whose names are these: the firstborn Ethema, the second Feila, the third Zelfa. And Zebul gave to the firstborn all that was around the land of the Phoenicians, and to the second he gave the olive grove of Ekron, but to the third he gave the tilled lands that were around Ashdod. And he gave them husbands, that is, to the firstborn Elisefan, to the second Odihel, but to the third Doel. (29:2) . . .
>
> . . . then the sons of Israel were celebrating Passover, and they commanded the sons of Benjamin, saying, "Go up and get wives for yourselves, because we cannot give you our daughters. For we made a vow in the time of our anger, but let it not happen that one tribe be blotted out from Israel." And the sons of Benjamin went up and seized for themselves wives and built for themselves Gabaon and began to dwell there. (48:3)

Finally, for all its ribaldry, the famous story of the three youths proclaims that a man "loves his wife more than his father or his mother" (1 Esd 4:25),[15] while texts such as the *Sibylline Oracles* (3:594, 767–795) and the *Testament of Abraham* (A10:3) picture the ideal Jewish life as one centered around marriage and family.

All these ideas go back, of course, to the "oneness of flesh" first described in the Genesis myth: "Therefore a man leaves his father and his mother and clings to his wife, and they become one flesh" (Gen 2:24).[16] As William Loader notes, "The Genesis myth will have meant more than new kinship for many, but carried with it the sense of union and intimacy which is universally attested where loving engagement thus finds its fulfillment."[17] Furthermore, Second Temple Judaism places a great deal of emphasis on the blessing found at Gen 1:28, "Be fruitful and multiply," which Second Temple Jews turned into a commandment.

Both Gen 1:28 and 2:24 were interpreted by Jews of the Second Temple era to teach that sex is only for procreation and should be confined to marriage. Jews share the idea with Plato (*Leg.* 840d–e; *Rep.* 5), which betrays the influence of Greco-Roman thought on Second Temple writers.[18] Sexual deviance, then, is any kind of sex that doesn't lead to procreation. Pseudo-Philo, for example, reports that an angel of the Lord gave instructions to Manoah to go and have sex with Eluma so she could give birth to Samson (42:7; cf. 58:3–4). There's also the exhortation in Pseudo-Phocylides to marry and so pay nature back for its generosity with offspring: "Do not remain unmarried, lest you die nameless. Give nature her due, you also, beget in your turn as you were begotten" (175–176).[19] Moreover, the author of the *Testaments of the Twelve Patriarchs* turns Rachel into a model of someone who desires sexual intercourse only for procreation: "For he perceived that she wanted to lie with Jacob for the sake of children and not merely for sexual gratification" (*Testament of Issachar* 2:3). And the patriarch Naphtali instructs his sons to view sex with their wives as an expression of the commandment to love one's neighbor as oneself (Lev. 19:18):

> The commandments of the Lord are double, and they are to be fulfilled with regularity. There is a time for having intercourse with one's wife, and a time to abstain for the purpose of prayer. And there are two commandments: Unless they are performed in proper sequence they leave one open to the greatest sin. It is the same with the other commandments. So be wise in the Lord and discerning, knowing the order of his commandments, what is ordained for every act, so that the Lord will love you. (Testament of Naphtali 8:7–10)

All these texts suggest that ejaculation for the purpose of procreation in any context other than marriage is wrong. Josephus (37 C.E.–100 C.E.), for example, insists that sexual intercourse occur only between a wife and a husband: "From the hire of a prostitute let no sacrifices be paid; for the Deity has pleasure in naught that proceeds from outrage, and no shame could be worse than the degradation of the body. Likewise, if one has received payment for the mating of a dog, whether hound of the chase or guardian of the flocks, he must not use thereof to sacrifice to God" (*Jewish Antiquities* 4.206). By writing these words, Josephus sets himself against Roman norms, which allowed men to have sex with other women under their control outside of marriage and with prostitutes.[20] Additionally, he utilizes Deut 23:18 to condemn female prostitution as immoral and shameful. By implication, contraception is also rejected. For most Jews of the Second Temple era, then, the purpose of sex is procreation, an idea they share with their Greco-Roman neighbors. As Walter Wilson notes, "In early Judaism, as in all traditional societies, children were a barometer of success."[21]

Philo and Procreationism

The most fervent advocate of this new sexual program of Procreationism is Philo of Alexandria. As Kathy L. Gaca reminds us, "Philo's sexual principles are part of an innovative agenda for social order that borrows from Plato and the Pentateuch, makes sense only in relation to both, and yet represents neither without noteworthy transformation."[22] This is particularly the case in Philo's reinterpretation of the tenth commandment, "You shall not desire" (*ouk epithumēseis; On the Decalogue* 142, 173–174; *On the Special Laws* 4.78). In his reinterpretation, desire (*epithumia*) not only signifies any inclination to defy God's will, but becomes overtly sexual. Uncontrolled desire means sexual pleasure, which Philo sees as the greatest source of individual and social corruption.

Philo is so adamant about procreation that he declares eunuchs banned from God's people (*On the Migration of Abraham* 69), and he chastises Jewish men who marry barren women (*On the Special Laws* 3.34).[23] His new sexual program is based on two major criteria by which he distinguishes lawful from unlawful sexual acts. First, he asks whether the sexual act is engaged in for pleasure or for procreation. If for pleasure, it's unlawful. Next he asks whether the sexual act entails rebellion against God or apostasy. Sexual behavior is licentious (*lagneia*) when it exceeds its strictly reproductive function within marriage.[24] For Philo, the origin of all wrongdoing is a person's innate sexual desire and its tendency toward excessive pleasures. As he states in *On the Special Laws:* "So great then and transcendent an evil is desire (*epithumia*), or rather it may be truly said the fountain of all evils. For plunderings and robberies and repudiations of debts and false accusations and outrages, also seductions, adulteries, murders and all wrongful actions, whether in things sacred or things profane, from what other source do they flow?" (4.84). Like any good Greco-Roman philosopher, Philo blames women for the introduction of desire into the world, for they are lesser creatures in the one-sex model. In *On the Creation of the World,* he conjectures that man was unaware of his sexual appetite until he met his other half:

> But when woman too had been made, beholding a figure like his own and a kindred form, he was gladdened by the sight, and approached and greeted her. She, seeing no living thing more like herself than he, is filled with glee and shamefastly returns his greeting. Love (*erōs*) supervenes, brings together and fits into one the divided halves, as it were, of a single living creature, and sets up in each of them a desire for fellowship (*koinōnias*) with a view to the production of their like (*eis tēn tou homoiou genesin*). And this desire (*pothos*) begat likewise bodily pleasure (*tōn sōmatōn hēdonēn*), that pleasure which is the beginning of wrongs and violation of law, the pleasure for the sake of which men bring on themselves the life of mortality and wretchedness in lieu of that of immortality and bliss. (151–152)

In Philo's universe, just as in Augustus's, a woman's sexual appetite is greater than a man's. Pleasure is feminized as the "biblical whore" (*pornē*): "So pleasure comes languishing in the guise of a harlot or a courtesan . . . she grins and giggles; her hair is dressed in curious and elaborate plaits; under her eyes are pencil lines; her eyebrows are smothered in paint; she revels perpetually in the warmth of the bath; her flush is artificial" (*On the Sacrifices of Cain and Abel* 20–21; cf. *On the Special Laws* 3.8).[25] The only antidote to this Jezebel is, as Gaca puts it, to "adopt the norm of procreationism to prevent sexual desire from ever getting its rebellious way again."[26]

In his biographies of Abraham, Joseph, and Moses, Philo depicts the biblical patriarchs as prime examples of the kind of reproductive sexual behavior God's people must imitate in order to restrain their sexual desire. Abraham sleeps with his slave girl Hagar out of duty and for the purpose of reproduction, not pleasure. As Sarah says to him, "But do not let the trouble of my barrenness extend to you, or kind feeling to me keep you from becoming what you can become, a father, for I shall have no jealousy of another woman, whom you will take not for unreasoning lust (*hēn ou di epithumian alogon axē*) but in fulfillment of nature's inevitable law (*nomon de phuseōs*)" (*On the Life of Abraham* 249). Moreover, Abraham believes that Isaac should sleep with Rebecca only for the procreation of children. Commenting on Gen 24:2, Philo asks, "Why does he say, 'Place thy hand under my thigh'? Being about to bind him by an oath concerning the betrothal, he bids him place his hand close to the place of generation, indicating a pure association and unpolluted marriage, not having sensual pleasure as its end but the procreation of legitimate children" (*Questions and Answers on Genesis* 4.86). Of course, Philo is allegorizing. No literal reading of Gen 24:2 would conclude that it's about procreation.[27] As Gaca writes, "According to Philo, therefore, the patriarchs lived by the procreationist rule and thereby set the example of properly restrained sexual devotion to the biblical God."[28]

But Philo is also well aware of the fact that sexual desire can be so powerful that it will indeed corrupt a perfectly good Jewish marriage. In fact, husbands can engage in illicit sex with their wives if they do it excessively because it feels so good:

> Now even natural pleasure (*phusin hēdonē*) is often greatly to blame when the craving for it is immoderate and insatiable, as for instance when it takes the form of voracious gluttony, even though none of the food taken is of the forbidden kind, or again the passionate desire for women shown by those who in their craze for sexual intercourse behave unchastely, not with the wives of others, but with their own. (*On the Special Laws* 3.9)

He even rules out Antipater's belief that married couples can engage in sexual relations for friendship.[29]

What ultimately concerns Philo is his belief that unrestrained eros will lead to lawlessness. It's one thing for sexual behavior to be licentious; it's another for it to be lawless. Beyond the wickedness of licentious sexual behavior lies an "even greater evil" (*On the Life of Moses* 1.295–296). This "greater evil" is eros taking such a hold in a Jew's life that it leads to idolatry and ultimately the abandonment of God and God's laws. That's why proper restraint of sexual desire is so important since appetitive sexual desire is the leading cause of Jewish failure in the Second Temple era. It's as if Philo is admonishing Jews to stop "screwing with God's laws."[30] Furthermore, we might say that for Philo, idolatry is a sexually transmitted disease. The only way to prevent its spread is a prophylactic of Procreationism.

Adapting the Scriptures

Even though Jews view their scriptures as "sacred," this doesn't mean those scriptures cannot be changed. In no way is a Second Temple Jew a modern fundamentalist. When Jews retell famous biblical stories, they update them for their audiences and for their own purposes. Unlike some modern Christians who view the Bible as an infallible, unchanging text, Second Temple Jews allow for much more flexibility in how their sacred stories are appropriated into new contexts.[31] A remarkable instance is the retelling of the Genesis creation stories in Jubilees, written somewhere around the early to mid-second century B.C.E. Copies survive in Ge'ez, a language of the Ethiopic church. A few fragments of the original Hebrew version exist in the Dead Sea Scrolls, so we can assume that Jubilees circulated rather widely during the Second Temple era.[32]

The author of Jubilees merges the creation accounts found in Genesis 1 and 2. Like the Genesis narratives, the author declares that on the sixth day God created humankind as one man and one woman. Additionally, the author mentions that the primary task of humanity is to rule over all of creation: "And after all of this, he created man—male and female he made them—and he gave him dominion over everything which was upon the earth and which was in the seas and over everything which flies, and over beasts and cattle and everything which moves upon the earth or above the whole earth. And over all this he gave him dominion" (2:14). What's conspicuously absent from Jubilees is any claim that man and woman are made in God's image, nor does the author suggest that God

48

wants them to reproduce. At 3:4–5, for example, Adam is brought to Eve, and, as in Gen 2:24, the two become "one flesh." But unlike other writers, the author of Jubilees doesn't view Gen 2:24 as an affirmation of the goodness of sex. So what is it? It seems to have some other purpose, which is never stated.[33]

The author of Jubilees isn't the only one to remove the commandment "be fruitful and multiply." Josephus also omits it, which may betray the fact that he's directly influenced by Jubilees. In his *Jewish Antiquities*, he retells the creation stories of Genesis, stripping them to their bare minimum. Noting that God made the animals male and female, he simply adds, "On this day also He formed man" (1.32). Nothing else is said. There's no reference to making humanity in God's image, to ruling over creation, or to being fruitful and multiplying.

Josephus also reports on God's response in Gen 2:20–23 concerning the creation of woman. Not once does he mention Adam's poetic utterance upon seeing Eve—"bone of my bone, flesh of my flesh"—nor does he declare that the two became "one flesh." There's also no reference to "nakedness," and later, when it does appear, it's unrelated to sexuality: "So they covered themselves with fig-leaves, and, thus screening their persons, believed themselves the happier for having found what they lacked before" (*Jewish Antiquities* 1.44). There seems, then, to be a shift in the Second Temple period regarding the meaning of the commandment "be fruitful and multiply." It looks like Josephus and the author of Jubilees downplay the commandment's significance, opening up asceticism as a viable option. In any case, to anyone who has read the Torah in its entirety, it's clear that asceticism is a valid, temporary option for priests and others who have taken certain vows. It's also required during particular seasons of the year and throughout certain lifecycles. But it's not the norm.

Several portions of the Torah reveal that there are times when an Israelite should abstain from sexual relations. In the book of Leviticus, the Mosaic law forbids sexual relations with a woman during her monthly period, though this law is clear that ritual impurity doesn't imply moral failure (18:19).[34] Instead, ritual impurity is incurred by not performing morally required acts (e.g., begetting lawful children or burying the dead). Additionally, Israelites can take a Nazarite vow, which means that they must not cut their hair and must abstain from drinking wine, and possibly from having sex, so as to dedicate themselves to God for a specified period of time (Num 6:1–21).[35] Furthermore, all contact with the dead is prohibited. Essentially, the Nazarite vow consecrates an Israelite to the Lord. Though it doesn't say so in the Hebrew, the Greek of the Septuagint makes it clear that the Nazarite vow brings devotees into a state of religious purity, which is thought to mean temporary abstention from sexual intercourse for the duration of the vow.[36]

Exodus 19:15 commands Israelite men to abstain from sexual intercourse for three days in preparation for God's gift of the giving of the law at Mount Sinai: "And he said to the people, 'Be ready for the third day; do not go near a woman.'" As one scholar says, "It is a measure of Moses' extraordinary intimacy with God at Sinai that he abstained miraculously for forty days even from pure foods, from bread and water."[37] Moreover, the Torah maintains that on Yom Kippur, held on the tenth day of the seventh month, the entire nation of Israel is to "afflict" or "humble" itself (Septuagint *tapeinōsate*), a command that appears to have been universally understood as a "technical term for fasting in the Priestly Code."[38]

Yom Kippur is a particularly interesting case study, since different Jewish groups disagree about when the tenth day falls and about the purpose of the day.[39] The author of Jubilees interprets Yom Kippur as a fast day, making it a time of penance (5:17–18). Abstention from forbidden foods appears to have been widely observed. Moreover, authorities impose harsh measures so that people will avoid temptations to assimilation.[40] During the rabbinic period, however, preparation for Yom Kippur involves abstaining from intercourse immediately beforehand, as well as ritual washing of one's body and clothing.[41] As Richard Finn suggests, "This was probably common practice earlier."[42]

What these texts tell us is that sexual abstention in the Hebrew Bible is understood to be temporary. The norm is to take Gen 1:28 seriously and propagate the earth, even though some writers, such as Josephus, start shifting its emphasis. Having said that, we shouldn't dismiss the fact that a greater intensity is placed on sexual purity and abstention in the Second Temple era as Jews reread their sacred texts and appropriate particular forms of Greco-Roman moral discourse into their theology.

An interesting case of abstention is Judith's refusal to remarry. The book of Judith, written in the early part of the first century B.C.E., is a fictional tale about the assassination of the general Holofernes by the heroine of its title.[43] Judith, who is emblematic of personal piety and Jewish identity, not only fasts throughout the year (8:6), but she also refuses offers of marriage in order to remain a widow until her death. When she dies, she leaves her money to members of her husband's family and her own:

> Many wished to marry her, but she gave herself to no man all the days of her life from the time her husband, Manasseh, died and was gathered to his people. Her fame continued to increase, and she lived in the house of her husband, reaching the advanced age of one hundred and five. She set her maid free. And when she died in Bethulia, they buried her in the cave of her husband, Manasseh; and the house of Israel mourned her for seven days. Before she died, she distributed her property to the relatives of her husband, Manasseh, and to her own relatives. (16:22–24)[44]

Roman readers would view Judith with distinction, since her actions are worthy of the epithet *univira*. But it's impossible to know whether or not this book circulated among non-Jewish audiences.

Essenes and the Dead Sea Scrolls: A Case for Celibacy

The most forthright example of sexual abstinence among Jews of the Second Temple era is seen in the practices of the Essenes. Philo, Pliny the Elder, and Josephus mention two branches of this community that lived, primarily, at Khirbet Qumran by the Dead Sea until the Romans annihilated them in 68–70 C.E.[45] Pliny the Elder (23 B.C.E.–79 C.E.) describes the Essenes as a "solitary tribe" (*gens sola*) of men who lived by the Dead Sea. In *Natural History*, he characterizes the Essenes as world-weary fugitives from society whose sexual abstinence, like their refusal of monetary commerce, is symbolic of a retreat from ordinary human exchange brought about by "dismay at others' lives":

> Lying on the west of Asphaltites, and sufficiently distant to escape its noxious exhalations, are the Essenes, a people that live apart from the world, and [are] marvelous beyond all others throughout the whole earth, for they have no women among them; to sexual desire they are strangers; money they have none; the palm trees are their only companions. Day after day,

however, their numbers are fully recruited by multitudes of strangers that resort to them, driven thither to adopt their usages by the tempests of fortune, and wearied with the miseries of life. Thus it is, that through thousands of ages, incredible to relate, this people eternally prolongs its existence, without a single birth taking place there; so fruitful a source of population to it is that weariness of life which is felt by others. (5.15)

Philo portrays the movement as a Greek philosophical sect.[46] In *That Every Good Person Is Free*, he points out that the Essenes withdraw from cities because they want to avoid the corrupting influences of urban life:

These men, in the first place, live in villages avoiding all cities on account of the habitual lawlessness of those who inhabit them, well knowing that such a moral disease is contracted from associations with wicked men, just as a real disease might be from an impure atmosphere, and that this would stamp an incurable evil on their souls . . . they devote all their attention to the moral part of philosophy, using as instructors the laws of their country which it would have been impossible for the human mind to devise without divine inspiration. (12.76–80)

In another work, he notes that the Essenes don't hold private property, which is proof that they're not held captive by the passions. Being able to resist the passions explains why no children are in the movement:

At all events, there are no children among the Essenes, no, nor any youths or persons only just entering manhood; since the dispositions of all such persons are unstable and liable to change . . . no one among them ventures at all to acquire any property, whatever of his own, neither house nor slave, nor farm, nor flocks and herds, nor any thing of any sort . . . but they bring them together into the middle as a common stock . . . And they all dwell in the same place, making clubs and societies, and combinations, and unions with one another. (*Hypothetica* 11.3–5)

Indeed, Philo describes the Essenes as "lovers of frugality and moderation, and averse to all sumptuousness and extravagance as a disease of both mind and body" (*Hypothetica* 11.11).

Like Philo, Josephus depicts the Essenes as an ascetic philosophical sect. One can find them in almost every town throughout Palestine, and one can distinguish them by the fact that they "practice holiness" (*semnotēta askein*) by dismissing pleasures and excelling in "self-control" (*enkrateia*). Additionally, the Essenes avoid marriage, not because of any inherent evil in the institution, but to escape the licentiousness of women: "They do not, indeed, on principle, condemn wedlock (*ton gamon*) and the propagation thereby of the race, but they wish to protect themselves against women's wantonness (*tōn gunaikōn aselgeias*), being persuaded that none of the sex keeps her plighted troth to one man (*tēn pros hena pistin*)" (*Jewish War* 2.121). In order for the sect to survive, Josephus points out that they adopt other men's children: "They shun pleasures (*hēdonas*) as a vice and regard temperance and the control of the passions (*tois pathesin*) as a special virtue. Marriage (*kai gamou*) they disdain, but they adopt other men's children, while yet pliable and docile, and regard them as their kin and mould them in accordance with their own principles" (*Jewish War* 2.120). A second group does marry but restricts sexual activity to procreative purposes:

> There is yet another order of Essenes, which while at one with the rest in its mode of life, customs, and regulations, differs from them in its views on marriage. They think that those who decline to marry cut off the chief function of life, the propagation of the race, and, what is more, that, were all to adopt the same view, the whole race would very quickly die out . . . They have no intercourse with [their wives] during pregnancy, thus showing that their motive in marrying is not self-indulgence (*hēdonēn*) but the procreation of children (*alla teknōn chreian gamein*). (*Jewish War* 2.160–161)

The Dead Sea Scrolls, written and preserved by the Essenes, provide a slightly different interpretation of the ascetic patterns described by Josephus, Pliny the Elder, and Philo. Scrolls such as the *Community Rule* or *Manual of Discipline* concern themselves with members of the group advancing in holiness through strict ritual purity and penitential fasting. Sexual abstinence is a basic requirement in order to maintain the level of purity appropriate to living in the Qumran community. Like Josephus, the *Damascus Document* also distinguishes between married and celibate members of the community: "And if they reside in camps in accordance with the rule of the land, and take women and beget children, they shall walk in accordance with the law and according to the regulation of the teachings according to the rule of the law, as he said: *Num 30:17* 'Between a man and his wife, and between a father and his son'" (*CD* VII.6–7).

According to Finn, "It is plausible, though not certain that the [celibate] belong to a distinct camp of 'perfect holiness,' a sectarian branch who maintain a higher level of ritual purity within the community than that required of others."[47] If Finn is right, this would explain the bodies that have been discovered at Qumran. Though archaeologists have unearthed the bodies of more than one thousand adult males, they have found the remains of only eleven women and five children.[48]

Other texts, such as the *Temple Scroll,* prescribe sexual abstinence within the confines of the city of Jerusalem: "And a man who lies with his wife and has an ejaculation, for three days shall not enter the whole city of the temple in which I shall cause my name to dwell" (11Q19 XLV.11–12). The purpose of this law is to avoid defiling the holy city and its temple through "uncleanness." According to Hannah Harrington, Essenes can't have intercourse on the Sabbath.[49] As the *Damascus Document* asserts, "And whoever approaches to have illegal sex with his wife, not in accordance with the regulation, shall leave and never return" (4Q270 XI Frag. 7 col. I). Of course, the nature of the crime isn't specified, and as Finn notes, "Some stipulations within the texts are obscure."[50] Harrington, however, makes the plausible case that the offense mentioned here is "sexual intercourse for pleasure" rather than for procreation.[51]

Second Temple Judaism's Gender Hierarchy

Despite the position taken by the writers of the Dead Sea Scrolls and others, celibacy wasn't the norm in the Judaism of the Second Temple period. As we've already seen, the imperative to "be fruitful and multiply" pervades most of the Jewish literature of the Second Temple era. Celibacy was almost always temporary and usually reserved for special circumstances.

Be that as it may, the scrolls uphold the traditional gender hierarchy of the ancient world, showing once again that gender hierarchy was part of the broader cultural pattern of the ancient Mediterranean world.[52] In the book of *Instruction,* written in Hebrew in the early second century B.C.E., we find an unusual case of rules being addressed directly to a woman.[53] The woman in question is probably the wife of the *mebin* or his daughter. The book of *Instruction* urges her to honor her husband, though admittedly, the lines of the text are poorly preserved:

Like a father honor your fa[*ther-in-l*]aw Do not depart from his heart and
. . . all the day long and in his bosom (is) [*your*] cove[*nant* . . .] lest you ne-
glect a ho[*ly*] covenant . . . And one who is hostile to you (lit. "your soul")
and . . . a w[*i*]fe fore[*ver* . . . *You will no longer live*] in the house of [*your*]
ori[*gins*]. Rather in your covenant you [*will be faithful* . . . *You will become*] an
object of praise in the mouth of all men ...... from the house of (your) birth.
(4Q415 Frag. col. II)[54]

More extensive instructions are given to husbands. These directions refer
more than once to "his womb," the assumption being that, since husband
and wife are now "one flesh," all she has is now his:

If you would marry a wife in your poverty, learn the causes of [. . .] from
the secret way things are. When you are united, live together with your
fleshly helper [. . . For as the verse says, "A man should leave] his father
and his mother [and adhere to his wife and they will become one flesh"
(Gen 2:24).] He has made you ruler over her, so [. . .] He did not give
[her father] authority over her, He has separated her from her mother,
and unto you [He has given authority . . . He has made your wife] and
you into one flesh. He will take your daughter away and give her to another, and your sons [. . .] But you, live together with the wife of your
womb, for she is the kin of [. . .] Whosoever governs her besides you has
"shifted the boundary" of his life [. . .] He has made you ruler over her, for
her to live the way you want her to, not adding any vows or offerings [. . .]
Turn her spirit to your will, and every binding oath, every vow [. . .] annul-
ling the utterance of your mouth, and forbidding the doing of your will
[. . .] your lips, forgive her, for your sake do not [. . .] your will [. . .] your
lips, forgive her, for your sake do not [. . .] your honor in your inheritance
[. . .] in your inheritance lest [. . .] the wife of your womb and shame [. . .]
(4Q418 Frag. 8–10)[55]

As we can easily see, throughout the book of *Instruction* occur allusions to
the fact that the husband rules over the wife. Furthermore, her origin is
found in man, an argument that also figures prominently in 1 Corinthians
11. None of this should surprise us since, as I noted in chapter 1, the ancient world is based on the one-sex model, which is meant to reinforce
gender hierarchy. As Loader points out, "[The book of *Instruction*] clearly
sees the man as the head of the partnership, typical of society at the
time."[56]

Controlling Women

The reason Jewish literature of this period suggests that the husband rules over his wife is that, like many Greco-Roman authors, Jewish authors thought women were deceitful, with no control over their passions. The *Testament of Reuben*, for example, notes that women lack self-control and are therefore dangerous: "Indeed, the angel of the Lord told me and instructed me that women are more easily overcome by the spirit of promiscuity than are men. They contrive in their hearts against men, then by decking themselves out they lead men's minds astray, by a look they implant their poison, and finally in the act itself they take them captive" (5:3–4). All women want is sex, and they can't control themselves. They're willing to do anything they can to fulfill their desires. Knowing that women are seductresses, a man should avoid them at all costs. One shouldn't even gaze at them so as not to be taken in by their beauty: "Do not devote your attention to a woman's looks, nor live with a woman who is already married, nor become involved in affairs with women" (3:10).

A perfect example of their sirenlike qualities is found in Tamar's seduction of Judah, which symbolizes women's ability to conquer even kings with their deceit: "And the angel of the Lord showed me that women have the mastery over both king and poor man: From the king they will take away his glory; from the virile man, his power; and from the poor man, even the slight support that he has in his poverty" (*Testament of Judah* 15:5–6). In fact, some Jewish literature of the Second Temple era goes so far as to blame women for the seduction of the Watchers in Genesis 6:

> For it was thus that they charmed the Watchers, who were before the Flood. As they continued looking at the women, they were filled with desire for them and perpetrated the act in their minds. Then they were transformed into human males, and while the women were cohabiting with their husbands they appeared to them. Since the women's minds were filled with lusts for these apparitions, they gave birth to giants. For the Watchers were disclosed to them as being as high as the heavens. (*Testament of Reuben* 5:6)[57]

Women's peccadillos lead the author of the *Testament of Reuben* to comment, "Women are evil, my children, and by reason of their lacking authority or power over man, they scheme treacherously how they might entice him to themselves by means of their looks" (5:1). A similar point is made by Ben Sira, who proclaims, "From a woman sin had its beginning, and because of her we all die," which is likely a reference to the biblical Eve (25:24). This sounds similar to Augustus telling the Roman Senate, "Women . . . if we could . . . we would live without them."

Because women spell danger, they must be controlled. Philo, for example, contends that women's minds are weak, which is why they're unable to control their passions. It's incumbent upon men to exercise control over them in order to guide them to a more rational existence and to order their households properly:

> For no one in the house of a wise man is ever slow to perform the duties of hospitality, but both women and men, and slaves and freemen, are most eager in the performance of all those duties towards strangers . . . For how could they ever have endured to enter a human habitation at all, unless they had been certain that all the inhabitants, within, like the well-managed and orderly crew of a ship, obeyed one signal only, namely, that of their master, as the sailors obey the command of the captain? (*On the Life of Abraham* 109, 116)

> But the other portion we may leave to the race that is never free, but which is of slavish disposition, of which class was the man who said, 'I have loved my Lord'; that is to say the mind which is the master in me; 'and my wife,' that is to say, the outward sense which is dear to him, and the housekeeper of his passions; 'and my children,' that is to say, the evils which are the offspring of them; 'I will not depart free.' (*Who Is the Heir?* 186)

A similar position is taken in the Wisdom of Jesus Ben Sira, a work written in Hebrew in the early second century B.C.E. by a teacher and sage. His grandson later translated the work into Greek. Ben Sira claims that since daughters are barely able to contain their sexual passions, they are likely to engage in inappropriate sexual behavior:

> A daughter keeps her father secretly wakeful,
> and worry over her robs him of sleep;
> when she is young, lest she do not marry,
> or if married, lest she be hated;
> while a virgin, lest she be defiled

or become pregnant in her father's house;
or having a husband, lest she prove unfaithful,
or, though married, lest she be barren.
Keep strict watch over a headstrong daughter,
lest she make you a laughingstock to your enemies,
a byword in the city and notorious among the people,
and put you to shame before the great multitude.
Do not look upon any one for beauty,
and do not sit in the midst of women;
for from garments comes the moth,
and from a woman comes woman's wickedness.
Better is the wickedness of a man than a woman who does good;
and it is a woman who brings shame and disgrace. (42:9–14)

At 26:10–12 he adds:

> Keep strict watch over a headstrong daughter,
> lest, when she finds liberty, she use it to her hurt.
> Be on guard against her impudent eye,
> and do not wonder if she sins against you.
> As a thirsty wayfarer opens his mouth
> and drinks from any water near him,
> so will she sit in front of every post
> and open her quiver to the arrow.

The Goodness of Sex and Marriage in the Eschaton

Interestingly, Ben Sira also celebrates the goodness of sexuality, using all sorts of sexual imagery for the feminine Wisdom. He says she lures the obedient into her secret chambers, where she invites them to sow and plow in her field (4:15, 6:19). And she commands them to hold her and not let her go (6:27). For all Ben Sira's warnings about the deceitfulness and folly of women, he affirms sexual attraction: "The beauty of a good wife in her well-kept home is like the noonday sun shining in the Lord's sky. Her beautiful face and attractive figure are as lovely as the light from the sacred lamp stand in the Temple, and like its gold shaft set on its silver base are her shapely legs and strong ankles" (26:13–18).

More erotic are the voyeuristic passages in the Song of Songs in which a young man gazes on the beauty of a woman: "My beloved is like a gazelle or a young stag. Behold, there he is behind the wall, gazing through the windows, looking through the lattice" (2:9; cf. Sir 24:16–22, 51:23–24). These images go back to the book of Proverbs, where feminine Wisdom, a figure who sets out to entice men into an intimate relationship with herself, is contrasted with the strange woman Folly, who is described as an adulteress and a prostitute (e.g., Prov 9:1–6). In later rabbinic Judaism, feminine Wisdom becomes the beloved Torah given to Moses at Mount Sinai.[58]

An exception to Procreationism that scholars sometimes cite is from 6 Ezra, a Jewish apocalyptic work written around 100 C.E.:

> Let him that sells be like one who will flee; let him that buys be like one who will lose; let him that does business be like one who will make a profit; and let him that builds a house be like one who will not live in it; let him that sows be like one who will not reap; so also him that prunes the vines, like one who will not gather the grapes; them that marry, like those who will have no children; and them that do not marry, like those that are widowed. (16:41–46)

Giorgio Agamben, for example, points out the numerous parallels between 6 Ezra and Paul in 1 Cor 7:29–32.[59] If 6 Ezra 16:41–46 were authentic, it would be one of the exceptional texts from the Second Temple era that promotes an ideology against Procreationism. It would also demonstrate that it wasn't just the Essenes who shunned marriage. But 6 Ezra 16 is one of four chapters that unknown Christian writers added to the book in the second half of the third century. Thus it reflects the attitudes of Christians of that time, not those of Second Temple Jews in the late first century.

Other writers proclaim that there will be no such thing as marriage in the future. Book 2 of the *Sibylline Oracles*, for example, declares that in the age to come there will be "no marriage, no death, no sales, no purchases" (2:238). In the *Testaments of the Twelve Patriarchs*, there exists not one single reference to a future with marriage, sexual relations, or procreation. The *Testament of Levi* says that God will open the gates of paradise; he will remove the sword that has threatened since Adam and will allow the saints to eat of the tree of life. The spirit of holiness shall be upon them (18:10–11). But there's no mention of marriage or sexual relations. Similarly, the *Testament of Dan* proclaims:

> And the saints shall refresh themselves in Eden; the righteous shall rejoice in the New Jerusalem, which shall be eternally for the glorification of God. And Jerusalem shall no longer undergo desolation, nor shall Israel be led into captivity, because the Lord will be in her midst [living among human beings]. The Holy One of Israel will rule over them in humility and poverty, and he who trusts in him shall reign in truth in the heavens. (5:12–13)

Once again, there's no mention of marriage or sex in the eschaton.

Conclusion

Overall, most of the texts of Second Temple Judaism declare marriage and sex to be a good and necessary thing; the command to propagate features regularly throughout the literature of the period (e.g., *1 En.* 67:13, 65:12; *2 En.* 42:11, 71:37; *Sib. Or.* 1:65; *Ps.-Phoc.* 176). As we've seen, some writers celebrate sexual desire, as long as that desire leads to procreation (Josephus, *Jewish Antiquities* 1.67). By and large, the strategies developed in Jewish literature of the Second Temple era privilege the home, marriage, and procreation. This shows just how widespread certain broader cultural patterns were in the ancient world. Like Augustus, the commitment of Second Temple Judaism, especially among the literature of the upper classes, is mostly to heteronormativity, which means that men dominate women. As Martin Goodman maintains, "the kind of Jews likely to pick up such Greek ideas were of course precisely, like Josephus, the ruling class whose status was in question."[60] The critique of modern heteronormativity by Charlotte Bunch applies equally, then, to Augustus and to some of the literature of Second Temple Judaism, which was written by upper-class men: "[Heteronormativity] assumes that every woman is heterosexual; that every woman is defined by and is the property of men. Her body, her services, her children belong to men. If you don't accept that definition, you're a queer—no matter who you sleep with; if you do not accept that definition in this society, you're a queer."[61] Later she adds, "The original imperialist assumption of the right of men to the bodies and services of women has been translated into a whole variety of forms of domination throughout this society. And as long as people accept that initial assumption—and question everything *but* that assumption—it is impossible to challenge the other forms of domination."[62]

Interestingly, there's very little on women, marriage, the family, or sexuality in the literature of Second Temple Judaism that would not please Augustus and fit nicely with his legislation and agenda, especially by those authors representing the upper classes. As Loader states, "[To procreate] was also the official Roman agenda set by Augustus, who required all men and women of fertile age to marry and bear children."[63] Much of the literature of the Second Temple era makes the same hegemonic cultural claims as the Augustan marriage legislation, except for the Essenes, who were not part of the ruling class.[64] Like Augustus's laws, much of this literature enforces the binary men/women, and as we saw with the Augustan legislation, it reduces women's bodies to the function of reproduction, except in very rare circumstances. In other words, the strategy created by the majority of the literature of Second Temple Judaism is largely one of control, which is often the case when women's sexuality is reduced to procreation.[65] Perhaps, then, Foucault was right when he surmised that no sexuality is free from its cultural constraints, nor is it free from the law. As Judith Butler reminds us, "Sexuality and power are coextensive, [which] implicitly refutes the postulation of a subversive or emancipatory sexuality which could be free of the law."[66]

But it would be unfair to ascribe to all of Second Temple Judaism the ideology of Procreationism. As I've already noted, the Essenes upheld asceticism over and against the dominant ideology of Procreationism. Furthermore, none of the extant literature tells us whether or not everyday Jews subscribed to the tenets of Procreationism. In fact, I wonder why so many modern Christians continue to misuse the term "Judeo-Christian" in a way that suggests that all Jews, ancient and modern, believe and practice Procreationism when they clearly do not.

As we join the world of early Christianity, things will slowly start to move in the direction of asceticism. Though Procreationism will still be with us in the form of New Testament texts that promote the household, something new will also arise. As we'll discover, many early Christian writers begin to emphasize a kind of antifamily ideology, which promotes singleness as an alternative to a procreative strategy. This doesn't mean, however, that early Christianity was any less hegemonic than Augustus or some of the literature of the Second Temple era.

CHAPTER THREE

NEW TESTAMENT

Conflicting Ideologies of the Family

The question posed by language analysis of some discursive fact or
other is always: according to what rules has a particular statement
been made, and consequently according to what rules could other
similar statements be made? The description of the events of discourse
poses a quite different question: how is it that one particular statement
appeared rather than another?

—*Michel Foucault*

Two ideologies concerning marriage and sex pervade the New Testament
writings. One ideology codifies a narrative that argues against marriage
and, perhaps, sexual intercourse, and the other retains the basic cultural
values of the upper classes of the Greco-Roman world. I call these two ideologies "profamily" and "antifamily." Though many scholars try to smooth
out the differences, these two ideologies compete with one another through
no fault of their own.[1] In other words, they compete with each other because they were, rightly or wrongly, given a place in the canon of Christian
scripture. What's of particular interest to me is that these two ideologies
created headaches for later Christians. In fact, I would argue that modern

Christianity still wrestles with the purpose and meaning of marriage and sex because of the competing family ideologies present in the New Testament. Additionally, many modern Christians on both the left and the right seem unwilling to acknowledge the impasse these two ideologies created. In other words, things aren't as consistent as we'd like them to be.

In this chapter, I examine key texts from the New Testament that represent both the profamily and antifamily ideologies. For the sake of clarity, I proceed in a somewhat chronological fashion based on when critical scholars believe certain texts were written.[2] I start with 1 Thessalonians, 1 Corinthians, and Mark, for example, because the vast majority of critical scholars maintain that these texts are earlier than Matthew, Luke, 1 and 2 Timothy, and Titus. I also proceed in this way because I want the reader to see, contrary to some scholarly thinking, that Christianity didn't start out as an egalitarian movement promoting sex, equality, and marriage only to devolve into a cesspool of misogyny by the end of the first century C.E.[3] In fact, as I demonstrate in the next chapter, Christians kept debating which of the two New Testament ideologies was "orthodox" up until the time of the Jovinian controversy in the fourth century.

One thing I don't do in this chapter is claim that Christianity is better than or superior to Judaism or the ideals of the Greco-Roman world, though I do believe Christianity "persists in pushing an increasingly supersessionist line."[4] Be that as it may, Christianity wouldn't have arrived at any of its conclusions without Second Temple Judaism or Greco-Roman thought. As I pointed out in the introduction, citing Michel Foucault, "The so-called Christian morality is nothing more than a piece of pagan ethics inserted into Christianity."[5] Additionally, I'm not at all interested in setting up Christianity as the liberator of Judaism.[6] Even though Christianity is my tradition, it's not my place to say whether or not it offers a more compelling answer to questions of sexuality and marriage than Judaism. In fact, I don't believe it's my place to offer answers to many of the questions I raise in this chapter. Instead, I offer analysis.[7]

Throughout this chapter, my goal is to explore the two competing ideological discourses found in the New Testament. Whether the New Testament writers meant to or not, the texts they wrote are our primary evidence, and ultimately, these texts created certain realities that Christians to this day still have to negotiate.[8] In my opinion, the aftereffects of the profamily and antifamily ideological strategies were likely unintended. In other words, I don't think Paul set out to create an entire theology of marriage when he penned 1 Corinthians 7, nor do I believe that he was consciously thinking of the Augustan marriage legislation when he downplayed the role of marriage and sex in a couple of his letters written to Greeks and Romans in the empire. Instead, what we're dealing with in these narratives are contingencies, which are, perhaps, more obvious to us than they were to their original authors. As M. M. Bakhtin reminds us, "Antiquity itself did not know the antiquity that we know now."[9] But as we'll see in chapters 4 and 5, "historical accidents" from two thousand years ago still affect us today.[10]

Paul's Antifamily Ideology

Paul, apostle to the gentiles, wrote the earliest instructions about sex and marriage in the New Testament around the year 50 C.E. In his letter to the Thessalonians, he tells his Greek audience that the Jewish God is the only "true and living God," Jesus is God's son, God is angry with the world because of idolatry, Jesus had been crucified and raised from the dead, and he will return soon to rescue those loyal to him from divine wrath (1 Thess 1:9–10). This is Paul's basic message and one example of what Christians preached to their neighbors in the Roman Empire.

Like many other Jews, Paul links sexual immorality and being gentile.[11] It's not surprising, then, that he spends time in his letters trying to correct gentile sexual ethics by attempting to bring them in line with Jewish sexual ethics.[12] A case in point is 1 Thess 4:1–8, a text that's addressed to men only.[13] Of particular importance are verses 3–7:

> For this is God's will, your sanctification; keep yourselves away from *porneia*. Each of you should know how to control his own vessel in holiness and honor, not in the passion of desire, like gentiles who do not know God. Let no one take advantage or cheat his brother in this matter, because the Lord is the avenger concerning all these things, just as we told you before and bore witness. For God did not call you to uncleanness, but in holiness.

Paul regularly warns his communities to avoid *porneia*. As we will see shortly, *porneia* plays a major role in Paul's correspondence with the

Corinthians.[14] Here, Paul isn't correcting any kind of sexual misbehavior but warning against it. Of course, it's virtually impossible to translate *porneia* into English. For most Greek speakers, it was simply the word they used for prostitution. The most common word for "prostitute," for example, was *pornē*, a "sex worker."[15] This is particularly common with Jewish writers, who used *porneia* for things like fornication, adultery, any form of oral sex, same-sex intercourse, allowing the woman to be "on top" or penetrating a man, or a man being penetrated in any way by either a man or a woman.[16] So it's very likely that Paul warns Greek men in the Thessalonian church to stay away from any kind of sexual impropriety.[17]

Another difficulty with this passage is the clause "Each of you should know how to control his own vessel in holiness and honor, not in the passion of desire, like gentiles who do not know God." The major problem here centers on the word "vessel" (*skeuos*). Since it's ambiguous, it could mean a man's wife or his sexual organs. Though I think it refers to a man's penis, the scholarship is evenly divided on the meaning of "vessel." So it seems best to allow the term's meaning to remain opaque.[18]

To understand what Paul is doing, we might ask what he means by (1) in holiness, (2) in honor, and (3) not in the passion of desire. Some help is gained by turning to 1 Pet 3:7, which encourages men to "give honor (*timē*) to their wives" as coinheritors of the gift of life "so that your prayers may not be hindered." Of course, there's no way to tell whether or not Paul has the same thing in mind as the author of 1 Peter.[19] What seems most plausible is to take Paul at his word and argue that verses 4–5 mean what they say. Dale Martin puts it best when he declares, "For Paul, even the experience of sexual desire and passion was something he expected from 'the gentiles' and that also he tried to preclude from Christian experience, even in the experience of sex itself."[20] Martin's idea is that Paul may have had the notion of a sexual inclination or urge that's not a full-blown desire. The former might then be acted on, but the latter should be avoided. In other words, Paul accepts sexual intercourse as long as desire (*epithumia*) isn't involved.[21] This means, then, that Paul doesn't have the most positive view of sex, though one could argue that Philo vies with Paul for title of "most negative."

Paul strengthens his lack of enthusiasm for sex with desire by omitting something modern readers of 1 Thessalonians and Paul's other writings often ignore. Nowhere does he state that the purpose of marriage is pro-creation, which would be expected of him as a good Jew. In fact, in all of his letters, he only twice identifies two parents and their children—Rufus and his mother (Rom 16:13) and the man sleeping with his "father's wife" (1 Cor 5:1–5). Children appear to be an afterthought with Paul, putting him at odds with the larger Greco-Roman world and its belief that women and men marry in order to procreate. One scholar is so mystified by Paul's lack of attention to procreation among married couples that he hypothesizes that two of Paul's fellow workers, Prisca and Aquila, must have had children even though there's no evidence for this (1 Cor 16:19, Rom 16:3–4).[22]

In what is our earliest text on sex and marriage in the New Testament, Paul's claims are predicated on his apocalyptic worldview.[23] At 1 Thess 4:13, Paul turns his attention to something that was troubling the Thessalonians: Some members of their community had died. Apparently, Paul didn't expect this to happen, since he seems to have thought he and many others would be alive when Jesus returned at the parousia (cf. 1 Cor 15:52).[24] The Thessalonians are asking a very practical question: "What will happen to the members of our community who have died before the return of Jesus?" In all honesty, it looks as if Paul forgot to mention the resurrection of the dead when he first preached to the Thessalonians. At 4:14–15, for example, he tells them: "For since we believe that Jesus died and rose again, even so, through Jesus, God will bring with him those who have died. For this we declare to you by the word of the Lord, that we who are alive, who are left until the coming of the Lord, will by no means precede those who have died." Additionally, Paul adds what we might call a "timetable of events," which he apparently forgot to mention earlier: "For the Lord himself, with a cry of command, with the archan-gel's call and with the sound of God's trumpet, will descend from heaven, and the dead in Christ will rise first. Then we who are alive, who are left, will be caught up in the clouds together with them to meet the Lord in the air; and so we will be with the Lord forever. Therefore encourage one another with these words" (4:16–18).

In the next section, Paul returns to a theme he has already taught the Thessalonians: the imminent parousia, or what Christians later call "the second coming." There is, as Paul says, nothing else to tell them (5:1).

What Paul does here is remind the Thessalonians that the "day of the Lord" will be soon and that they should not worry about those who have died because they'll be raised from the dead at the parousia. All the Thessalonians need to do is continue living holy, sober lives (5:5–8).[25]

At the start, then, the earliest text in the New Testament amalgamates sexual ethics with the sudden return of Jesus. Perhaps it's this suddenness that caused Paul to render a rather negative judgment of sex and marriage; perhaps the imminence of the parousia had nothing to do with Paul's evaluation of sex and marriage. It's impossible to tell. Whatever the case, Paul's strategy is so negative that it has no place for children within it, which many scholars fail to note. In fact, what's conspicuously absent from 1 Thessalonians is a statement such as "the purpose of marriage is procreation," which would have been the norm in Second Temple Judaism and the Roman Empire. Moreover, it's what the Thessalonians would have likely expected Paul to say since early Christianity adapted to the social world around it.[26] But he says nothing about procreation. Instead, he thinks that sex is permissible as long as it occurs without desire. And by extension, I would argue that he says nothing about children to the Thessalonians because he doesn't view procreation as the purpose of marriage.

It would be nice if Paul would clarify his thinking for us, but he tends to convolute it even more in the Corinthian correspondence written a few years after 1 Thessalonians. To be fair, scholars haven't helped the matter much, so it's not entirely Paul's fault. Some scholars are so baffled by what Paul says in 1 Corinthians 7 that they insist he must have had procreation in the back of his mind when he wrote this chapter, because it's unfathomable for a Jew like Paul to think of marriage and sex without thinking of procreation.[27] The problem is, Paul never mentions procreation anywhere in the Corinthian correspondence. But this hasn't stopped some scholars from reading 1 Corinthians 7 and declaring it the most important chapter in the New Testament for questions on marriage and procreation.[28] What Paul doesn't say about procreation and marriage, however, may be just as important as what he does say about these topics.

By far, 1 Corinthians 7 is the longest text in the New Testament covering the topics of sex and marriage. There are two things we need to keep in mind when analyzing it: (1) The passage ends up implicating Paul in all kinds of contradictions in his teaching on marriage, sex, divorce, and remarriage, and (2) apologizing for what Paul says is unnecessary.[29] What he says is what he says.

The passage starts out with what is now almost universally accepted as a quotation from a previous letter the Corinthians wrote to Paul that is now lost (7:1b).[30] The Corinthians ask Paul, "Is it right or not for a husband to have sex with his wife?" The only real debate concerns whether or not the quotation originated with the Corinthians or with Paul.[31] In my opinion, this debate is irrelevant because, as we'll see, Paul agrees with the sentiment that it is not good for a man to have sex with his wife.[32]

Paul proceeds, in verse 2, to state the purpose of marriage and the meaning of sex within marriage. Because of the temptation of *porneia,* "Each man should have sex with his own wife and each woman her own husband." As in 1 Thessalonians, Paul never suggests that the purpose of marriage is procreation. Furthermore, the only purpose he sees for sex within marriage is the prevention of *porneia.* As one scholar puts it: "Sex within marriage was not the expression of desire, proper or improper; rather it was the prophylaxis against desire."[33] Paul will return to this idea in verse 5, but before he does, he discusses the conjugal duties of wife and husband.

At 7:3–4, Paul declares that the husband and the wife do not own their own bodies. The wife's body belongs to her husband, just as the husband's body belongs to his wife. Additionally, each owes the other their conjugal rights. Many who have read Paul's advice interpret it as revealing his egalitarian views. In fact, verses 3–4 are often thought to espouse a unique doctrine of "mutuality" unprecedented in the ancient world in which wife and husband are equals.[34] Philip B. Payne, for example, writes:

> The strikingly egalitarian understanding of the dynamics of marital relations expressed in Paul's symmetry throughout this passage is without parallel in the literature of the ancient world. It is all the more impressive because it is focused on the marriage relationship, a relationship that traditionalists regard as intrinsically hierarchical based on the "created order." Against a cultural backdrop where men were viewed as possessing their wives, Paul states in 7:2, "let each woman have her own husband." Against a cultural backdrop where women were viewed as owing sexual duty to their husbands, Paul states in 7:3, "Let the husband fulfill his marital duty to his wife." It is hard to imagine how revolutionary it was for Paul to write

in 7:4, "the husband does not have authority over his own body, but his wife does."[35]

Actually, what Paul says here isn't that revolutionary, for, as I noted in chapter 1, there are parallels to be found in the ancient world, particularly in the writings of Musonius Rufus.[36] But just because Paul says what he says in verses 3–4 doesn't mean he's a proponent of equality. It also doesn't mean that he's a proponent of marriage in general. This is wishful thinking on the part of some modern scholars.

Throughout 1 Corinthians, numerous passages presuppose gender, cosmic, and material hierarchies. In 1 Corinthians 15, for example, Paul defends the specific doctrine of the resurrection of the body by demonstrating that the universe is constructed on a kind of cosmic hierarchy. There are different "fleshes" for humans, animals, birds, and fish (15:39). Here, Paul creates a hierarchy in descending order, which his audience easily would have recognized. Next, he changes his term from "flesh" to "body" because the next hierarchy is made up of cosmic entities: sun, moon, and stars, with even the stars having different levels of "glory" in their bodies (15:40–41). Again, these cosmic entities are listed in a descending order of importance, though most Greco-Roman writers would have put stars higher up on the list.

If scholars would look beyond chapter 7 to chapter 11, they would easily see that no matter what Paul says in 1 Corinthians 7, he still upholds the traditional Greco-Roman gender hierarchy in 1 Cor 11:2–16.[37] In verse 7, he clearly states that man is the "reflection" (*doxa*—which could mean "glory") of God and woman is the "reflection" (or "glory") of man. The language Paul uses here is hierarchical, which means that he doesn't think women and men are equal. In verse 8, he explains: "For man is not of woman, but woman of man." Furthermore, he adds, "And man was not created because of woman but woman because of man" (v. 9). Once again, to those in the ancient world this line of reasoning would imply hierarchy since only those in the lower classes are said to exist for the sake of others in the higher classes.[38]

Daniel Boyarin nicely summarizes Paul's theory of gender as found in 1 Cor 11:2–16.[39] As he points out, Paul isn't ashamed to say that (1) every man's head is Christ, but a woman's head is man (v. 3); (2) woman is the reflection of man . . . woman originates from man . . . woman was created for man, not man for woman (vv. 7–9); and (3) in the Lord there's neither woman without man nor man with woman . . . everything comes from God (vv. 11–12).⁴⁰ Again, there's no need to apologize for Paul. What he says is what he says.

Throughout the next several verses of 1 Corinthians 7, Paul is clear that he thinks remaining single (*agamos*) is better than getting married. Though he doesn't specifically command it, his wish is that the Corinthians be like him—presumably, "single" (vv. 6–7). But his wish is not merely a wish, considering that he reinforces it by telling the unmarried and the widows how good it is for them to remain single like him (v. 8). In fact, the only reason people should get married is if they lack self-control: "It is better to marry than to burn with passion (*parousthai*)" (v. 9).⁴¹ None of what Paul says here can be considered a ringing endorsement of marriage. His ideology is antifamily since he declares that marriage is for those who lack self-control (*enkrateia*) and for those tempted by *porneia*. Apparently, marriage is not about procreation, mutual care, or fulfilling a particular Roman law. Instead, it's about preventing sexual immorality.

In verses 10–15, Paul turns to the question of divorce. He goes back and forth in these verses about what his opinion is and what's a "charge from the Lord" (e.g., vv. 10–12). Interestingly, Paul tells us in verse 11 that if a wife separates from her husband, she should remain unmarried (*agamos*). Here he seems to be adding his own interpretation to what he thinks is a command from the Lord: "To the married I give this charge (not I, but the Lord): the wife should not separate from her husband (but if she does, she should remain unmarried or else become reconciled to her husband)." Later on, he'll tell those married to "unbelievers" that if their unbelieving spouses leave the marriage, let them leave (vv. 12–16).

What seems to be holding all of Paul's logic together is his basic principle that the Corinthians should "live the life assigned to them by the Lord" (vv. 17, 20).⁴² If a Corinthian is circumcised, he should remain so (v. 18). If, on the other hand, a Corinthian is uncircumcised, he shouldn't try to get circumcised (v. 19). For Paul, these things no longer matter: "For neither circumcision counts nor uncircumcision, but keeping the commandments of God." It seems that by implication Paul likely thinks, "If you're married, remain married; if you're single, remain single—but I would prefer it if all of you were like me," which is exactly what he says later on in verse 27: "Are you bound to a wife? Do not seek to be free. Are you free from a wife? Do not seek a wife."

As in 1 Thessalonians, Paul's apocalyptic mindset is partially responsible for what he says in 1 Corinthians 7. At 7:25, Paul turns his attention to the "betrothed" (*parthenōn*). He has nothing specific from the Lord to tell them, but he suggests that in light of the "present distress" (*enestōsan anagkēn*), the betrothed should not go ahead and get married. The "present distress" is very likely Paul's belief that the present world will end soon with the return of Jesus at the parousia.[43] At 7:31, Paul couldn't be any clearer: "For the present form of this world is passing away." As he has done throughout 1 Corinthians 7, he once again shows that he's not in favor of marriage: "From now on let those who have wives live as though they had none" (v. 29); however, he also softens his position somewhat by adding that those who marry "have not sinned" (v. 28).

The real problem Paul sees with marriage is that it leads to anxiety (*merimna*), which is something he wants to spare the Corinthians from experiencing (v. 32). That the married life causes anxiety is a common trope among Hellenistic philosophers, so Paul's critique of marriage is hardly original.[44] Essentially, the married person's loyalty is divided between spouse and God: "But the married man is anxious about worldly things, how to please his wife, and his interests are divided. And the unmarried or betrothed woman is anxious about the things of the Lord, how to be holy in body and spirit" (vv. 33–34). Once again, Paul's preference is clear: "He who marries does well; he who refrains does better" (paraphrasing v. 38).

As Paul closes out chapter 7, he implicates himself in a few inconsistencies. At 7:39–40, he returns to the topic of widows, which he previously addressed at 7:8–9. There he told the unmarried and widows to remain single and marry only if they couldn't control their passions. At 7:39–40, however, he seems to have no problem with widows remarrying as long as they marry another follower of Jesus: "A wife is bound to her husband as long as he lives. But if her husband dies, she is free to be married to whom she wishes only in the Lord." Perhaps realizing what he just said, he adds verse 40: "Yet in my judgment she is happier if she remains as she is." He closes 1 Corinthians 7 with the rather enigmatic, "And I think that I too have the Spirit of God."

Even though Paul's statements on marriage and sex are hardly organized in a systematic fashion, the ideology he creates in 1 Thessalonians and the Corinthian correspondence clearly indicates that he is antimarriage.[45] If anything, the authentic Paul's attitude toward marriage seems closer to that of Cynic philosophy than it does to anything in Judaism or Stoicism, for even the conservative Essenes knew that some members of their celibate sect would have to marry if the group were to survive.[46] But Paul seems convinced that procreation is irrelevant since Jesus will return soon.[47]

What's far from clear in 1 Thessalonians 4 and 1 Corinthians 7 is whether or not Paul meant to create a set of rules for early Christians to follow. I highly doubt that he thought he was producing holy writ that would last for generations, considering his certainty of an imminent parousia. Again, most of what he says is contingent; however, contingency often produces opposition to something, whether an author means for it to or not. In this case, Paul's advice created a strategy of power that challenged marriage itself.[48] This part of Paul's strategy is rarely appropriated in modern Christian debates about the family on the left or the right in modern American society, though, as we'll see, it was taken seriously by Paul's contemporaries, who either agreed with him or disagreed vigorously. This means, of course, that Paul does not—and did not for that matter—get to have the last word on the subject of marriage and sex in a Christian context.

Mark: Jesus, Marriage, and Divorce

About ten to fifteen years after Paul wrote to the Corinthians, someone composed a work that is now known to us as the Gospel of Mark.[49] Though no one knows who wrote this text, it, along with Paul's writings, constitutes our earliest witnesses to early Christian thinking.[50] Though Mark is a narrative centered on the theme of Jesus as the suffering Son of God (1:1), it contains an antifamily theme which maintains that family divisions and even marital separations occurred within the families of those who responded to Jesus's message.[51] We can easily see that this is the case in Jesus's teaching on divorce.

At Mark 10:2–12, Jesus makes what at first seems like a straightforward pronouncement on divorce:

And Pharisees came up and in order to test him asked, "Is it lawful for a man to divorce his wife?" He answered them, "What did Moses command you?" They said, "Moses allowed a man to write a certificate of divorce and to send her away." And Jesus said to them, "Because of your hardness of heart he wrote you this commandment. But from the beginning of creation, 'God made them male and female.' 'Therefore a man shall leave his father and mother and hold fast to his wife, and the two shall become one flesh. What therefore God has joined together, let no one separate.'" And in the house his disciples asked him about this matter. And he said to them, "Whoever divorces his wife and marries another commits adultery against her, and if she divorces her husband and marries another, she commits adultery.

Because this tradition occurs in Matthew, Luke, Q, and 1 Corinthians 7 with variations, it's virtually impossible to reconstruct what Jesus actually said.[52] Mark's text has an unqualified moral prohibition against divorce, which is likely as close as we'll ever get to what Jesus really taught. In fact, both Mark and Paul assume that either a wife or a husband has the legal right to initiate a divorce. In contrast, another early text, the hypothetical Q source, seems to assume the right is only the man's: "Everyone who divorces his wife, and marries another, commits adultery, and he who marries a divorcée commits adultery" (as in Luke 16:18).[53]

Even though the texts disagree, Mark sets Jesus's comments on divorce in the context of a dialogue with the Pharisees after the Pharisees question Jesus about divorce. The debate centers on how to interpret the Mosaic law, particularly Deut 24:1–4, which permits a husband to end his marriage by presenting his wife with a certificate of divorce.[54] Jesus supports his view with an allusion to Gen 2:24 at Mark 10:9: "Therefore what God has joined together let no one separate (*chōrizō*)."[55] In an aside to his disciples, Jesus categorically prohibits divorce and remarriage (Mark 10:10–12).[56] As Kathleen Corley maintains, "His comments . . . suggest that both men and women could initiate divorce proceedings, and thus be equally culpable of adultery."[57]

When Matthew's narrative takes over Mark's narrative, Matthew adds the famous "exception clause" for cases involving adultery or illicit sex (*porneia;* Matt 5:32, 19:9).[58] The author also complicates matters by adding an admittedly difficult-to-interpret saying about those who have "made themselves eunuchs for the sake of the kingdom of God" (Matt 19:12). The most likely interpretation of this saying is that the best way to avoid divorce and adultery is to avoid marriage and procreation altogether.[59]

The strategies created by Mark and Matthew reveal that divorce and separation were facts of life among Jesus's followers. But their strategies also show that early Christians found Jesus's teaching on marriage and divorce to be problematic and difficult. There was, in other words, no one definitive opinion on the subject, which, as we'll see, changes even more in the second and third centuries.

The Return of the Household

Mark, writing between 65 and 70 C.E., presents us with a Jesus who prohibits divorce and remarriage, while Matthew, writing between 85 and 90 C.E., presents us with a Jesus who disapproves of divorce, makes an exception in cases involving *porneia*, yet finds the overall remedy to divorce in remaining single. Both these discourses, in their own ways, uphold ideas already present in the antifamily ideologies encoded in 1 Thessalonians 4 and 1 Corinthians 7. But this is only one side of the story. Other writers in the New Testament create a different familial ideology that ultimately resists the claims of Paul and the authors of Mark and Matthew.[60]

Critical scholars maintain that Paul didn't write all the letters attributed to him in the New Testament.[61] They usually assume that Ephesians and Colossians were written by later disciples of Paul, while others have argued that the so-called Pastoral Epistles may have been written by individuals who opposed Paul.[62] Something rather intriguing occurs in both Ephesians and Colossians in what scholars call the *Haustafeln*, or "household codes." To understand the issues, it's easiest to look at the household code found at Eph 5:22–6:9.

A disciple of Paul likely wrote Ephesians several years after Paul's death; most scholars place it anywhere between 70 and 80 C.E. It was addressed to the "saints in Ephesus" (1:1), though the words "in Ephesus" aren't found in the earliest and best Greek manuscripts. Most scholars think the original letter was probably a "circular letter," meaning that it was sent to more than one place. The major theme of the letter is the unity and reconciliation of creation through the agency of the church and, in particular, its foundation in Christ as the will of the Father. At 4:1–3, for example, we read: "As a prisoner of the Lord, then, I urge you to live a life worthy of the calling you have received. Be completely humble and gentle; be patient, bearing with one another in love. Make every effort to keep the unity of the Spirit through the bond of peace." And at 5:1–2: "Therefore be imitators of God, as beloved children. And walk in love, as Christ loved us and gave himself up for us, a fragrant offering and sacrifice to God." From 4:17 to 6:20 the author of the letter offers practical advice on how to live a holy, pure, and Christ-inspired life.

The message of unity focuses on the organization of the household. This, of course, is nothing new since the household was the major focal point of life for Jews as well as Greeks and Romans.[63] Beginning at 5:22, the author of Ephesians organizes the household in a strikingly hierarchical fashion. Wives in the community must submit to their husbands (5:22).[64] A husband is the head of the wife even as Christ is the head of the church (5:23). As the church submits to Christ, wives should submit to their husbands (5:24). Of course, husbands must love their wives and give themselves up as Christ gave himself up for the church (5:25). Ultimately, husbands should love their wives as they love themselves (5:33).

As the household code continues, children, a subject never discussed in the authentic letters of Paul, suddenly appear. The author commands children to obey their parents: "'Honor your father and mother' (this is the first commandment with a promise), 'that it may go well with you and that you may live long in the land'" (6:1–3). The code also tells fathers not to "provoke their children to anger" but to raise them wisely with discipline and instruction (6:4).

Moreover, it addresses slaves. They must obey their "earthly masters with fear and trembling," because they are "slaves of Christ" (6:5–6). Masters should avoid threatening their slaves. The rationale here is simple: Christian slaves and Christian masters have another master in heaven. As the author of Ephesians puts it, "There is no partiality with him" (6:9). So something has changed in the relationship between slaves and masters because of their mutual relationship with Jesus.

When compared with other ancient household codes, the *Haustafel* in Ephesians is somewhat different. The classic example of an ancient

Haustafel, upon which the code in Ephesians is likely based, is the Aristotelean code.[65] Part of it reads:

> Now that it is clear what are the component parts of the state, we have first of all to discuss household management (*oikonomia*); for every state is composed of households (*ex oikiēn*). Household management falls into departments corresponding to the parts of which the household in its turn is composed; and the household in its perfect form consists of slaves and freemen. The investigation of everything begins with its smallest parts, and the primary and smallest parts of the household are master and slave, husband and wife, father and children; we ought therefore to examine the proper constitution and character of each of these three relationships, I mean that of mastership (*despotikē*), that of marriage (*gamikē*) . . ., and thirdly the progenitive relationship (*teknopoihtikē*) . . . There is also the department which some people consider the same as household management and others the most important part of it . . .: I mean what is called the art of getting wealth. (*Politics* I 1253b 1–14)

Like the code at Eph 5:22–6:9, the Aristotelean code addresses three pairs and focuses on the topic of submission. Three major differences exist between the code in Ephesians and that of Aristotle: (1) The concern for money, for household income, is absent in Ephesians. (2) Aristotle mentions masters, husbands, and fathers before slaves, wives, and children. Moreover, he addresses only the male—the master, husband, and father. The code in Ephesians addresses wives before husbands, children before parents, and slaves before their masters. And (3) there's no discussion in Ephesians about the city, which features prominently in Aristotle's writings. This is because early Christians were concerned with the house, not the city.[66]

If we compare Eph 5:22–6:9 with 1 Thess 4:1–8 and 1 Corinthians 7, it's clear that something has changed, especially for the followers of Paul who were still alive a decade or two after his death. What's noticeably different is that the author of Ephesians no longer explicitly views marriage as a prophylaxis against *porneia*. Furthermore, there's a blanket assumption in Ephesians that Christian households now include children. Finally, the emphasis Paul once placed on the imminence of the parousia has disappeared.[67] The question for us is, "What happened in those ten to twenty years after Paul's death that caused his followers to rethink his antifamily message?"

Robert Grant, in an analysis of 1 Corinthians 7, suggests that Paul and the Corinthians were well aware of the Augustan marriage legislation, given the obvious romanization of Corinth. He declares that the Augustan laws were of prime importance for Paul, noting that Roman imperial policy agreed with Paul's attempts to regulate sex among Christians at Corinth.[68] There's also a variation of this argument that runs like this: Paul's advice in 1 Corinthians 7 is a direct assault on the values promoted by the Augustan marriage legislation.[69] I would agree that what Paul says in 1 Thessalonians 4 and 1 Corinthians 7 is the exact opposite of what appears in Augustus's marriage legislation. The problem with these kinds of analyses, however, is that they assume that Roman family law was well known outside the city of Rome.[70] On the contrary, the evidence suggests that it wasn't well known at all.

I seriously doubt that the Corinthian Christians knew anything about the Augustan marriage legislation.[71] What they did know, though, were basic societal structures that they took for granted every day, such as the hierarchical nature of the ancient household. It's easy to imagine that local societal pressures forced Christians to start rethinking the antifamily ideology that Paul created. Was this political? I doubt it. Was it calculated? I don't think so. Instead, in light of the fact that Jesus hadn't returned as expected, followers of Paul realized that they had to survive. Survival meant no longer thinking of marriage as a defense against desire. Instead, marriage for Pauline Christians became what it had always been about—procreation. Moreover, survival meant a kind of conformity, which is a normal pattern for fledgling groups that begin to grow in number and influence.[72]

The results of these survival strategies are of grave importance. In fact, later followers of Paul created a second, competing narrative—a second, competing ideology—with the one found in 1 Thessalonians 4 and 1 Corinthians 7. The author of Ephesians, writing later and also in Paul's name, extended the male, patriarchal ideology of the Greco-Roman household to the Christian household. As one scholar notes, this is rather insidious, since the author conflates "the superior male's role with that of God and Christ in relation to the church."[73] The role of the husband significantly expands to the point that there's an amalgamation between the husband's authority and Christ's authority. But an even more explicit and pronounced version of this strategy comes from the Pastoral Epistles.[74]

Three letters make up the Pastoral Epistles: 1 Timothy, 2 Timothy, and Titus. As Francine Cardman notes, "The Pastoral Epistles model the churches' ministries on the patriarchal order of the Roman household, expanding the household codes of Ephesians and Colossians and applying them to the 'household of God' (1 Tim 3:15)."[75] Traditionally, these letters were ascribed to Paul, but modern scholarship is overwhelmingly convinced that Paul didn't write any of them even though they bear his name.[76] In fact, some recent scholarship suggests that even though these letters were written in Paul's name, their main purpose was to refute certain things Paul said in his authentic writings.[77]

The author of the Pastoral Epistles, written in the first half of the second century, writes to early Christians in order to encourage hierarchical family structures within the ancient church and to encourage bishops and deacons to have only one wife (1 Tim 3:2–12). Much of what we find in these letters looks strikingly compatible with Augustus's marriage legislation, though, once again, we shouldn't assume that these laws were known outside the city of Rome. Be that as it may, Augustus, if he had still been alive, would have preferred the profamily ideology of the Pastoral Epistles over the antifamily ideology found in 1 Thessalonians 4 and 1 Corinthians 7.

Early in 1 Timothy, the readers and hearers of this letter are instructed to pray for "emperors and all in authority" (2:2). Though this may echo Paul's authentic comments in Rom 13:1–7, other parts of 1 Timothy seem at odds with the apostle to the gentiles. At 2:11, for example, women are told that they may not pray or speak. Instead, they must learn "in silence and submission." The author's rationale for this remark is that women are gullible creatures, just like the biblical Eve. Additionally, their main function is to produce children—not for the state, but for the church. In fact, the author makes a rather strange remark in which he insists that women can be saved through the act of bearing a child (2:15).[78]

The church is also turned into a patriarchal household (3:5, 15). This will have a huge effect on single women since women without husbands are problematic because they don't fit into the typical structures of a Greco-Roman house. To remedy this situation, the author encourages young women to get married, while simultaneously encouraging older widows to find various roles in the church under the authority of its male leaders rather than getting remarried (5:3–16).[79] They cannot, in other words, be allowed to be independent of or outside patriarchal authority. Slaves find similar treatment in these letters; they, too, are told not to expect much from Christianity for their servitude (6:1–2).

One scholar deems the Pastoral Epistles to be the "familial hijacking of the apostle Paul."[80] The Pastorals change Paul's antifamily ideology found in 1 Thessalonians 4 and 1 Corinthians 7 so that it supports traditional Roman values by making it profamily. Again, there's no way of knowing whether or not the Augustan marriage laws were familiar to anyone who wrote, read, or heard the Pastoral Epistles, but the instructions in these letters support the ideological values of those laws. Marriage, for example, is now central to being a Christian; the purpose of marriage is procreation. Augustus would have approved.

It didn't take long, however, until other Christians challenged the profamily ideology of the Pastorals, attempting a return to Paul's antifamily ideology. As I noted in the introduction, power and resistance often go hand in hand: "Power is a relation between forces, or rather every relation between forces is a power relation . . . Force is never singular but essentially exists in relation with other forces, such that any force is already a relation, that is to say power."[81] This seems to be precisely the pattern Christianity is following in the first and second centuries: There's power, the antifamily ideology, followed by resistance, the profamily ideology, followed by more resistance, and a return to the antifamily ideology. As Cardman explains, "Between the time of the Pastorals and the end of the second century, the rapidly evolving Christian movement began to develop a more complex infrastructure to meet the needs of expression and to establish authoritative teachers."[82]

A major challenge to the Pastorals comes from a noncanonical text written around the same time known as the *Acts of Paul and Thecla*. The plot of this narrative is straightforward and simple. The heroine, Thecla, an upper-class woman, finds herself enamored of the ascetic message of the apostle Paul. He urges young men and women to keep themselves virgins, to avoid sex entirely, to reject marriage, and to devote themselves to celibacy (7). What's at stake here isn't marriage per se but "the virgin life," or "sexual renunciation."

In the *Acts of Paul and Thecla*, a revivified Paul also claims that the only way people can experience the resurrection is if they remain virgins and celibate. Not surprisingly, such a message didn't sit well with Thecla's maternally approved fiancé, Thamyris. When Thamyris discovers that Thecla broke off their engagement because of her newfound commitment to Paul's message of celibacy, he becomes enraged:

> Thamyris rose up early in the morning full of jealousy and wrath and went to the house of Onesiphorus with the rulers and officers and a great crowd with cudgels, and said to Paul: "You have destroyed the city of the Iconians, and my betrothed, so that she will not have me. Let us go to the governor Castellius!" The whole crowd shouted: "Away with the sorcerer! For he has corrupted all our wives." And the multitude let themselves be persuaded. (15)

Because of Thecla, Paul finds himself in familiar territory—jail. Thecla, love-struck, visits him, and the narrative takes on erotic tones similar to those found in Greek novels such as *Leucippe and Clitophon*.

When Thecla's family and Thamyris discover her alone with Paul in his cell, the situation escalates into a full-scale public confrontation. Obviously, they assume the worst: Paul and Thecla are having an affair. Again, they bring the two before the governor, who questions Thecla: "Why won't you marry Thamyris according to the law of the Iconians?" Thecla stands looking steadily at Paul (20). After a few moments of intense silence, her mother, Theocleia, cries out: "Burn the lawless one! Burn her that is no bride in the midst of the theater, that all the women who have been taught by this man may be afraid!"

A cycle of martyrdom and miracle ensues.[83] God intervenes and saves Thecla. Like a devoted lover, she follows Paul into exile. Eventually, the two arrive at Antioch where another man falls madly in love with her. Going before the governor once more, she's condemned, this time to the beasts. But once again, God saves her. Next, she follows Paul to Myra, where she converts the proconsul himself.

Throughout, the clear enemy is the household. As Kate Copper writes, "The challenge by the apostle to the householder is the urgent message of these narratives, and it is essentially a conflict *between men*" (italics in the original).[84] In fact, conflict pits male heads of households against all other potential members of households—women, girls, and young men—on the other side with Thecla. The men understand what's at stake: They themselves insist that if Christianity and Thecla succeed, it means the destruction of their households.[85]

The story concludes with a triumphant Thecla. She baptizes herself in a huge vat of killer seals, she promises to cut her hair like a man's, and she dresses herself like a man. For her faithfulness, a rich widow rewards her so she and her mother can become independent and self-sustaining. In other words, Thecla will no longer need to depend on a man for financial support. Like Virginia Woolf, she finally has a room of her own. Freed from family and household, she leaves Paul in order to become an apostle just like him. She spreads the Christian message of the ancient household's demise and establishes alternative communities of Christian ascetics. In later Christian tradition, she is remembered as a saint.

Scholars of early Christianity interpret the story of Thecla as a tale about a young woman using chastity as a form of power: "Thecla resists the social and political powers of her day and overcomes Paul's objections to her ministry."[86] Her story casts light on the ambiguities of women's authority in second-century churches. In other words, the *Acts of Paul and Thecla* is powerful ideology meant to subvert another powerful ideology. Its original intention might have been to subvert the power of the state, but second-century Christian women probably read it as a subversion of male hierarchical authority in the church. Whatever way we choose to read it, it's clearly antifamily ideology in the spirit of the authentic Paul.

We'll never know whether texts like Ephesians and 1 Timothy purposely set out to counter things Paul wrote to the Thessalonians or the Corinthians. Likewise, we'll never know whether the antifamily statements in Mark and Matthew were purposely written to counter the profamily statements of other Christian writers. Through the act of canonization, however, two competing strategies now exist side by side in the New Testament. One of these strategies, which represents the authentic Paul as well as Mark and Matthew, is antifamily, antimarriage, antihousehold, and antiprocreation. The other strategy, which represents the Pastoral Epistles, is the exact opposite. What's of particular interest, since any history of the past is also a history of the present, is that many modern Christians in the United States appropriate only the later strategy in their discussions of marriage and the family. As we'll see in the next chapter, many Christians, generations after the New Testament writers, were largely in favor of the first strategy, preferring asceticism to marriage. What this means is that early Christianity had nothing of the modern idolatry of the family and patriotism. As Martin correctly observes, the dominant ideology of early Christianity "is certainly no form of nationalism—unless it is the nationalism of the kingdom of God. Indeed, in this kind of Christianity, people have put all their eggs (literally, we may think, if we are thinking ovaries) in one basket: the kingdom of God."[87]

CHAPTER FOUR

EARLY CHURCH

The Battle Begins

> Copulation and mirrors are abominable. The text of the encyclopedia
> said: For one of those gnostics, the visible universe was an illusion or
> (more precisely) a sophism. Mirrors and fatherhood are abominable
> because they multiply and disseminate that universe.
> —*Jorge Luis Borges*, Labyrinths

As the first century passes into the second, things change. Second- and
third-generation Christians take over the household codes of Ephesians
and Colossians, which serve the needs of the family.[1] Suddenly, Christians
find themselves concerned with the functioning of economic and social
efforts. Unless married Christians and other members of the Christian
house live in harmony, all is lost. As Susanne Heine notes, Christians
begin to adapt to the social reality in which they find themselves.[2] We see
this assimilation to the broader culture at 1 Tim 2:2, where someone writing in Paul's name admonishes Christians to pray for rulers in order that
the rulers may lead peaceful, quiet lives that are "godly and dignified in
every way." Much more blunt is 1 Pet 2:17: "Honor everyone. Love the
brotherhood. Fear God. Honor the emperor." Within twenty-five to fifty

years, the ethics of second- and third-generation Christians begin to appear much more compatible with the tenets of the Augustan marriage laws.[3] For the sake of survival, early Christians redefine their family ideologies as they socialize themselves into the world of the Roman Empire.

Yet second- and third-generation Christians wrestle with familial ideologies, until sexual renunciation becomes the norm by 300 C.E.[4] Christian males of this period partake in the deeply ingrained social practice of all men in the ancient world, using women, to borrow a phrase from Claude Lévi-Strauss, "to think with," as they try to work out the seeming contradictions created by Paul, the writers of the gospels, and other writers of the New Testament.[5] Since the church fathers think scripture contains paradoxes but not contradictions, they try to harmonize the diversity that confronts them instead of pointing out the contradictory voices, as would modern critical scholars.[6] The task is not an easy one, since scripture forces the fathers to reckon with a wide variety of competing narratives and ideologies. Ultimately, the Bible compels them to create newer discourses and strategies based on the previous ones. The circle is unending, and some of their decisions remain with us to this day.

This chapter examines the development of the antifamily and profamily strategies found in the New Testament. Here I limit myself to an analysis of Tatian and his "encratite" argument, Clement's emerging ecclesiastical sexual ethics, and Epiphanes's so-called libertine Christianity, which regards Platonic and early Stoic sexual principles as the right models for a Christian way of life. Next, I demonstrate how all of these ideas coalesce in the writings of John Cassian, who, according to Michel Foucault, is the quintessence of late antique sexual morality.[7] These texts reveal that throughout Christianity's beginnings, the two ideological strategies created by the New Testament writers compete with each other until the monastic movement declared the celibate life to be the norm over and against Jovinian and his followers, who viewed the married life as equal to the ascetic one.[8] This means, of course, that when the fathers of the patristic period and late antiquity confront the value of marriage and childbearing in the Jewish scriptures, they insist on a radical difference between Jewish and Christian sexual ethics. As I contend, they place sexuality on par with Hebrew ritual practices, forcing some Christians to argue that many Jewish rituals were now sub-Christian with the coming of Christ. In other words, the fathers wouldn't understand our modern term "Judeo-Christian," which is often used to describe the "biblical" heritage of the United States.

Tatian: Marriage Is Porneia

Some time between the years 155 and 160, Tatian the Assyrian met Justin Martyr in Rome.[9] Most scholars agree that Tatian converted to Christianity between 150 and 155, prior to his first meeting with Justin. Before this pivotal encounter, Tatian spent about a decade among the Greeks in search of "the truth." After Justin's death, Tatian remained in Rome and established his own school, where Rhodon became one of his most famous pupils.

Because of Tatian's heterodox Christology and extremist views on marriage and celibacy, the Roman church expelled him around the year 172.[10] As W. H. C. Frend remarks, Tatian was an "uncompromising rebel."[11] After a few years of trying to find a captive audience, Tatian returned to the East around 175 or 177. There he set up another school where he taught his own brand of Christianity until he died at sixty-five or seventy years of age. At the time of his death, he had already left an indelible mark on the growing Christian movement.

Centuries later, Michael the Syrian, patriarch of Antioch from 1166 until his death in 1199, crafted the following sketch of Tatian:

> [Tatian] became inclined to the blasphemy of the followers of Saturnilos [*sic*] and Marcion . . . like the followers of Valentinos. He acts stupidly and spoke of invisible aeons, and he called legitimate marriage adultery. And he collected and mixed a gospel and he called it Diatessaron . . . And from him the heresy of the Encratites sprang up. And there were tracts in which he was showing that Christ was from the seed of David. (*Chronicle* 6.5)[12]

For my purposes, it's Michael the Syrian's charge of Encratism that's most important.[13] *Enkrateia* means "restraint, abstention, or self-control."[14] Broadly speaking, encratites were early Christians who rejected sexual intercourse, meat, and wine.[15] But, as William Petersen points out, "Encratism is a poorly-defined movement with no clear boundaries."[16] Whether or not Tatian was the father of Encratism is debatable, but a profound distaste for marriage and procreation permeates his extant writings.[17]

In one of those writings, *Address to the Greeks,* we discover an apology with three aims: First, Tatian asks the rulers of the Roman Empire to tolerate Christians; second, he defends Christianity by castigating everything Greek; and third, he establishes the superiority of Christianity to Greek culture by "proving" that Moses is older than Plato. While doing all of these things, he also provides an astringent critique of procreation and marriage. As he says: "I have no desire to rule, I do not wish to be rich; I do not seek command, I hate *porneia* (*porneian memisēka*), I am not driven by greed to go on voyages . . . I do not boast of my good birth" (11.1).[18] Furthermore, he insists that unlike Sappho, whom he calls a "lewd, love-sick female," all Christian women are "chaste, and the maidens at their distaffs sing of divine things more nobly than that damsel of yours" (33).[19]

In the *Fragments,* Tatian pronounces "all sexual intercourse impure" (3). As he says, "If any one sows to the flesh, of the flesh he shall reap corruption; but he sows to the flesh who is joined to a woman; therefore he who takes a wife and sows in the flesh, of the flesh he shall reap corruption" (3). Additionally, he deems marriage "a defilement," echoing the sentiments of Marcion and Saturninus (4).[20]

Irenaeus, the bishop of Lyons (130–202 C.E.), condemns Tatian and charges him with Encratism:

> . . . the ones called Encratites, issuing from Saturninus and Marcion, preached abstinence from marriage . . . and they have introduced [dietary] abstinence from what they call "living things" . . . They likewise deny the salvation of him who was the first formed [Adam]. But this last idea was recently invented among them, when a certain Tatian first introduced this blasphemy. He was an *auditor* of Justin . . . and exalted at the prospect of being a teacher, and puffed up as if he were superior to everyone else, he created a unique doctrine. Like those who follow Valentinus, he expounded an account of invisible Aeons; and like Marcion and Saturninus, he said marriage was corruption and fornication. But denying the salvation of Adam was his own doing. (*Against Heresies* 1.28.1)[21]

For Irenaeus, Tatian's rejection of marriage presents a problem since it brought an accusation against the God of Gen 1:27–28, who, in Irenaeus's view, favored procreation (1.28.1). As Kathy L. Gaca asserts: "Pragmatically speaking . . . it makes good sense for God to issue a procreative mandate. If he were not accorded the power to regenerate his people and yet required their exclusive devotion, he would likely be short-lived and impotent in his religious influence, a lonely eunuch in the kingdom of God."[22] But for Tatian, sexuality is a false ideology, a "false consciousness," from which God is entirely removed.[23]

It may well be that Tatian understands Paul and his antifamily ideology better than some church fathers upon whom we bequeath the modern epithet "orthodox." In his reading of 1 Corinthians 7, for example, Tatian points out that for Paul, no sexual activity is safe to practice. In a fragment from *On Perfection According to the Savior,* Tatian insists that marriage (*gamos*) is *porneia* and that Paul links sexual activity to uncontrolled, Satanic fornication (fr. 5). In other words, sex enslaves one to the devil: "Paul permits them [Christian marital sexual relations] in so disapproving a manner that he in effect prevents the practice. By agreeing that [the couples] after their prayers may come together in the union of sexual corruption because of Satan and their lack of self-control (*akrasia*), Paul has revealed that the one who would follow this advice is enslaved . . . to a state of being uncontrolled (*akrasia*), to sexual immorality (*porneia*), and to the devil."[24] The only solution is to renounce any and all sexual activity.[25]

Of course, Encratism isn't exclusive to Tatian and his followers. As we've already seen, certain Jewish groups, such as the Essenes, shunned marriage, and the Torah permits the taking of a Nazarite vow, which entails eschewing wine and strong drink, along with any contact with corpses and cutting one's hair. In fact, if John the Baptist had lived into the second and third centuries, he too might have been charged with "Encratism" since his clothing, diet, and withdrawn life in the wilderness indicate an ascetic lifestyle (Matt 3:1–6).[26] Furthermore, the book of Acts demonstrates that Christianity from the very beginning had certain ascetic—and, for that matter, encratitic—tendencies. We see this in the communistic lifestyle depicted in Acts for the Jerusalem church (2:44–45; 4:32, 34–37; 5:1–11). We also see it in a request by a young Christian in Alexandria to the Roman governor there, Felix, that he be permitted to castrate himself to emulate Jesus's words at Matt 19:12 (Justin, *First Apology* 19.2–3).[27] It may well be, then, that Tatian understands the New Testament's antifamily ideology better than Irenaeus. Indeed, one scholar suggests that Tatian is simply a victim of time and place. Had he lived in the fourth or fifth century, he probably wouldn't be known as a heretic for his views on marriage. Instead, he might have been deemed a saint.[28] Frend also reminds us that Tatian had been attracted to Christianity because it was a "protest religion."[29] For him, Christianity was "an effective counter to the emptiness, pride, and injustice of the Greco-Roman world as he [Tatian] had experienced it."[30] Not surprisingly, as Christianity became more and more like Roman imperial culture, Tatian found himself unimpressed with a religion "that was prepared even on its own terms to live with the world."[31]

Clement: Normalizing Ecclesiastical Sexual Ethics

In the late second century, Clement settled in the city of Alexandria to cultivate a friendship with and to benefit from the instruction of the Christian Stoic Pantaenus.[32] Pantaenus was in charge of a catechetical school in Alexandria, and when he died at the close of the century, Clement became head of the school, continuing the policies and methods practiced by his master. One of Clement's most famous works is titled the *Paidagōgos*, a term difficult to translate into English. It is usually rendered as *Christ the Educator*, but *paidagōgos* can mean anything from "leader of children" to a "slave who conducted the children of the household back and forth from school, and later, the slave, usually an educated one, who supervised their training and the formation of their characters."[33]

The *Paidagōgos* makes up part of a trilogy, which begins with the *Protreptikos*, commonly called *An Exhortation to the Greeks*, and is followed by the *Paidagōgos* and the *Strōmateis*, known as the *Miscellanies*. All three books are a comment on the same subject: "Therefore, the all-loving Word, anxious to perfect us in a way that leads progressively to salvation, makes effective use of an order well adapted to our development; at first, He persuades, then He educates, and after all this He teaches" (*Paidagōgos* 1.1.3). Not surprisingly, part of a Christian's education includes instruction in marriage.[34]

Book Two of the *Paidagōgos* contains an entire chapter devoted to the subjects of wedlock and sexual intercourse. "It remains for us now to consider the restriction of sexual intercourse to those who are joined in wedlock" (2.10.83). Pointing to Gen 1:28, Clement argues that it is the duty of all Christians to be fruitful and multiply.[35] This means that the goal of married couples is procreation. John Boswell calls this position the "Alexandrian Rule," which means that "to have sexual intercourse for any purpose other than generating children is to violate nature."[36] The best way to fulfill that goal is by having a large family, "just as a hope of a crop drives the farmer to sow his seed, while the fulfillment of his hope is the actual harvesting of the crop" (2.10.83).[37] Simultaneously, Clement also places limits on sexual intercourse.[38]

Reinterpreting Deut 14:7, "Do not eat the hare nor the hyena," Clement suggests that God "does not want man to be contaminated by their traits nor even to taste of their wantonness, for these animals have an insatiable appetite for coition (2.10.83)."[39] Moreover, he maintains that the prohibition against eating the hare is "nothing else than a condemnation of pederasty" (2.10.83). Later on he declares, "the mysterious prohibition [of Moses] in reality is but counsel to restrain violent sexual impulses, and intercourse in too frequent succession," which include relations with a pregnant woman, pederasty, adultery, and lewdness (2.10.88). As David G. Hunter notes, "In Clement's own lexicon of desire . . . the term *epithumia* became irrevocably associated with the unrestrained use of sex advocated by the libertines, and *enkrateia* was proposed as the orthodox Christian alternative."[40] In other words, *enkrateia* (self-control) is Clement's ideological antidote to out-of-control sexual desire.

Echoing Paul in 1 Corinthians 7, Clement also argues for sex without passion.[41] He calls sexual pleasure a "disoriented way" and notes that pleasure sought for its own sake—even within the bonds of marriage— "is a sin and contrary both to law and to reason" (2.10.89). This kind of thinking leads Clement to ask whether a Christian should marry at all. Additionally, it forces him to decide whether he thinks sexual intercourse is a good or bad thing.

The mere fact that Clement has to ask whether or not a Christian should get married leads him to conclude, "Now if we have to consider whether we may marry at all, then how can we possibly permit ourselves to indulge in intercourse each time without restraint, as we would food, as if it were a necessity?" (2.10.94). He believes that coitus takes away a person's strength, and he quotes with approval the sophist Abdera, who calls sexual intercourse, "a minor epilepsy," declaring it an incurable disease.

Even though Clement depends on Paul and the Hebrew prophets to provide the framework for his marital ideology, "he imposes a far more restrictive sexual decorum than they do for God's woman to stand by her man."[42] Wives, for example, must never take the initiative in the sexual act. During that act, she belongs under the man, since she is subordinate to him (3.94.5). And a husband must never ejaculate in a part of his wife's body other than her vagina, and then only for procreation.[43] This means, of course, that Clement forbids all forms of oral and anal sex acts. In fact, he even links excessive sexual desire within marriage to adultery.[44] Christians suffer "prostitute passion" (*hetairikon pathos*) if they make love for any reason other than marital reproduction: "Sexual pleasure is a prostitute passion because it represents the whore incarnate and her son, Aphrodite and Eros" (2.98.3).[45]

Book Three of Clement's *Miscellanies* is another important work that covers marriage and sex. A major theme of *Miscellanies* is self-discipline (*sōphrosynē*), a topic also relevant to the Greco-Roman moral philosophers.[46] For Clement, "Self-discipline means disdain of the body, following obedience to God." It applies not just to sexual matters, "but to everything else for which the soul lusts improperly, because it is not satisfied with the bare necessities" (3.1.4). This leads Clement to assert that Christians who are able to abstain from sexual intercourse should be admired and blessed by the Christian community because they are exemplary Christians. Additionally, he notes that monogamy should be praised. Those Christians who marry only once should be respected, echoing the Roman praise of the *univira* (3.80.3). A Christian may marry a second time, but only if the first spouse has died. Clement condones no more than one remarriage, no matter the circumstances (3.82.4–5).[47]

Many scholars conclude that Clement develops a "middle ground" in his sexual ethics.[48] But this is hardly the case. Instead, he creates something new. As Gaca puts it: "Clement develops his innovative and influential piecework of Christian sexual rules from Greek philosophical and biblical sources, including the Pythagoreans, Plato, several later Stoics, Philo, the Septuagint Pentateuch and Prophets, Paul, and a few passages from Matthew and John."[49] His pastiche offers two choices to unmarried Christians: (1) They remain single and presumably chaste, and (2) if they're going to be sexually active, they must marry other Christians and engage in sex only for procreation. Sex with *epithumia* is out of the question.

Clement's new family ideology is a paradigm shift, marking "the change in Christian sexual morality from the early views we see in Paul and Matthew to the ecclesiastical views of the developing church."[50] Essentially, he provides the foundation for ecclesiastical sexual ethics, which will become the *new* standard among the church fathers until the rise of the monastic movement: Have sex only for reproduction and not for adultery or pleasure. But any honest reading of Clement reveals that he is closer to Tatian than often supposed.[51]

For Clement, God rescues Christians from the need to fully renounce the sex act. Jesus came into the world to save humanity from pleasures and desires (3.44.4, 3.94.3). In place of uncontrolled sexual desire, God grants Christians a higher level of "natural impulses" (*hai tēs phuseōs orexeis*) for procreation (3.82.1). As a consequence, Christians desire only that which is sexually "appropriate," namely, legitimate Christian children. They reject, then, any sexual activity that is "harmful" (3.69.2). Gaca refers to this as "prophylactic grace," which may very well be a good title for Clement's familial ideology. But prophylactic grace also means that Clement is hostile toward sex in general, especially when the deed is done for pleasure. John Ferguson, for example, maintains that "Clement's ideal is not to feel sexual desire, and to let sexual union be determined wholly by will."[52] John Oulton and Henry Chadwick claim that Clement's ideal is for the Christian "not to feel anything at all" during sex.[53] Though it's true that Clement does not believe Tatian's claim that all sexual intercourse is in thrall to "fornication and the devil" (3.82.1), he grants absolution from sexual desire only to married Christian procreationists. His position, then, is far from the modern "Judeo-Christian" ideal of sex being for both pleasure and procreation.

Epiphanes: Liberated Sexual Ethics

A completely opposite view, one of sexual freedom and liberation, is found in Epiphanes's *On Justice*, which is preserved piecemeal in Clement's *Miscellanies*. According to Clement, Epiphanes was born in the late first or early second century and died around the age of seventeen

(3.5.1–3). Irenaeus associates Epiphanes with the Carpocratians, but this claim is questionable (*Against Heresies* 1.25).[54]

Epiphanes upholds Plato's proposals in *Republic* 5 and early Stoic political theory, both of which call for a radical, communitarian sexual model of society.[55] As Clement notes, "The followers of Carpocrates and Epiphanes think that wives should be common property" (*Miscellanies* 3.5.1). Additionally, Epiphanes promotes other communist principles such as the sharing of property. Of this, Clement relates, "The righteousness of God is a kind of universal fairness and equality" (3.6.1). Though a community of wives and common property may seem odd to modern Christians who have been socialized into thinking that marriage is between one man and one woman and private property is a virtue, Epiphanes builds his ideological system on biblical principles. In the book of Acts, for example, the author commends the first disciples of Jesus for their shared communal property:

> They devoted themselves to the apostles' teaching and fellowship, to the breaking of bread and prayers. Awe came upon everyone, because many wonders and signs were being done by the apostles. All who believed were together and had all things in common; they would sell their possessions and goods and distribute the proceeds to all, as any had need. Day by day, as they spent much time together in the temple, they broke bread at home and ate their food with glad and generous hearts, praising God and having the goodwill of all the people. And day by day the Lord added to their number those who were being saved. (2:42–47)[56]

Moreover, Jesus teaches his disciples to give all their goods to the poor, rather than keeping their material belongings for themselves (Matt 19:16–31; Mark 10:17–31; Luke 18:18–30). As one scholar suggests, "Epiphanes' communal sexual model of society was a pragmatic attempt to impart a more enduring basis to the inchoate communal customs of Jesus' first followers by grounding them in the sexual reforms of Zeno, Chrysippus, and Plato."[57] But how does Epiphanes's communitarian plan work?

First, following Plato, Epiphanes emphasizes that men must renounce owning individual wives and instead practice communal sexual mores:

> He brought female to be with male and in the same way united all animals. He thus showed righteousness to be a universal fairness and equality.

But those who have been born in this way have denied the universality which is the corollary of their birth and say, "Let him who has taken one woman keep her, whereas all alike can have her, just as the other animals do." (*Miscellanies* 3.8.1–2)

For Epiphanes, justice is "sharing in common on a basis of equity (*koinōnia tis met' isotētos*)" (3.6.1, 3.8.2). One of the most unjust things is the ownership of private possessions, and the worst offense is men's claim to individual wives. This is why he says that the "law" (*nomos*), which commands men to take wives, "entered" (*pareiselthein*) the world as original sin (3.7.2–3).

Epiphanes also challenges the tenth commandment, which prohibits men from coveting their neighbor's wife and property (Exod 20:17; Deut 5:21). Christian monogamy intensified the meaning of this rule. For church fathers such as Clement, the tenth commandment meant that a Christian wife could not leave her husband and marry another man without being labeled an adulterer. For Epiphanes, the tenth commandment can't possibly represent God's true position. In fact, he calls the commandment "laughable" (*geloioteron;* 3.9.3). As Gaca maintains, "If this biblical sexual rule of social order were to become the law of the land, it would induce Christians to turn their backs on the communal heritage of the apostles."[58] Epiphanes's solution is to add the teachings of Plato and the early Stoics to Christianity. In other words, Christians need to abolish marriage and the household. As he relates, "There is no distinction between rich and poor, people and governor, stupid and clever, female and male, free men and slaves" (3.6.2).

Clement's reaction to Epiphanes is quite striking. Not only does he find Epiphanes's argument dangerous, he labels his ideas "fornicating justice" (*hē pornikē dikaiosuē;* 3.10.1). In fact, he believes that Epiphanes should be excommunicated from the Christian community, asking "How can this man still be reckoned among our number when he openly abolishes both law and gospel?" (3.8.5). But what all of this tells us is that two viable options existed for Christians in the second and third centuries: (1) the prophylactic grace and ecclesiastical sexual ideology of Clement, and (2) the libertine, communitarian option of Epiphanes. Both were "live" options, though neither view would become the church's eventual ideological state apparatus.

Cassian: Bringing the Pieces Together

The "battle for chastity" begins with John Cassian (360–435 C.E.), who disguises Origen's ideas on chastity for a new Latin audience.[59] In the early 380s, Cassian enters the monastery near the Cave of the Nativity in Bethlehem with his older friend Germanus (*Institutes* 3.4; *Conferences* 1.1). It didn't take long for the two friends to go to Egypt, to Panephysis, a monastery near the mouth of the Nile. From there, they travel to Scetis and Kellia. After 399, Cassian moves to Constantinople, where he serves as a deacon. Given his proficiency in Greek and Latin, he serves on John Chrysostom's diplomatic staff, taking dictation at the time of Chrysostom's downfall in 404 to Pope Innocent in Rome (Palladius, *Dialogue* 3). By 419, he becomes a priest in Marseilles, where he founds and directs two religious communities, one a monastery (perhaps Saint Victor) and the second a convent (perhaps Saint Savior's).[60] While there, Cassian articulates an account of monastic life, indebted to Evagrius, for local bishops and monks, such as Castor, bishop of Apta Julia. Additionally, he acknowledges his debt to the teachings of Basil and Jerome.[61] He writes his account of monastic life in the *Institutes* and the *Conferences*, both composed during the 420s.[62] Though Cassian writes the two works for monks, much of his advice is for married Christians. As Foucault observes, "These new fashions in monastic sexual mores, the build-up of a new relationship between the subject and the truth, and the establishment of complex relations of obedience to the other self all form part of a whole whose coherence is well illustrated in Cassian's text."[63]

Since Cassian advocates strict celibacy for monks, it's no surprise that he slams the door shut on any possible healthy sex for married Christians.[64] Gone are the days of Clement and his prophylactic grace. In Cassian's writings, married Christians either commit to celibacy within marriage or separate from their spouses in order to undertake the monastic life.[65] To illustrate one of these options, Cassian tells a story about Abba John, who stands in awe of an exorcist's immense power and efficacy. After several failed attempts on the monk's part to rid a man of a demon, Abba John encounters a layman who easily defeats the demonic spirit. Upon witnessing this event, John asks the layman what he did to deserve such grace. Cassian reports the following answer: "He confessed that twelve years previously he had been forced by the pressure and command of his parents to take a wife, although he had wanted to profess the monastic life. Although even now no one was aware of it, he kept her a virgin and treated her as a sister" (*Conferences* 14.7.4–5). The man's story strikes Abba John with such intensity that he publicly acknowledges that the man's example of chastity is not for everyone. Still, he admires it: "Although Abba John would speak of this situation with the highest admiration, nonetheless he did not encourage any of the monks to try it out, knowing that many things which have been rightly practiced by some have led others who imitated them into great danger, and that what the Lord has bestowed by a special favor upon a few cannot be seized upon by all" (14.7.5). As Columba Stewart notes, Abba John "regards this proximity to temptation as a particularly heroic form of chastity and does not recommend it to others, echoing repeated ecclesiastical condemnation of such practices."[66]

Cassian tells another story about Abba Joseph, who argues that the allowance of marriage for the sake of populating the world has been superseded with the coming of the gospel. Abba Joseph declares, "Now that the end of the ages is at hand and the multiplication of the human race has been completed, that ancient freedom with regard to many wives and concubines had rightly to be cut off as quite unnecessary, thanks to gospel perfection." He even declares that Gen 1:28 is no longer binding on Christians. Indeed, what might be called the "age of the Synagogue" has given way to the "age of the Church," in which "blossoms of angelic virginity . . . spring forth and the aromatic fruits of chastity . . . grow sweetly" (17.19.1–2).

In the final *Conference*, Cassian tells us about Abba Abraham, who "used to have a wife in the wanton 'passion of lust'" (24.26.6). Over time, Abraham persuades his wife to live a celibate lifestyle and enter the cenobitic community. As he relates, "The woman is the same, but the value of the love has grown a hundredfold." Even the most cursory reading of the story reveals that the married state is inferior to a life lived in celibate devotion to God.

Though we hear nothing more of Abraham's story, Cassian echoes its themes in greater detail in a narrative about Abba Theonas, a story that typifies the dominant attitude toward marriage and celibacy among at least elite Christians in the fourth century. According to Cassian, Theonas, a married man, visits a monastery to offer the first fruits of his harvest. While at the monastery, he overhears an admonition on the superiority of grace over law (21.4.2). In fact, the voluntary renunciation of lawful goods is encouraged for the sake of divine love. Inspired by the exhortation to renunciation and perfection, Theonas decides to follow the gospel's message of chastity. He returns home and urges his wife to join him. His attempts fail: "But although he persisted unremittingly in beseeching thus, his inflexible spouse would not give her consent to him, saying that she could never abstain from conjugal relations in the flower of her life, and that if she were abandoned by him and committed some sin it would have to be imputed to him instead for having broken the bonds of marriage" (21.9.1). Theonas counters his wife's protests with a diatribe on the "weakness and instability" of human nature. As he declares, "It would be dangerous to entangle over an extended period in carnal desires and labors" (21.9.1). In other words, since he has heard the call to a virtuous life, he has no other choice but to obey. "The greatness of perfection belonged to every age and to both sexes, and all the members of the Church were urged to scale the heights of lofty virtue by the Apostle, when he said: 'Run in such a way as to obtain'" (21.9.2).

Abba Theonas is left with only one option: divorce. As Cassian declares, "And if he was unable to have the blessing of joining Christ's company with his wife, he preferred to be saved even at the expense of one member and as it were to enter the kingdom of heaven crippled, rather than to be condemned with a sound body" (21.9.2). Next Theonas reinterprets the law of Moses, arguing that if Moses permitted divorce because of "hardness of heart," why would Christ not allow it because of a desire for chastity (21.9.3)? "Clearly, then, just as the word of the gospel condemns those who break the bonds of marriage by the crime of adultery, so also it promises hundredfold rewards to those who, on account of a love for Christ and a desire for chastity, have rejected the yoke of the flesh" (21.9.4).

Unimpressed, Theonas's wife rejects his offer of marital virginity: "Despite these and other such words the woman's attitude was unbending, and she remained obstinate and unyielding." Theonas concludes: "If I am unable to keep you from death, neither shall you separate me from Christ. It is safer for me to be divorced from a human being than from God" (21.9.4). In the end, he flees to a monastery to find his salvation.

With all of these stories—and many others like them—Cassian tries "to contrast the multiple cares of marriage with the single focus and freedom from worldly distraction of his ideal of chastity."[67] But in the process, he creates a hierarchy of sexual virtues. As Stewart writes: "Virginity is the most perfect form of Christian life. The practice of celibacy by those who are not virgins comes a close second, with sexual activity in marriage ranked lower as a 'lawful' compromise, and other sexual activity, whether heterosexual or homosexual, beyond the pale."[68]

Jovinian and Jerome: The Conflict Ends

What we are witnessing from the second and third centuries to the fourth and fifth centuries is an evolution in Christian thinking about marriage and sex, at least among the elite. As J. N. D. Kelly puts it:

> From the second century onwards a widening stream of such [ascetic] essays had been published by Christian writers . . . They all draw on a common fund of ideas and expound, though with widely differing nuances, what is essentially the same doctrine. This is that marriage is, on the most favorable interpretation, a poor second best; virginity is the original state willed by God, and sexual intercourse came in only after the Fall. The underlying presuppositions are that the sexual act is intrinsically defiling, and that indulgence in it creates a barrier between the soul and God. If one is married, it is better to abstain from intercourse; a second marriage betokens regrettable carnal weakness.[69]

An exception is Jovinian, a Roman Christian. Sometime around the year 390, he teaches not the superiority of the married state, but that those who marry and have sex are equal in the eyes of God to virgins and celibate members of the church.[70] Of course, many New Testament writers proclaim the same thing. Titus and 1 and 2 Timothy, for example, all promote ancient Christian "family values," placing great importance on marriage and childrearing. But things change. As Dale Martin relates, "The opposite point of view, which valued celibacy over marriage, gradually became the more dominant position in late ancient Christianity."[71] The conflict, though, continued between Jerome and Jovinian.

Scholars refer to the clash between these two men as the "Jovinian controversy." Jovinian's arguments stem from a popular book he wrote that sets out the case for Christian marriage. Jerome preserves the content of this book in his writings. Jovinian maintains that all baptized Christians are of equal spiritual and moral status. It does not matter whether they're married, widowed, or celibate—they're equal by virtue of their baptismal initiation into the church community. He also contends that Christians who fast are not superior to those who do not. Thus, ascetic practices do not make one a better Christian. Additionally, he argues that at the last judgment, all Christians who have persevered in the faith will receive an equal reward regardless of how abstemious they have been.

The church hierarchy condemns Jovinian and his followers. In the year 393, for example, Pope Siricius calls a synod to study Jovinian's views on marriage. The synod rejects them, excommunicating him along with a number of his associates. As a result, Siricius writes a letter to the Italian bishops labeling Jovinian a "heretic" and calling him and his followers "the authors of a new heresy and blasphemy."[72] Additionally, he proclaims that the Jovinianists are "wounding Catholics, perverting the continence of the Old and New Testaments, interpreting it in a diabolical sense; by their seductive and deceitful speech they have begun to destroy no small number of Christians and to make them allies of their own insanity." David G. Hunter notes that Pope Siricius's letter is a watershed moment in the life of the church: "Siricius's letter marked the first time in the history of Christianity that the superiority of celibacy over marriage was officially defined as doctrine, and conversely, that its denial was labeled as 'heresy.' Siricius's letter, therefore, marked a distinctive hardening of boundaries in the later fourth century, the moment at which a previously implicit Christian consensus about marriage and celibacy reached a consequential degree of explicitness."[73] Now with the power of the seat of Peter, the inferiority of marriage becomes a doctrine. The antifamily ideology of some of the New Testament writers becomes the de facto winner.

After their excommunication from the Roman church, Jovinian and his followers move to Milan, where things go from bad to worse because they encounter the powerful Bishop Ambrose (later Saint Ambrose). Ambrose convenes a synod and confirms both the condemnation of Jovinian's views and his excommunication. Simply put, Pope Siricius and one of the most respected church fathers condemn as "heresy" the idea that marriage is equal with celibacy.

Jerome is Jovinian's chief nemesis. In 393, he viciously responds to Jovinian's defense of marriage with his *Against Jovinian*, a work so damaging to marriage that many of Jerome's friends attempted to remove the book from circulation. In fact, Jerome's harangue wasn't well received even by members of the clergy, even though they agreed with him.[74]

In *Against Jovinian*, Jerome points out that he and others realize that scripture says marriage is a good thing. He points to Heb 13:4, which says, "Marriage is honorable and the bed undefiled," and Gen 1:28, which proclaims, "Increase and multiply and fill the earth." He even calls the Genesis text "God's first judgment" (1.3). But he promptly adds, "Just as we accept marriage, we prefer virginity, which is born of marriage" (1.3) In other words, the entire reason virginity exists is because of marriage—and Christians should prefer virginity to marriage.

Jerome bases part of his argument on his belief that Adam and Eve were originally virgins (1.16). Chastity is to be preferred because before the fall, Adam and Eve didn't engage in sexual intercourse. It was only after what he calls "the sin" that they were married and had sex. It doesn't take long to realize the implications of what Jerome is saying. He links "the sin" of the fall with sexual intercourse, a popular idea that continues to this day. Sex is bad because it contributed to humanity's rebellion against God.

He also upholds what many scholars term "spiritual marriages." In these kinds of marriages women remain with their husbands in wedlock but refrain from sexual relations. As he says, "I do not deny that widows are blessed who remain in the state of widowhood after their baptisms; nor do I detract from the honor of those women who remain with their husbands in sexual abstinence" (1.33). Indeed, he even declares that these women have a "higher reward" than married women "who comply with the marriage duty." As with Cassian's hierarchy of sexual virtues, the virgin holds a special place. "To undertake virginity is for the many, to stick with it is for the few" (1.36). Yet those who "stick with it" receive a great reward, for he believes that virgins start out on this earth as others will be in the resurrection: "If it is promised us that we shall be as the angels (however, among angels there is no difference of sex), either we shall be without sex, as the angels are, or assuredly, as is plainly attested, we may be resurrected in our own sex but shall not perform the sexual function" (1.36). The question, then, is, "Why have sex in the here and now when one can be as one will be in the resurrected state by being chaste?"

Ultimately, Jerome and other church fathers must insist on a "radical difference between Jewish and Christian ethics."[75] Sexuality is placed on a par with Old Testament ritual practices. In other words, Jerome and many others find themselves in positions in which they're forced to argue that Jewish rituals, like keeping kosher, were valuable only for their time and were essentially sub-Christian and outdated with the coming of Christ. This also includes the Jewish injunction—recognized as a command by Jerome—to "be fruitful and multiply." By the fourth and fifth centuries, its time had passed.

Conclusion

Since we've come a long way in this chapter, covering several centuries of Christian history, it's important to recall that every discourse discussed here is an ideology—a strategy of power. Though none of the church fathers may have meant for this to happen, their discourses on the superiority of celibacy eventually led to the invention of new social institutions, which is what ideological state apparatuses do. Ultimately, by privileging the celibate life over the married life, consecrated female communities and organized monasteries began appearing throughout the Roman Empire. Even though Christians would continue to get married and to procreate, the better life—the "more Christian life"—was now found among monks and nuns. They were closer to God than the man and woman who decided to marry out of desire or lust.

But we should also keep in mind that the church had a financial stake in its popularity among the governing authorities. As the Christian movement grew, it became attractive to some wealthy women who adopted the celibate lifestyle. Perhaps these women felt that this was their way of subverting the cultural norm of getting married in order to procreate; perhaps they felt the celibate life guaranteed them more freedom than the average Roman life for women. Whatever the case, wealthy women adopting a celibate life, and with no descendants to care for, willed massive amounts of money to ecclesiastical and charitable projects.[76] These women might become powerful patrons, taking dozens of virgins from less affluent backgrounds under their protection and bringing them into their households.[77] In other words, celibacy wasn't just a theological tenet, it was political and economic. If celibacy wasn't openly confronting the ideological discourses of the Roman Empire, it was helping create wealth for the church.

A question, though, lingers as this chapter comes to a close. As I've noted, in modern parlance some Christians often speak of "Judeo-Christian values," a term that usually includes a preference for marriage and the creation of children. Some politicians in the United States have called such values the "bedrock" of our country, and profamily advocates react whenever they perceive these traditional "family values" threatened by either abortion or gay marriage. Yet I'm left to wonder whether "Judeo-Christian" is the right term. Aren't many of these profamily advocates modern followers of Jovinian? Wouldn't they have been condemned by no less than Saint Jerome or Pope Siricius? Since I believe that every history of the past is also a history of the present, I turn now from the ancient world and its empire to the modern world and its empire.

CHAPTER FIVE

THEN AND NOW

Reification

Capitalism does not structurally require patriarchal gender asymmetry,
but historically it has made use of the institution of marriage and the
heterosexual norms it regulates to reproduce gendered divisions of labor
both in and outside the family.
—*Rosemary Hennessy*

I'm often asked, "Why are you interested in the subjects you explore in
your book?" I think people ask me this because I don't look like someone
who would be interested in the intersection between gender, sex, and religion. That is, I look rather conservative, dressed in a pair of khakis or
gray flannel pants, paired with a repp tie and navy blazer. People who
know me well, however, understand what I mean when I jokingly say,
"Don't let the sweater vest fool you." My close friends and family members concur that the sweater vest is worn by a very complex, socially liberal individual.

Complicating matters is my religion. I'm a devout Catholic, but I also
struggle with the injustices perpetrated in the name of Jesus. To illustrate
what I mean, I quote from one of my favorite theologians, Herbert

McCabe. In his book *Law, Love and Language,* McCabe eschews the binary liberal/conservative Christian, opting, instead, to describe what he terms a "radical christian [*sic*]":

> In every age, I suppose, there will be conservatives who cling to a formula-
> tion arrived at in an earlier time and are hence at odds with the present,
> and there will be liberals in reaction against such conservatism who will
> frequently be merely conforming to this world. Both of these seem to me
> to be distortions of christianity, but the genuine radical christian will al-
> ways be accused by each side of belonging to the other. This is not in the
> least because he is a "moderate," but because he is opposed to both sides,
> seeing both as basically conformist—the one conforming to a past, the
> other to a present world.[1]

He continues by describing, what in his mind, is the authentic Christian:

> The christian reaches out beyond this world towards a future world of
> freedom, towards real communication between men [and women] and
> therefore full human life. Such freedom, he will maintain, can never be an
> achieved static condition; it is only possible in a dynamic reaching out to-
> wards the Father. Man becomes fully human only by transcending human-
> ity in divinity.[2]

These brief sentences reflect some of my beliefs, practices, and struggles and partly answer the question of why I'm interested in the subjects I write about in this book.

As I have said, "A history of the past is a history of the present." Discourses are never closed. Furthermore, honest historians know that they choose to study a particular topic because they have a personal, vested interest in it. Although I've tried to be objective in this book and suspend any second-order judgments, I know that they're probably lurking in the background. To borrow words from Gilles Deleuze, I've been more of a "map-maker" than a "historian."[3] But the reader should keep in mind that my maps are not about mirroring the terrain. Instead, my main concern has been contingencies—the accidents of history. I don't see a logical, linear development, for example, between the Augustan marriage legislation and Paul's proclamation that marriage is a prophylactic against *porneia.* I don't believe that Paul ever intended to create a sexual ethic that went against the Greco-Roman norm, but paradoxically, that's exactly what he did. What I've been doing, then, throughout this work is general history instead of total history.

Total history looks for overarching principles that govern the development of an epoch. In contrast, general history eschews the "totalizing" theme, concentrating instead on describing differences, transformations, continuities, mutations, and so forth.[4] If a theme is governing this work, it's related to how biopower creates discourses that control things like sex, marriage, and procreation; as Michel Foucault states, "It will be granted no doubt that relations of sex gave rise, in every society, to a deployment of alliance."[5] One of the clearest alliances throughout history is the amalgamation of marriage and procreation.[6] As we've seen, tied to this alliance are politics and power, as well as the exchange and transfer of wealth and property.[7] And this isn't just the case with secular legislation such as the Augustan marriage laws. It's also true of ecclesiastical proclamations.

As I turn to the present, it's important to note that modern power masks itself in ways not so different from how ancient power masks itself. As Foucault notes, "Power as a pure limit set on freedom is, at least in our society, the general form of its acceptability."[8] Modern power "masks itself by producing a discourse, seemingly opposed to it but part of a larger deployment of modern power."[9] In this chapter, I aim to *unmask* modern forms of power that use Christianity in the service of policing modern society in the United States. As I'll make clear, I'm particularly troubled by certain claims that marriage and procreation can save our world; additionally, I'm equally troubled by constant references to the term "Judeo-Christian" to back up this kind of argument.[10] My task, as I conceive it, is to "push and jab" at modern ideas and make them yield their ideological content "to make manifest the ways in which their authors seek to present their highly constructed arguments as 'natural' interpretations, obvious to all 'rational' people."[11] I don't pretend to have any answers to the things that I unmask.[12] Indeed, I find myself in agreement with Thomas Aquinas, who believed that there are questions that have to be asked but that cannot be answered.[13] With that in mind, I turn to the modern while acknowledging that the past is somehow still with us.

Fagan and the Heritage Foundation: Marriage and Capitalism

Modern legal analyses of marriage suggest that there are two competing views when it comes to the question "What is marriage?"[14] In their article of the same name, Sherif Girgis, Robert P. George, and Ryan T. Anderson point out that one view is labeled "conjugal" while the other is termed "revisionist." The conjugal view is defined as "the union of a man and a woman who make a permanent and exclusive commitment to each other of the type that is naturally (inherently) fulfilled by bearing and rearing children together."[15] In the conjugal view, the purpose of marriage is reproduction, which is behavioral: "Marriage is valuable in itself, but its inherent orientation to the bearing and rearing of children contributes to its distinctive structure, including norms of monogamy and fidelity."[16] Those people who define marriage along these lines link the welfare of children to a stable marriage between a man and a woman, arguing that such "traditional" marriages are important to the common good. Thus, states should recognize, regulate, and protect these kinds of marriages because they're beneficial to society in general.

The revisionist view declares that "marriage is the union of two people (whether of the same sex or of the opposite sexes) who commit to romantically loving and caring for each other and to sharing the burden and benefits of domestic life."[17] This view maintains that if two people love one another, their union will be enhanced by "whatever forms of sexual intimacy both partners find agreeable."[18] Accordingly, the government should protect and recognize all forms of marriage, because it has "an interest in stable romantic partnerships and in the concrete needs of spouses and any children they may choose to rear."[19]

Some people argue that the conjugal view is simply another way of talking about a view of marriage that many major religions support. But this may not be entirely true. Girgis, George, and Anderson, for example, offer a different point of view: "Although the world's major religious traditions have historically understood marriage as a union of man and woman that is by nature apt for procreation and childrearing, this suggests merely that no one religion invented marriage."[20] But I think this is somewhat inaccurate. Even when nonreligious arguments have been made for the conjugal view of marriage, they have usually been made by members of conservative think tanks who have deeply held religious beliefs.

Patrick Fagan is a case in point. Fagan is a senior fellow and director of the Marriage and Religion Research Institute at the Family Research Council, a conservative Christian organization. In an article titled "The Wealth of the Nations Depends on the Health of Families," Fagan argues that whether one is religious or not, the U.S. economy is best served by the conjugal view of marriage.[21] He notes that before the sexual revolution in the 1960s, "the United States was the world's heavyweight champion in economic productivity and earnings." Citing his colleague Henry Potrykus, Fagan reasons that divorce, which became much more acceptable after the sexual revolution, reduced the annual growth rate of the economy by at least one-sixth since the mid-1980s. Thus the current U.S. economic crisis is not due to, for instance, two wars, lack of government regulations, or Wall Street greed, but to a decline in the number of traditional marriages and an increase in the divorce rate.

Citing no religious literature, Fagan asserts: "A productive household does not simply happen when parents beget a child. The foundation for a productive household begins with marriage. Other arrangements cannot measure up, not for the child, not for the couple, not for society, and certainly not for the economy." Interestingly, Fagan believes that the first place a child learns about capitalism and a healthy market-based ideology is in a traditional marriage: "The child learns about the marketplace when he first sees his parents taking care of the family's material needs, earning, saving, and investing in the home and the children's education." He goes on to say that as a child—and by this he means a male child—starts giving back to society, he'll mimic the capitalist system he learned from his parents. In fact, Fagan declares that the marketplace depends on traditional marriages and stable families, because "stockbrokers and life-insurance salesmen know where strength lies too: Their biggest markets are married couples, though Wall Street has yet to figure out the macroeconomic implications."

According to Fagan, the biggest threat to the market system is premarital sex and divorce. "Who would ever have thought that chastity is tied to the growth rate of the American economy?" Fagan asks. Citing research from the conservative think tank the Heritage Foundation, Fagan believes there's a direct link between the number of sexual partners a person has before marriage and the divorce rate. Singling out women, he writes: "Always-monogamous women have much more stable marriages. For women ages thirty to forty-four, one non-marital sexual partner (usually before marriage) correlates with a huge drop in the likelihood of staying married, from 80 percent for the monogamous woman, down to 54 percent for the one-extra-partner woman."[22] It seems that Fagan might agree with many of the ancient writers we've examined in previous chapters and declare that women are weak, deceitful creatures whose libidos are out of control. In fact, a major part of his argument sounds nothing like Jesus, Paul, or many of the early church fathers, but more like the Augustan legislation and Greco-Roman moral philosophy. He believes that the "core strategy" for forming "great workers for the economy" depends on healthy, traditional marriages that produce children. As he reckons, "Not only does [the traditional marriage] produce the greatest average human capital for the marketplace; it also produces the best citizens for the *polis* and the common good." But as Martha Albertson Fineman notes, "This extremely and highly questionable 'family values' perspective is based on faulty and incomplete social science and disingenuously compares idealized nuclear families with those of single mothers already in trouble."[23]

Part of what I find so perplexing about Fagan's argument is that I can't tell whether he's more interested in stable families or a stable capitalist economy. Additionally, he contrasts the stalwart economy of the United States before the sexual revolution with that of Spain, Italy, and Greece today. He singles out these countries, along with the finance ministers of the European Union, because he believes they have failed to acknowledge that the "economy-altering implications" of economic change in the EU are directly related to a lack of stable, traditional marriages that produce children for the workforce. I'm somewhat troubled by the fact that Fagan specifically points to Spain, Italy, and Greece. Doesn't he know that two of these countries are majority Catholic and the other Greek Orthodox? Given that the Family Research Council is largely controlled by fundamentalist and evangelical Protestants, I find myself asking whether the critique of Spain, Italy, and Greece isn't just about stable, traditional marriages that produce children, but about something unstated—something else entirely.

Perhaps he finds Catholic and Orthodox forms of Christianity inferior to specific forms of evangelical Protestantism.

The Heritage Foundation also argues for a conjugal view of marriage without any reference to religious texts. Anyone familiar with the thinking of any of the fellows of this conservative organization knows, however, that religion—particularly fundamentalist Christianity—is at the core of many of the foundation's beliefs about government and society. I've had numerous encounters with members of the Heritage Foundation at their prolife rallies. Though the speakers claim they're just making an economic and philosophical case against abortion, they usually begin their talks by praying to Jesus and asking him to send more prolife Christians into the House, the Senate, the Supreme Court, and the White House. In fact, at a rally I attended held at Wright-Patterson Air Force Base—an odd venue for so-called prolifers—a speaker from the Heritage Foundation referred to President Barack Obama as a "baby killer," comparing him to Herod in the New Testament.[24] Thus I think it's safe to say that when speakers associated with the Heritage Foundation claim they are making economically based arguments, not religiously based ones, they're masking their true intentions. Apparently, they have forgotten that lying is a sin.

In a pamphlet titled "What You Need to Know About Marriage: Questions and Answers Driving the Debate," the Heritage Foundation defines marriage as (1) bringing a man and a woman together as husband and wife to be father and mother to any children their union produces; (2) a system based on the biological fact that reproduction depends on a man and a woman and the reality that children need a mother and a father; and (3) the building block of all human civilization. For members of the Heritage Foundation, marriage has "public, not just private, purposes," which sounds quite similar to Augustus and his legislation.[25]

What concerns the Heritage Foundation most are the recent challenges to the 1996 Defense of Marriage Act (DOMA) and to Proposition 8 passed in 2008 by voters in California.[26] According to the foundation's literature: "Marriage has been weakened by our culture of convenience. This demotes marriage to little more than emotional intensity or legal privileges."[27] Interestingly, the fellows at the Heritage Foundation declare that marriage is about the needs of children rather than the "desires of adults." So the U.S. government must protect traditional marriage because "it is an institution that benefits society in a way that no other relationship does."[28] Members of the foundation fear that redefining marriage would (1) hurt children because decades of social science show that children do better when raised by a married mom and dad; (2) further separate marriage from the needs of children, which would ultimately force the government to intervene more often with ever-growing welfare programs; (3) put a new principle into the law—that marriage is whatever emotional bond that government says it is; and (4) push out traditional views on the family, leading to the erosion of religious liberty. This last fear is particularly noteworthy, since the Heritage Foundation argues that citizens of Canada, Massachusetts, and Washington, D.C., are already seeing this happen before their eyes.

Anne Wilson: Catholicism and the Heteronormative Family

A similar position is taken by Anne Wilson in the conservative publication *Catholic Update*.[29] Like the Heritage Foundation, she's afraid that if marriage is redefined, society will crumble: "As we witness the rapid change in public opinion and decisions about who can 'marry' in court cases, we are watching the binding of society unraveling."[30] For her, something dramatic happened after 2001. Citing a Pew Research poll, Wilson notes that in the year 2000 only 40 percent of those identifying themselves as Catholic favored allowing couples of the same sex to marry. Fourteen years later, a similar poll showed that 57 percent of Catholics favored allowing couples of the same sex to marry.

Wilson believes that these changes of attitude were prompted by a society that today allows couples to choose from "an unending table of contents of relationship options—including living together or choosing a partner of the same gender."[31] She contrasts today's attitudes with those she learned from elementary school readers when she was a Catholic schoolgirl in the 1970s: "Bright illustrations accompanied stories that taught us not only how to read, but also what family life was like . . . for most people—a father, a mother, and their children."[32] The vignettes these readers taught reinforced "family values" in her and many of her schoolmates and weaved in bits and pieces of what it meant to live a sacramental life.

Citing Gen 2:18 and 2:24, *Gaudium et Spes,* and the *Catechism of the Catholic Church,* Wilson declares that the Catholic Church teaches that the purpose of marriage is twofold: (1) to be procreative and perpetuate God's gift of life, and (2) to be unitive, joining spouses together in an intimate, affirming, and complementary bond.[33] She also contends that further support is found for the Catholic Church's position throughout the New Testament writings, though she is quite selective in which writings she refers to. Citing Mark 10:6–8, which she presumably believes goes back to the historical Jesus, Wilson argues that Jesus tackled tough issues, such as divorce, going so far as to challenge the traditional Jewish customs of his day. In a rather clever hermeneutical move, she maintains that while Jesus challenged traditional Jewish views on divorce—which were presumably not tough enough for her—he "fully supported and reiterated the laws of God about the composition of marriage."[34] Here she takes as a defense of traditional marriage between a man and a woman Mark's words, "But from the beginning of creation, 'God made them male and female. For this reason a man shall leave his father and mother [and be joined to his wife].'" And I suspect she thinks Jesus also taught that the husband and wife should marry in order to procreate, though, as I have pointed out in chapter 3, Jesus never taught that the purpose of marriage is procreation.

Next, Wilson turns to the wedding at Cana, where Jesus blesses the marriage of a man and woman by working his first public miracle (John 2:1–11). Sidestepping any of the issues of the historicity of the fourth gospel, she puts a lot of emphasis on verse 11: "Jesus did this at the beginning of his signs in Cana in Galilee and so revealed his glory, and his disciples began to believe in him." Instead of seeing this text as an allusion to the Eucharist or to the exodus story, Wilson concludes, "It is unlikely that Jesus would have chosen to begin to publicly reveal his divine power at a wedding if he did not believe in an unchanging definition of the composition of marriage."[35] But in the fourth gospel Jesus also begins his public ministry by cleansing the temple. So, based on the same logic, why doesn't Wilson view this event as a condemnation of ecclesiastical hierarchy?

These two texts, Mark 10:6–8 and John 2:1–11, are the only ones Wilson uses to defend her "biblical" understanding of the Catholic Church's position on traditional marriage. I find it particularly odd that she leaves out the writings of Paul, Ephesians, Colossians, Revelation, the Gospel of Luke, and the Pastoral Epistles in her construction of what marriage is in the New Testament.[36] If she really believes that redefining the traditional meaning of marriage has global implications, what does she do with the fact that Paul already redefined it? Not to mention the fact that Matthew deconstructed Mark's construction of Jesus's statements on divorce and remarriage. Wilson doesn't seem to realize that she, too, is deconstructing the multiplicity of voices in the New Testament concerning marriage.

USCCB: Regulating Heteronormativity in the Church

Regrettably, many U.S. bishops in the Catholic Church have done the same thing as Wilson in their official statements on marriage and sexuality. In November 2003, the U.S. Conference of Catholic Bishops (USCCB) wrote "Between Man and Woman," a document that approved a restatement of long-held Catholic beliefs on marriage.[37] I'm particularly interested in this document because it's one of the most recent, authoritative ecclesiastical statements that (re)defines marriage in the United States. The report from the U.S. bishops is said to be a response to a growing movement in U.S. society to recognize homosexual unions as legal, married unions. Perhaps the bishops were prescient, since within a few months of the publication of "Between Man and Woman," the Massachusetts Supreme Judicial Court ruled that same-sex unions can be equated with marriage.

The introduction to "Between Man and Woman" states that the U.S. bishops are offering "basic truths" to help people understand Catholic teaching about marriage and "to enable them to promote marriage and its sacredness." Then follows the question, "What is marriage?" The bishops declare that marriage is "instituted by God." It is a "faithful, exclusive, lifelong union of a man and a woman joined in an intimate community of life and love." Within a marriage, a man and a woman are equal, but the bishops contend that equality doesn't mean they're the same. Instead, husbands and wives complement one another, and "this complementarity, including sexual difference, draws them together in a mutually loving union." Furthermore, this union should always be open to procreation (cf. *Catechism of the Catholic Church* [*CCC*] nos. 1602–1605).[38]

For the U.S. bishops, these "truths" about marriage are present in the "order of nature" and can be perceived "by the light of human reason." They also declare that these truths have been confirmed by divine revelation in sacred scripture. Like Wilson, the U.S. bishops seem to think that the Bible speaks with a unified voice on marriage and sexuality.

According to "Between Man and Woman," marriage comes from "the loving hand of God, who fashioned both male and female in the divine image" (Gen 1:27). Citing with approval Gen 2:24, the bishops maintain that it is natural for a man "to leave his father and mother and cling to his wife." The man recognizes the woman as "bone of my bone and flesh of my flesh" (Gen 2:23). God blesses marital unions and commands a husband and wife to "be fruitful and multiply" (Gen 1:28). Next, Jesus reiterates these truths from Genesis in Mark's Gospel. There he declares, "But from the beginning of creation, 'God made them male and female. For this reason a man shall leave his father and mother [and be joined to his wife], and the two shall become one flesh'" (10:6–8). Notably absent is any reference to the redaction of this text in Matthew's Gospel.

The texts in Mark and Genesis lead the U.S. bishops to assert, "Marriage is both a natural institution and a sacred union because it is rooted in the divine plan of creation." Additionally, they reiterate the fact that the Catholic Church has always taught that a "valid marriage" of baptized Christians is a sacrament (i.e., "a saving reality"). The sacrament of marriage is modeled on Jesus's love for his church, demonstrated in Eph 5:25–33. "A true marriage in the Lord with his grace will bring the spouses to holiness. Their love, manifested in fidelity, passion, fertility, generosity, sacrifice, forgiveness, and healing, makes known God's love in their family, communities, and society" (cf. *CCC* nos. 1612–1617; 1641–1642). A Christian understanding of marriage "confirms and strengthens" the human value of a marital union. In fact, just like the Heritage Foundation, the U.S. bishops reason that traditional marriage is the best thing for society as a whole: "Across times, cultures, and very different religious beliefs, marriage is the foundation of the family. The family in turn, is the basic unit of society. Thus, marriage is a personal relationship with public significance." In particular, traditional marriage is best for raising children; it is only in a stable, loving relationship of a mother and a father that a child can be raised in a healthy, normal manner. (Of

course, one might query whether Jesus had a "healthy, normal" upbring-
ing, since Catholic tradition holds that Joseph died when Jesus was a
teenager, forcing Mary to raise him alone from that time.)

In Catholic theology, the marital union serves the common good.
Everyone benefits from traditional families. The bishops are so insistent
on this point that they invoke the argument that if this were not so, state
laws would not recognize the importance of heteronormative marriages:
"The state rightly recognizes this relationship as a public institution in its
laws because the relationship makes a unique and essential contribution to
the common good." A traditional marriage is so sacred that it functions as
a "domestic church" (*Lumen Gentium* no. 11). This is why marriage can't be
redefined—or so the U.S. bishops contend. As an institution, marriage is
regulated by civil laws and ecclesiastical laws, but because it originates
from God, neither the church nor the state "can alter the basic meaning
and structure of marriage." But it seems to me that this is exactly what
"Between Man and Woman" is doing—redefining the meaning and structure of marriage, especially marriage as understood and defined by
church fathers such as Clement of Alexandria and John Cassian.

Marriage and the U.S. Supreme Court: Searching for a Definition

Turning to the secular world, one finds that defining and understanding the meaning and purpose of marriage has reached the highest court
in the land. I'm speaking of the Supreme Court case *Obergefell v. Hodges,*
which, though not specifically about heterosexual marriage, provides us
with several definitions and redefinitions of marriage in the United States
because of questions regarding the legality of same-sex marital unions.
Oral arguments before the court took place April 28, 2015.[39]

Throughout the hearings, the subject of marriage and its alliance to
procreation came up more than one might expect for a court case based
on the rights of same-sex couples. In fact, it's accurate to say that procreation became "that thing" which made heteronormative marriages "different" from same-sex marriages. I'm particularly interested in the
debates between Justices Elena Kagan, Sonia Sotomayor, and Ruth
Bader Ginsburg with John J. Bursch, the special assistant attorney general
of Lansing, Michigan, who argued against the legality of same-sex

marriages on the grounds that same-sex couples cannot procreate, as he put it, in "the natural way." What follows are some highlights from the court hearings.

After a few questions from Justice Stephen Breyer, Bursch declares that "the marriage institution did not develop to deny dignity or to give second class status to anyone. It developed to serve purposes that, by their nature, arise from biology" (43). Playing on the "conjugal" and "revisionist" views of marriage as I've defined them above, Bursch reasons that even without marriage, men and women would procreate because that's what they're biologically programmed to do. In contrast, he maintains that revisionists argue "that marriage is all about love and commitment." According to Bursch, states have no interest in a definition of marriage that's all about love and commitment.

In an attempt to unmask what Bursch is actually saying, Justice Kagan points out that in his legal briefs, Bursch argues that since same-sex marriages cannot lead to procreation, they are fundamentally flawed in some way (44). Kagan, rightly in my opinion, declares that what Bursch and others are arguing for is state regulation of procreation. She asks Bursch, "Are you saying that recognizing same-sex marriage will impinge upon that State interest, will harm that State interest in regulating procreation through marriage?" To which Bursch baldly replies, "We are saying that, Your Honor" (44).

From here a rather heated exchange ensues between Bursch and Justices Kagan, Sotomayor, and Ginsburg. Ginsburg wants to know why Bursch thinks redefining marriage to include same-sex couples will threaten the benefits heterosexual couples receive. As she notes, "They would have the very same incentive to marry, all the benefits that come with marriage that they do now" (44). Bursch protests that Justices Kagan and Ginsburg don't understand what he's saying (perhaps because they are "only" women?). His argument—or so he claims—is based on a "societal understanding" of marriage, a "dictionary definition which has existed for millennia" (49). Moreover, he claims that he's thinking of ideas that are "much bigger" and broader than those of Kagan and Ginsburg. Ultimately, Bursch believes that if you change the basic definition of marriage, you do great harm to society: "And when you change the definition of marriage to delink the idea that we're binding children with their biological mom and dad, that has consequences" (45). Justice Sotomayor isn't impressed by this line of reasoning. She counters by asking Bursch what he thinks about all of the single moms and dads who have raised perfectly healthy children. Bursch is insistent, though, that plenty of scientific studies show that children from traditional marriages are far better off than children raised by single parents. Sotomayor counters that the evidence from these studies is shaky at best.

Later, Justice Kagan defines Bursch's position as "procreation-centered," another term for the conjugal view of marriage as opposed to the revisionist view, or the ideology of Procreationism that was pervasive among some Second Temple Jewish writers (see chapter 2). Kagan asks an important question about a hypothetical situation that could easily arise in a state that defines marriage on the basis of a "procreation-centered" view:

> Mr. Bursch, suppose—suppose this: Suppose that there's a State with a procreation-centered view of marriage of the kind that you're talking about. And it—you know, so emotional commitment and support, all of these, the State thinks are not the purpose of marriage and they want their marriage licenses to be addressed only to the things which serve this procreation purpose. And so they say, Well we're not giving marriage licenses to any—to anybody who doesn't want children. So when people come in and ask for a marriage license, they just ask a simple question: Do you want children? And if the answer is no, the State says, no marriage license for you. Would that be constitutional? (53).

This line of questioning doesn't sit well with Bursch. He's forced to admit that it wouldn't be constitutional for a state to ask anyone that question. But he's also insistent that there are plenty of people who enter a marriage not wanting any children who end up having them anyway. After a few forceful questions from Justice Kennedy, who has remained silent up to this point, Bursch finally gets around to answering the question of constitutionality. He reluctantly claims, "I think it would be an unconstitutional invasion of privacy to ask the question" (54). In order to clarify what Bursch just said, Kagan queries, "To ask if you want children is an unconstitutional invasion of privacy?" Again, Bursch responds, "I—I think that would be the case, yes" (54–55).

As has happened on more than one occasion, Justice Ginsburg provides one of the more lively—and humorous—moments of the deliberations.

Having heard Bursch's arguments, she asks the following hypothetical question, which is met with laughter: "Suppose a couple, a 70-year-old couple comes in and they want to get married. You don't have to ask them any questions. You know that they are not going to have any children" (55). This would seem like an entirely logical point, but Bursch is not yet willing to concede, saying, "Well a 70-year old man, obviously, is still capable of having children and you'd like [to] keep that within marriage." Additionally, he reverts to a previous argument of his, "But even if you applied some kind of heightened scrutiny, you know, again, many people get married thinking that they can't have kids or won't have kids, and they end up with children . . . [this] advances the State's interest" (55). As Kagan points out, for Bursch, all of this is based on natural reason—or perhaps some kind of natural law theory. It should be obvious to anyone. But it isn't.

What particularly concerns me about Bursch's argument is that he often claims that reason dictates that every culture for millennia has emphasized the conjugal view of marriage. As we've seen, this same point was made by the U.S. bishops in "Between Man and Woman" and by the Heritage Foundation, Anne Wilson, and Patrick Fagan. Bursch assumes, as do so many others, that the default position when it comes to marriage is that it's a union between a man and a woman, that its basic purpose is procreation, and that almost every society on earth has thought this since the beginning of time. Even liberal Protestant denominations that bless same-sex unions, such as some members of the Anglican Communion, maintain that marriage has a threefold purpose. According to the Anglican *Prayer Book,* marriage was ordained (1) for the procreation of children, (2) as a remedy against sin, and (3) as a means of mutual support.[40] But in previous chapters of this book, we've seen that many Christians didn't believe this at all.

Judeo-Christianity and the "Traditional" Family

In the world of politics, the position Bursch argues for is often referred to as part of the "Judeo-Christian" values upon which the United States was founded. The earliest use of the term dates to the 1820s, where it's first found in the missionary journal of Joseph Wolff.[41] According to the

Oxford English Dictionary, when originally coined, the term referred to Jews who had converted to Christianity. They were called "Judeo-Christians" or "Judeo Christians." But since the 1950s, the term has encompassed common beliefs of American Christians and Jews. In 1952, for example, President Dwight D. Eisenhower looked to the founding fathers of 1776 and declared: "All men are endowed by their Creator. In other words, our form of government has no sense unless it is founded in deeply felt religious faith, and I don't care what it is. With us of course it is the Judeo-Christian concept, but it must be a religion with all men created equal."[42]

Others have identified the term "Judeo-Christian" with historic religious traditions in the United States. Dennis Prager, a politically conservative Jewish columnist, contends that the concept of Judeo-Christian ethics does not rest on a claim that the two religions are the same. Instead, Judeo-Christianity promotes the idea that there is a shared intersection of values, brought to the United States by early European settlers, that is based on the Hebrew Bible (Torah).[43] The basis for what Prager argues goes back to the 1830s when Alexis de Tocqueville in *Democracy in America* described America's unique religious heritage, which it received from the Puritans: "The Americans combine the notions of Christianity and of liberty so intimately in their minds, that it is impossible to make them conceive the one without the other; and with them this conviction does not spring from the barren traditionary faith which seems to vegetate in the soul rather than to live." And he writes, "The principles of New England . . . now extend their influence beyond its limits, over the whole American world. The civilization of New England has been like a beacon lit upon a hill."[44]

When the term "Judeo-Christian" is used today, it often has something to do with the "traditional" family. American men and women are to refrain from having sex until they get married. After they marry, they should procreate. According to Ronnie Floyd, president of the Southern Baptist Convention (SBC) until June 2016, this is how it's always been. Speaking to about five thousand people attending a two-day meeting of the SBC in Columbus, Ohio, Floyd declared in reaction to the Supreme Court's ruling in favor of same-sex marriages, "I want to remind everyone today, humbly, the Supreme Court of the United States is not the final authority, nor is the culture itself, but the Bible is God's final authority about marriage and on this book we stand."[45] Floyd and other Southern Baptists adopted a resolution titled "On the Call to Public Witness on Marriage." In this document, they say that the SBC views marriage as "a covenanted, conjugal union of one man and one woman."[46] Additionally, they declare that marriage is a lifelong commitment that a man and a woman pursue in order to procreate. If this traditional understanding of marriage isn't upheld, the SBC intimates that "the flourishing of human civilization" may be in danger.

What's ultimately at stake here is the "Judeo-Christian" heritage of the United States. According to Richard Lee, the editor of *The American Patriot's Bible,* the Judeo-Christian heritage of the United States is based on seven principles: (1) the dignity of human life, (2) the traditional family, (3) a national work ethic, (4) the right to a God-centered education, (5) the Abrahamic covenant, (6) common decency, and (7) personal accountability to God. Regarding the traditional family, Lee maintains that traditional marriage is the "backbone of a healthy social order" and the "clear plan of God" based on Gen 2:21–24. This clear plan includes procreation, which a man and woman should do in order to produce children who will become "healthy, productive, and responsible citizens." As Lee reasons, "When God's definition of 'marriage' and 'family' are no longer respected, these institutions become meaningless." And like many before him, Lee declares that "world history has proven over and again that preserving the traditional family is vital to the future of any great nation."[47]

The problem with all of these assumptions—and that's what they are— is that hyphens used in terms such as "Judeo-Christian" create discontinuity. They are disruptive. In their book *The Hyphen: Between Judaism and Christianity,* Jean-François Lyotard and Ebehard Gruber point out that the hyphen in "Judeo-Christian" disunites what it appears to unite.[48] It isn't about continuity but discontinuity. We've seen this while comparing Second Temple Jewish sexual ethics, some of which are based on an ideology of Procreationism, with early Christian sexual ethics, which are by and large antifamily. In practical terms, what many U.S. commentators, scholars, and politicians miss when they use the term "Judeo-Christian" is that it implies a separation between Jewish and Christian ideologies of the family. Furthermore, not all Jews upheld the ideology of Procreationism. This means that although some people long for the return of what they think are Judeo-Christian sexual ethics in this country, they might really be longing for what could be called "neo-imperial-capitalist" sexual ethics, since our modern sexual ethics seem closer to Augustus's imperialism than they do to the ethics and ideologies of the early church.

We could explore many other examples, but whether they are Catholic, evangelical, fundamentalist, or philosophically and ideologically conservative, they all end up supporting the following statement: *All of human history has shown us that the best way for humanity to survive is through a traditional marriage in which a man and a woman create children in order to better society.* Apparently, this isn't just a biblical idea, but an idea that every human civilization agrees is the correct one. Without it, we're doomed to fail as a people. In fact, many U.S. institutions have turned this idea into what Louis Althusser calls an "ideological state apparatus" (see the introduction). Churches, think tanks, and certain political groups produce ideologies that individuals internalize.[49] As B. H. McLean notes, "Such institutions make the dominant ideology of a society . . . natural, whereas ideologies that differ from this norm are made to appear radical and unnatural."[50] But as I've been saying all along, the internalized sexual ideology of the United States isn't "Judeo-Christian."

If we believe in the United States's internalized sexual ideology—or if we assume those who proclaim it are experts—we might conclude that there have never been any dissenting voices to this ideological state apparatus. We might even conclude that the first real dissent appeared in the United States during the 1960s or sometime after the 1973 Supreme Court decision in *Roe v. Wade.* But we know better than that. As we've seen, working through layers of a particular period of history, one finds a very different story to be told.

One of the things I've attempted to demonstrate throughout this book is that sexuality is constructed by various cultures and groups. As I said in the introduction, sex is about power. That's probably the one constant of human civilization that's never changed, whether we're talking about the United States in the twenty-first century, the Augustan marriage legislation during the Roman Empire, or the world of the Bible. The other thing that we've seen with each ideology we've probed is that when sex and politics collide—or, better yet, when sex and patriotism collide—sex ends up serving the purposes of heteroreproductive sexuality.[51] This happens because far too many individuals past and present take it for granted that "what founds society . . . is heterosexuality."[52] Even the left seems to overlook the fact that it buys into the idea that patriarchy is the foundation of society. As Luce Irigaray remarks: "The patriarchal foundation of our social existence is in fact overlooked in contemporary politics, even leftist politics. Up to now *even Marxism has paid very little attention to the problems of the specific exploitation of women, and women's struggles most often seem to disturb Marxists"* (italics in the original).[53]

What I find surprising is that in the twenty-first century, a binary has been created that looks something like this:[54]

Traditional values	Revisionist values
Conjugal view of marriage	Revisionist view of marriage
Christian	Atheist
Republican	Democrat
Patriot	Traitor
Heterosexual	Homosexual
American	Un-American

The belief in American culture and in many American churches seems to be that the first individuals to come up with a third option challenging the binary are members of the modern LGBTQI movement. But Christians going all the way back to Jesus and Paul were already making antifamily statements that questioned the idea that the best thing for society was an ideology based on the traditional family. It almost seems disingenuous that certain groups of Christians don't recognize this fact. Why, in other words, has a modern-day pope not spoken *ex cathedra* declaring that the oldest Christian view of marriage maintains that sex is a prophylactic against *porneia* and has nothing to do with procreation? Why, in other words, are there only two ways of defining marriage in our culture—conjugal and revisionist? What about a third option that suggests married people need not have sexual relations? Or a fourth option that might lead to a motion being brought before Congress in which single people are pronounced superior to those who are married? My questions may seem absurd, but they are driven by my own archaeological investigation of a particular set of data found in the tells of history.

Having examined the layers of this data, I'm left to conclude a number of things. First, it's virtually impossible to discover the exact origins of our own sexual beliefs and practices. Admittedly, there are some parallels in the Bible, but there are also parallels with Greco-Roman philosophy and other movements that hardly enter into the discourses of some modern-day preachers, politicians, lawyers, and judges. Our closest ally, in fact, is Augustus, and not nascent Christianity. Second, if Christians were honest about their history, they would see that the definition of marriage has changed repeatedly as Christianity developed. Though I agree that marriage seems to be consistently defined as being between a man and a woman, the purpose of marriage changes from age to age. As we've seen, it wasn't always about procreation. Indeed, there was a time when those in powerful positions within the church thought that it was better to remain chaste and single than to marry. I can only imagine what would happen if that opinion became the default in American Christianity instead of the myth of the "traditional family" that's part of our conjoined "Judeo-Christian" heritage. Third, Christians today aren't Pauline, nor are they following Jesus when it comes to how they practice and understand marriage. If anything, they are Jovinianists, since they believe that marriage is just as good as—if not better than—remaining single. (And this is something both the left and the right seem to believe.) American Christian values, then, aren't "Judeo-Christian" because most Christians in the United States believe in the ideology of Procreationism, which benefits the empire. Fourth, if we've learned anything from this study, it's that the view that marriage has for millennia been defined as being between a man and a woman so they can procreate in order to develop good citizens for the state is wrong. The problem with this view—a view that has dominated far too many court cases in the United States—is that for the first five or six centuries of the existence of the Christian church, marriage was frowned upon, along with procreation. Yet I've never heard a modern Christian call John Cassian or Pope Siricius an enemy of the "traditional family." But from our vantage point, that's exactly what they were. Finally, we need to ask ourselves some honest questions about why so many people—religious and not religious—are obsessed with the idea of the "traditional family." What's lurking behind this powerful ideological belief?

If we think back to the ideas of Patrick Fagan noted above, we see that capitalism stands behind the narrative of the traditional family.[55] As Chrys Ingraham declares in her groundbreaking work on the wedding industrial complex, "Marriage primarily benefits groups that are not disproportionately represented among the poor and that are able to maintain goods and property."[56] Though Fagan is honest about this, others are not. Perhaps they don't know that behind their religious convictions skulks a particular economic conviction, or perhaps they don't want someone unmasking their ideology for what it really is: an ideological state apparatus that has been internalized by the masses. But with Fagan, it's easy to see that those who fight for the traditional family and the conjugal view of marriage are doing so because the best way to promote the common good is to ensure that capitalism is maintained as a guiding principle for future generations. And what's the best way to do this? Ensure that men and women marry and procreate.

NOTES

Note: For ancient sources, I have used the editions and translations most widely available in the United States: the Hebrew Bible, Septuagint, and New Testament from Deutsche Bibelgesellschaft (Stuttgart), the Loeb Classical Library (Harvard University Press), Patrologica graeca, Patrologia latina, Corpus Scriptorum, Sources chrétiennes, *Thesaurus linguae graecae* (electronic), and Library of Latin Texts (electronic). Unless otherwise specified, English translations of the church fathers are from the Ancient Christian Writers series.

Introduction

1. For a recent general discussion of ideologies, see Hall, "The Problem of Ideology," and the essays in Žižek, ed., *Mapping Ideology*.

2. Hirsch, *Validity in Interpretation*, 126.

3. Griffin, "*Urbs Roma, Plebs,* and *Princeps,*" 23. For an analysis of the Marxist concept of ideology, see McLean, *Biblical Interpretation*, 200–203; and Williams, *Marxism and Literature*, 55–71.

4. Martin, *The Corinthian Body*, xiv.

5. Drake, *Slandering the Jew*, 17.

6. Althusser, "Ideology and Ideological State Apparatuses." For recent critiques of Althusser's theory of ideology, see Bourdieu and Wacquant, *An Invitation to Reflexive Sociology*, 155–164 and 250–251; and Rehmann, *Theories of Ideology*, 147–178. For Althusser's defense of his theory, see his *Essays in Self-Criticism*.

7. A further development of Althusser's theory of ideology can be found in Pêcheux, "The Mechanism of Ideological (Mis)recognition."

8. Althusser, "Ideology and Ideological State Apparatuses," 96.

9. McLean, *Biblical Interpretation*, 209.

10. Althusser, "Ideology and Ideological State Apparatuses," 107–109.

11. Althusser, "Ideology and Ideological State Apparatuses," 107.

12. According to Jakobsen and Pellegrini, *Love the Sin*, 28, "heteronormativity," a term created by social theorists Lauren Berlant and Michael Warner, "describes the moral and conceptual centrality of heterosexuality in contemporary American life." It shouldn't be confused with "heterosexuality."

13. Althusser, "Ideology and Ideological State Apparatuses," 119.

14. McLean, *Biblical Interpretation*, 210.

15. Pêcheux, "The Mechanism of Ideological (Mis)recognition," 147.

16. For a discussion of power as a strategy, see Kendall and Wickham, *Using Foucault's Methods*, 49–50.

17. Deleuze, *Foucault*, 70.

18. Kendall and Wickham, *Using Foucault's Methods*, 49.

19. Williams, *Marxism and Literature*, 112.

20. This quotation is from the James Lecture at the Institute for the Humanities, New York University, 20 November 1980. It can be found in Foucault, "Sexuality and Solitude," 184.

21. Brown quoted in Foucault, "Sexuality and Solitude," 183.

22. McLean, *Biblical Interpretation*, 62.

23. Kendall and Wickham, *Using Foucault's Methods*, 24.

24. See Dean, *Critical and Effective Histories*, 93.

25. Dean, *Critical and Effective Histories*, 93–94.

26. Dean, *Critical and Effective Histories*, 93–94.

27. Gaca, *The Making of Fornication*, 4.

28. See Michel Foucault, "Genealogy of Ethics," in Rabinow, ed., *The Foucault Reader*, 244, 240.

29. Foucault, *The Use of Pleasure*, 20–21.

30. Gaca, *The Making of Fornication*, 5.

31. Gaca, *The Making of Fornication*, 5.

32. Gaca, *The Making of Fornication*, 6.

33. Harper's monograph is based on his research in his *"Porneia."* For an important critique of Harper, see Glancy, "The Sexual Use of Slaves."

34. For a history of uniqueness in historical positivism, see McLean, *Biblical Interpretation*, 58–59.

35. Smith, *Drudgery Divine*, 9–14.

36. Smith, *Drudgery Divine*, 38–39. Of course, one might argue that the real counterpart of similarity is difference. Difference, however, does not imply that early Christian ideas

are superior to Jewish or Greco-Roman ideas. See, for example, Welborn, "Paul and Pain."

37. Smith, *Drudgery Divine*, 40.

38. Mack, *A Myth of Innocence*, 4.

39. Taylor, "Introduction," 14.

40. Taylor, "Introduction," 14.

41. For the notion that sex is mediated by culture, see Golden and Toohey, "Introduction," 7.

42. Eidinow, "Sex, Religion, and the Law," 102–103.

43. *Ta aphrodisia* (the things of Aphrodite), the usual way the Greek referred to sexuality, comes from the Greek word *aphros* (foam).

44. Cf. Foucault, who writes, "The diverse schools of philosophy of the Hellenistic period proposed different solutions to the difficulties of traditional sexual ethics." See Rabinow, ed., *The Foucault Reader*, 389.

45. Foucault, *Use of Pleasure*, 209.

46. I completely agree with Jakobsen and Pellegrini, *Love the Sin*, 40, who maintain that the "Judeo-Christian" tradition is a myth.

47. In my opinion, it is only the Judean ruling class that upholds sexual ideological codes comparable to the sexual codes of the Roman Empire. Cf. Goodman, *The Ruling Class of Judaea*, 129, who writes, "But the kind of Jews likely to pick up such Greek ideas were of course precisely, like Josephus, the ruling class whose status was in question."

48. Agamben, *The Time That Remains*, 14, is correct when he states, "The feeble opposition that sets the classical world against Judaism reveals its shortcomings."

49. Cf. Goodman, *The Ruling Class of Judaea*, 130.

50. As Runions, *The Babylonian Complex*, 84, notes, "Christian interpretations claim authenticity and historicity through Judaism." Christianity, then, especially in its modern forms, is guilty of using Judaism for its own ideological ends.

51. Foucault, "The Battle for Chastity."

52. Cf. Hunter, *Marriage, Celibacy, and Heresy in Ancient Christianity*.

53. See Hunter, "Michel Foucault," 38–39.

54. On this point, see Rose, "Of Madness Itself."

55. Cf. Martin, *Sex and the Single Savior*, 121–124.

56. Lyotard and Gruber, *The Hyphen*, 14.

1. Augustus and the Roman Empire

1. From "Remarks Accepting the Presidential Nomination at the Republican National Convention in Dallas, Texas," 23 August 1984, unpaginated, http://www.reagan.utexas.edu/archives/speeches/1984/82384f.htm. Reagan also used this phrase in his 11 January 1989 farewell speech to the nation. The phrase itself entered the American lexicon in John Winthrop's 1630 sermon "A Model of Christian Charity." While still aboard the

Arbella, Winthrop encouraged the future inhabitants of the Massachusetts Bay colony to make their new home a light to the world—"a city upon a hill." In this case, the city on the hill became Boston.

2. Livy, *Periochae* 59, and Suetonius, *Aug.* 89.

3. The idea that women are creatures that men must endure goes far back into history. Hesiod (700 B.C.E.), for example, says in the *Theogony,* "Even so Zeus who thunders on high made women to be an evil to mortal men, with a nature to do evil" (600–601). Semonides of Amorgos (600 B.C.E.), in his poem *Women,* proclaims, "From the start, the gods made women different" (1). Later on, he echoes Hesiod, declaring, "Yes, Zeus made this the greatest pain of all: Woman" (98–99). In Euripides's *Hippolytus* (fifth century B.C.E.), Zeus is petitioned with, "Great Zeus, why didst thou, to man's sorrow, put woman, evil counterfeit, to dwell where shines the sun?" (616ff.). For more on these ancient Greek attitudes toward women, see Arthur, "Early Greece."

4. Suzanne Dixon, *Reading Roman Women,* 35, writes: "It is notable how little we do hear of female desire in Latin literature. Greek myth, drama, philosophy and even law-court speeches reveal a strong male vision of the terrifying female principle, directly related to uncontrolled female sexuality and probably to a deep-seated fear of the female reproductive organs."

5. For more on this topic, see Coontz, *The Way We Never Were.*

6. At the 2014 meeting, Mat Staver, for example, painted the Obama administration as more malicious than the government of Nazi Germany. Meanwhile, Michele Bachmann, Robert Dees, Gary Bauer, and Brigitte Gabriel dedicated their speeches to the threat of Islam, seeking religious freedom for Christians but not for Muslims in the United States. See Brian Tashman, Right Wing Watch, "Mat Staver: Third Party Needed to Stop Gay Marriage, Just Like With Slavery," unpaginated, 9 October 2014, http://www.rightwingwatch.org/content/mat-staver-third-party-needed-stop-gay-marriage-just-slavery. Another example is Tony Perkins of the Family Research Council, who linked the persecution of Christians in places like Iraq and Sudan to the supposed persecution of Christians in the United States as a result of gay rights and the Obama administration's policies. See Brian Tashman, Right Wing Watch, "Tony Perkins: 'Deadly Consequences' If Gay Rights Movement Succeeds," unpaginated, 30 September 2014, http://www.rightwingwatch.org/content/tony-perkins-deadly-consequences-if-gay-rights-movement-succeeds. For a thorough overview of the so-called values voters, see Posner, *God's Profits.*

7. Veyne, *The Roman Empire,* 37.

8. The modern historian is forced to reconstruct the laws from ancient references, which include, but are not limited to *Res Gestae* 6; Horace *Carmen Seculare* 4.5.21–24; Ovid *Fasti* 2.139; Dio 54.16; Suetonius *Augustus* 34; Ulpian 11.20; *Digest* 23.2; 44–46, also known as the Law of Citations. For a collection of the laws, see Jörs, "Ueber das Verhältnis der *Lex Iulia de maritandis ordinibus* zur *Lex Papia Poppaea*"; Riccobono, *Acta divi Augusti*; and Rotondi, *Leges publicae populi Romani.*

9. Cf. D'Angelo, "Gender and Geopolitics." D'Angelo convincingly argues that Philo is trying to outdo the piety of the strictest Romans in Augustan "family values."

10. Wallace-Hadrill, "Family and Inheritance in the Augustan Marriage Laws," 58.

11. Treggiari, "Social Status and Social Legislation," 889.

12. For an overview of Plato's eugenics program, see Gaca, *The Making of Fornication*, 48–57.

13. For more on the concept of utopia in Atwood's *The Handmaid's Tale*, see Weiss, "Offred's Complicity and the Dystopian Tradition."

14. Cooley, ed., *Res Gestae Divi Augusti*, 64. Augustus likely knew that he was building his reform program on ideas stretching back to the Gracchi, who also tried to address the problem of a declining population. See, for example, Nörr, "The Matrimonial Legislation of Augustus," 358.

15. Lintott, *The Constitution of the Roman Republic*, 117–119.

16. MacDonald, "Reading Real Women," 212, writes: "Historians have expressed doubts about the extent to which the Augustan marriage laws were effective in various parts of the empire among people at various echelons of society. At the very least, they reflect the unease among government officials about the deterioration of the household and point to tensions that were ready to erupt given the presence of a perceived social irritant."

17. For more on the Golden Age, see Galinsky, *Augustus*, 92–94; and Wallace-Hadrill, "The Golden Age and Sin in Augustan Ideology."

18. Cf. Cudjoe, *The Social and Legal Position of Widows and Orphans*, 17–26, who gives a vivid and horrifying depiction of Athenian casualties in the fifth and fourth centuries B.C.E. and their effect on Athenian society.

19. Raditsa, "Augustus' Legislation," 13:283.

20. Veyne, *The Roman Empire*, 38.

21. Eduard Fraenkel, *Horace*, 374, notes that the reference to the *lege marita* is an unambiguous allusion to the Augustan marriage legislation: "The legislation which is the theme of these lines is not concerned with technicalities of private or public law but goes straight to the roots of the life of human society."

22. The phrase "not to incur blame" refers to the Julian law against adultery formulated in 18 B.C.E.

23. Fraenkel, *Horace*, 20–21.

24. Syme, *The Roman Revolution*, 450.

25. Veyne, *The Roman Empire*, 37–38.

26. Corbett, *The Roman Law of Marriage*, 117–121.

27. Michel Foucault, *An Introduction*, 25, notes that the "policing of sex" isn't about a taboo per se, but about "the necessity of regulating sex through useful and public discourses."

28. Veyne, *The Roman Empire*, 37.

29. See Sanders, "A Birth Certificate."

30. Groen-Vallinga, "Female Participation," 300.

31. Beryl Rawson, "Adult-Child Relationships," 14, notes that if a child survives until its naming-day (*nominum dies;* eight days for girls, nine for boys), that child fulfills the requirements for the privileges due to parenthood (the *ius liberorum*) set out in the *lex Iulia et Papia.*

32. McGinn, *Prostitution, Sexuality, and the Law,* 79–80.

33. In *Epistles* 10.94, Pliny, for example, petitioned Trajan successfully on behalf of his friend Suetonius for a special dispensation that granted him certain privileges, without fulfilling the *ius liberorum.*

34. Rawson, "Adult-Child Relationships," 10.

35. McGinn, *Prostitution, Sexuality, and the Law,* 141.

36. Foucault, *An Introduction,* 83.

37. Edwards, *The Politics of Immorality in Ancient Rome,* 47–48.

38. Dixon, *Reading Roman Women,* 147.

39. This can be seen by looking at artistic representations of figures such as Gorgon and Medusa. See Africa, "The Mask of an Assassin."

40. Kampen, "Gender Theory in Roman Art," 14.

41. Suet. *Aug.* 73. The image of the ideal woman is also found in inscriptions. *CIL* I².1211 = 6.15346 = *ILLRP* 973 = CE 52 reads, "Stranger, I have little to say: stop and read / This is the ugly tomb of a beautiful woman. / Her parents called her Claudia by name. / She loved her husband with her heart. / She bore two children: one of these / she leaves on the earth, the other she buries under the earth. / Her speech was delightful, her gait graceful. / She kept house, she made wool. I have finished. Go!"

42. Examples include Plautus *Amph.* 839ff.; ps.-Sen. *Mon.* 105; Plautus *Aul.* 239, 492–493; Horace *Carm.* 3.24.21ff.; Terence *Ad.* 345–346; Sen. *Contr.* 1.6.6; Apuleius *Apol.* 92.

43. Dixon, *The Roman Mother,* 6. Because of mortality rates, a couple was lucky if their marriage lasted between ten and fifteen years. Helpful examples include *CIL* 6.16592, which was inscribed to the nurse Crispina, dead at age thirty, erected by her husband Albus in commemoration of their seventeen years of married life. Interestingly, poorer girls often married later than their rich counterparts. See Shaw, "The Age of Roman Girls at Marriage." Shaw argues that lower-class women in the Roman Empire tended to marry relatively late. He suggests that they probably married in their late teens and sometimes even in their early twenties. On modern debates about the age of marriage, see Fitzgerald, "Orphans in Mediterranean Antiquity and Early Christianity," 32–34.

44. Williams, "Some Aspects of Roman Marriage Ceremonies and Ideals," 24.

45. The original law of 18 B.C.E., the *lex Iulia de maritandis ordinibus,* allowed only a year's delay in remarrying for widows and six months for divorcées, but this was changed by the later *lex Papia.* For more, see Ulpian's *Rules* 14.

46. Dixon, *The Roman Mother,* 59.

47. Çsillag, *The Augustan Laws on Family Relations,* 89.

48. Ovid was so out of step with the reforms that he was banished from Rome in 8 C.E. because of his *carmen et error* (*Trist.* 2.207), an "innocent" misdemeanor that remains

mysterious despite the speculations of modern historians (cf. *Trist.* 3.5.49–52, 3.6.29–36; *Pont.* 1.6.21–26). See Green, "Carmen et error."

49. Alison Sharrock, "Ovid and the Discourses of Love," 154, relates: "Our gut reaction that love and sex are 'private' must be a triumph of optimism over experience, since not only our national laws but also our popular culture deny that this is so. Yet the belief remains."

50. Herbert-Brown, "Fasti," 126.

51. For more on this, see the epigraphical calendar, known as the *Pareneste* calendar, dated 6–9 C.E., in Degrassi, *Inscriptiones Italiae,* 141.

52. See Lape, "Heterosexuality," 33–34.

53. Gardner, *Women in Roman Law and Society,* 248.

54. Balsdon, *Roman Women,* 14.

55. Treggiari, "Women in Roman Society," 118–123. More recent estimates suggest six to nine children. See Skinner, *Sexuality in Greek and Roman Culture,* 351–352.

56. Rabinow, ed., *The Foucault Reader,* 389.

57. Harper, *From Shame to Sin,* 72.

58. Foucault, *The Care of the Self,* 151.

59. Gaca, *The Making of Fornication,* 86.

60. Musonius's thought is also rooted in Bryson Arabus's *Management of the Estate.* See Swain, *Economy, Family, and Society from Rome to Islam,* 31–35.

61. Cf. Bryson, *Management of the Estate,* 84, which reads, "When he takes the woman (in marriage), it is necessary that the man should begin by making her understand the reason he wanted her: that he did not want her for children without (also) caring for him and checking on his affairs during his presence, absence, health, and sickness, having custody of all his wealth and aiding him in all his affairs, and (for) her duties in respect of these, on account of the reasons we have explained." Furthermore, Bryson writes, "We have now explained the two purposes for which the woman is sought, i.e. children and the management of the estate" (88).

62. Cf. Bryson, *Management of the Estate,* 159: "A warning must be given to the boy about sexual intercourse or obtaining knowledge of any aspect of sexual intercourse or coming near it before he is married."

63. On the topic of Musonius's feminism, see Asmis, "The Stoics on Women"; Klassen, "Musonius Rufus, Jesus, and Paul"; and van Geytenbeek, *Musonius Rufus and the Greek Diatribe,* 67. For an important and balanced response to these works, see Engel, "The Gender Egalitarianism of Musonius Rufus" and "Women's Role in the Home and State." For additional bibliography, see Ramelli, *Hierocles the Stoic,* 108–111.

64. Cf. Lucillius (frg. 678–686), who writes in his poetry about the numerous flaws of women, which include extravagance and sexual infidelity. For him, these flaws are so great that they are grounds for a man to reject marriage outright.

65. Engel, "Women's Role in the Home and State," 284.

66. Veyne, *The Roman Empire,* 40.

67. Veyne, *The Roman Empire*, 46. Also see the discussion of Antipater in Deming, *Paul on Marriage and Celibacy*, 66–67. On pages 221–229, Deming provides a useful translation of part of Antipater's *On Marriage*.

68. Veyne, *The Roman Empire*, 47.

69. Skinner, *Sexuality in Greek and Roman Culture*, 197.

70. Cf. Bryson, *Management of the Estate*, 81–82.

71. Laqueur, *Making Sex*, 22.

72. Flemming, *Medicine and the Making of Roman Women*, 317.

73. One should recall that the woman's ovum was not discovered until 1827 by C. A. von Baer. For an overview of Galen's influence on modern medicine, one should consult Tempkin, *Galenism*.

74. Laqueur, *Making Sex*, 4–8. Byzantine and Arab physicians preserved Galen's treatises. They were handed down to students of medicine in the Renaissance and early modern Europe.

75. See the important discussion about Galen and female doctors in Flemming, "Gendering Medical Provision," 275–281.

76. Hankinson, "The Man and His Work," 2.

77. It should be noted, however, that somewhat earlier he described her chief nurse as "a most excellent woman." Boethus was Galen's patron. See Johnson, *Readers and Reading Culture*, 78–80, 85–86.

78. On Galen's female patients, see Mattern, *Galen and the Rhetoric of Healing*, 112–114.

79. For Galen's description of women as "rational animals," see *On the Doctrines of Hippocrates and Plato* V 742. Of course, his remark is a backhanded compliment, since he immediately says (following Plato), "men are superior in every employment and discipline."

80. Cf. Karl Marx's comment in his *Grundrisse*, in which he declares that reproduction is all about survival: "The aim of all these communities is survival; i.e. *reproduction of the individuals who compose it as proprietors, i.e. in the same objective mode of existence as forms the relation among the members and at the same time therefore the commune itself.* This *reproduction, however, is at the same time necessarily new production and destruction of the old form.*" Quoted in Elster, ed., *Karl Marx*, 205.

81. For more on the problems of the retention of seed, see Flemming, *Medicine and the Making of Roman Women*, 339.

82. Quoted in Parker, "Women and Medicine," 114. Cf. Galen 13.319–320; 8.417, 420, 424, 432; 16.178.

83. Galen is quoted in Parker, "Women and Medicine," 114.

84. Laqueur, *Making Sex*, 40.

85. For more on Herophilus, see von Staden, ed., *Herophilus*.

86. Laqueur, *Making Sex*, 28.

87. Laqueur, *Making Sex*, 28.

88. Flemming, *Medicine and the Making of Roman Women*, 355.

89. I borrow the term "baby factories" from Parker, "Women and Medicine," 122.

90. Parker, "Women and Medicine," 122.

91. Cooper, *The Virgin and the Bride*, 26.

92. Whitmarsh, *Greek Literature and the Roman Empire*, 41–45.

93. Morales, *Vision and Narrative*, 1.

94. Goldhill, *Foucault's Virginity*, 68.

95. For a detailed explanation, see Goldhill, *Foucault's Virginity*, 7–11.

96. Cf. Goldhill, *Foucault's Virginity*, 68–69.

97. Quoted in Zeitlin, "The Poetics of *Erōs*, 432.

98. Goldhill, *Foucault's Virginity*, 69.

99. For more on *ekphrasis*, see Morales, *Vision and Narrative*, 36–48.

100. Goldhill, *Foucault's Virginity*, 70.

101. Konstan, *Sexual Symmetry*, 63.

102. Konstan, *Sexual Symmetry*, 64.

103. Irigaray, "Interview 1," 50.

104. Morales, *Vision and Narrative*, 18.

105. Johns, *Sex or Symbol*, 61–73.

106. Harper, *From Shame to Sin*, 61.

107. Harper, *From Shame to Sin*, 61.

108. Morales, *Vision and Narrative*, 7.

109. Foucault, *The Care of the Self*, 228.

110. Foucault, *The Care of the Self*, 228.

111. Goldhill, *Foucault's Virginity*, 85.

112. Goldhill, *Foucault's Virginity*, 86. In the medical texts, for example, female pleasure during sex is hardly noted, and female desire is usually represented as desire for procreation.

113. Foucault, *The Care of the Self*, 229.

114. Konstan, *Sexual Symmetry*, 229.

115. Cooper, *The Virgin and the Bride*, 36.

116. Cooper, *The Virgin and the Bride*, 37.

117. Cooper, *The Virgin and the Bride*, 37.

118. Cooper, *The Virgin and the Bride*, 43.

119. Veyne, *The Roman Empire*, 36.

120. Veyne, *The Roman Empire*, 37.

121. Veyne, *The Roman Empire*, 38.

122. Veyne, *The Roman Empire*, 45.

2. Judaism

1. For an overview of sexuality in the Talmudic era, which is completely different from sexuality in the Second Temple era, see Boyarin, *Carnal Israel;* and Moore, *Judaism in the First Centuries of the Christian Era*, 2:119–140.

2. As David Daube, *The Duty of Procreation*, 3, makes clear, Gen 1:28 originally wasn't a commandment but a blessing. Furthermore, he points out that the influence of Greco-Roman thought on Second Temple Jews is the reason Gen 1:28 became a binding commandment on all Jews.

3. For an evaluation, see Loader, *Making Sense of Sex*, 9–10.

4. I borrow this term from Gaca, *The Making of Fornication*, 204. On the importance of procreation in Judaism, see Cohen, *"Be Fertile and Increase,"* 13, 27–35, 76–82, 125–140, 167–180.

5. Gaca, *The Making of Fornication*, 204.

6. For the date of Tobit, see Fitzmyer, *Tobit*, 50–55.

7. For important comments on these verses, see Moore, *Tobit*, 129–132.

8. Cf. LAB 29:2, where Zebul arranges husbands for the daughters of Kenaz.

9. This is the first historical mention of the marriage contract.

10. On the use of *porneia* in Tobit, see Jensen, "Does *porneia* Mean Fornication?" Also see Moore, *Tobit*, 238, who remarks, "Whether he intended it or not, Tobiah is certainly subscribing to the Essene ideal as described by Josephus: 'They stress pleasures as a vice and consider moderation and control of the passions as the essence of virtue.'"

11. Cf. b. Yebam. 39b. See Zimmerman, *The Book of Tobit*, 94.

12. Daube, *The Duty of Procreation*, 7.

13. Their children are mentioned in 14:12.

14. These lines are a paraphrase of Homer's *Odyssey* 6.182–184. They had become practically proverbial in antiquity.

15. For an analysis of this verse, see Myers, *I and II Esdras*, 53–57.

16. Sarna, *Genesis*, 23, observes, "To become 'one flesh' refers to the physical aspects of marriage, as though the separated elements seek one another for reunification."

17. Loader, *Making Sense of Sex*, 56.

18. For an overview of Plato's ideological program, see Levin, "Women's Nature and Role in the Ideal *POLIS*."

19. For parallels between these verses and Greco-Roman philosophical ideas, see van der Horst, *The Sentences of Pseudo-Phocylides*, 225–227.

20. Josephus also sets himself at odds with the Torah and most of the rest of the Hebrew Bible.

21. Wilson, *The Sentences of Pseudo-Phocylides*, 188.

22. Gaca, *The Making of Fornication*, 193.

23. For recent discussions of eunuchs in antiquity, see Kuefler, *The Manly Eunuch;* and Tougher, *Eunuchs in Antiquity and Beyond*.

24. See Belkin, *Philo and the Oral Law*, 219–220; and Heinemann, *Philons griechische und jüdische Bildung*, 267–268.

25. Cf. *The Tabula of Cebes* 5. For a discussion of *porneia* as rhetoric, see Drake, *Slandering the Jew*, 9–10. Drake is dependent on Knust, *Abandoned to Lust*, 17–22.

26. Gaca, *The Making of Fornication*, 215.

27. For other examples, see *On the Life of Joseph* 43 and *On the Life of Moses* 1.28.

28. Gaca, *The Making of Fornication*, 205.

29. See Antipater's *On Marriage* in Deming, *Paul on Marriage and Celibacy*, 221–229.

30. I borrow this phrase from Gaca, *The Making of Fornication*, 201.

31. For examples of this practice, see Kugel, *How to Read the Bible*, 1–46; and Visotzky, *Reading the Book*, 1–20.

32. For an overview of Jubilees, see VanderKam, *The Book of Jubilees*, 1–22.

33. Kugel, *A Walk Through Jubilees*, 37, conjectures: "This narrative scandalized the author of *Jubilees*, since it seemed to imply that God had first sought a mate for Adam from the animal kingdom and, only after seeing that Adam did not call any of the animals 'my wife' or 'woman' or something similar, decided to create a mate for Adam from his own 'rib' or 'side.' How could such a narrative square with the Torah's own prohibition of bestiality (Exod 22:18, Deut 27:21), not to speak of *Jubilees*' repeated warning against 'all impurity and fornication'?"

34. Levine, *Leviticus*, 122, writes, "This prohibition, which initiates the section on sexual activity other than incest, is distinctive in that it governs a man's sexual relations with his own wife."

35. There's considerable evidence that Jews of the Second Temple era undertook Nazarite vows. Usually, Jews of this period took the vow to be cured of an illness. One should note, however, that the destruction of the temple made it impossible for Nazarites to offer their hair as part of the vow. For additional details, see Chepey, *Nazarites in Late Second Temple Judaism*, 50–53 and 57–61. Also see Milgrom, *Numbers*, 44–50.

36. Chepey, *Nazarites in Late Second Temple Judaism*, 25–30.

37. Finn, *Asceticism in the Graeco-Roman World*, 41.

38. Muddiman, "Fast, Fasting," 2:773. Also see Propp, *Exodus 19–40*, 162–163.

39. Barclay, *Jews in the Mediterranean Diaspora*, 416.

40. For resistance to assimilation, see 3 Macc 7:11 and 4 Macc 1:32–35. Also see Barclay, *Jews in the Mediterranean Diaspora*, 434–437.

41. Harrington, *Holiness*, 111.

42. Finn, *Asceticism in the Graeco-Roman World*, 44.

43. For this date, see Levine, "Judith," 633.

44. See Levine, "Sacrifice and Salvation, 17–30."

45. For an overview of the Essenes in Philo, Pliny, and Josephus, see Taylor, *The Essenes, the Scrolls, and the Dead Sea*, 22–140.

46. On the Essenes as a philosophical sect, see Fitzgerald, "Cynics," "Epicureans," "Pythagoreans."

47. Finn, *Asceticism in the Graeco-Roman World*, 49.

48. Harrington, *The Purity Texts*, 14. For additional details, see Eschel et al., "New Data"; and Zias, "The Cemeteries of Qumran and Celibacy."

49. Harrington, *The Purity Texts*, 17.

50. Finn, *Asceticism in the Graeco-Roman World*, 49.

51. Harrington, *The Purity Texts,* 47.

52. Commenting on marriage in the Dead Sea Scrolls, Goff, *4QInstruction,* 33, declares, "The overriding concern is not simply that the bond of marriage be respected by the man and the woman, but also that dominion over the female be smoothly transferred from her father to her husband."

53. Goff, *Discerning Wisdom,* 49–53.

54. The English translation is from Goff, *4QInstruction,* 31. For an overview of 4Q415 2 ii, see Rey, *4QInstruction,* 138–143.

55. The English translation, with modifications, is from Wise, Abegg, and Cook, *The Dead Sea Scrolls,* 488–489.

56. Loader, *Making Sense of Sex,* 15.

57. For an excursus on the Watchers, see Collins, "Watchers."

58. For an analysis, see Reed, "How Semitic Was John?"

59. Agamben, *The Time That Remains;* and Wolbert, *Ethische Argumentation und Paränese in 1 Kor 7,* 122.

60. Goodman, *The Ruling Class of Judaea,* 129. Of course, one wonders whether members of the Judean elite conformed to Roman norms out of fear. Perhaps they felt like the Greeks whom Plutarch addresses: "Do not have great pride or confidence in your crown, since you see the boots of Roman soldiers just above your head" (*Precepts of State Craft* 813E). Or maybe some of the Jewish literature examined in this chapter imitates Roman sexual codes because of semblance. See, for example, Benjamin, "Goethe's Elective Affinities."

61. Bunch, "Not for Lesbians Only," 56. Quoting Monique Wittig, Butler, *Gender Trouble,* 157, relates that we often take for granted the fact that "what founds society, any society, is heterosexuality."

62. Bunch, "Not for Lesbians Only," 56. Cf. Rancière, *Hatred of Democracy,* 57, who writes, "Domination works through the distinction of the public, which belongs to everyone, and the private, where the liberties of all prevail."

63. Loader, *Making Sense of Sex,* 97.

64. Cf. Goodman, *The Ruling Class of Judaea,* 130.

65. For more on this, see Gimenez, "The Oppression of Women, 76.

66. Butler, *Gender Trouble,* 40.

3. New Testament

1. One such example of smoothing out these inconsistencies is Bailey, "Women in the New Testament."

2. By "critical scholars," I mean those scholars who feel no compulsion to accept certain dates or authors of texts as a matter of faith or doctrine related to the historical reliability of the Bible.

3. See the important remarks in Corley, *Women and the Historical Jesus,* 7–26.

4. Jacobs, "Dialogical Differences," 304.

5. Foucault, "Sexuality and Solitude," 184.

6. See the important statements in Kraemer, "Jewish Women and Christian Origins," 35–49.

7. Cf. Derrida, *Positions*, 52, who writes: "The work of my reading does not take this form. (When I try to decipher a text I do not constantly ask myself if I will finish by answering *yes* or *no*, as happens in France at determined periods of history, and generally on Sunday.)."

8. As Bakhtin, *Speech Genres*, 103, observes: "The text is the unmediated reality (reality of thought and experience) . . . Where there is no text, there is no object of study, and no object of thought either."

9. Bakhtin, *Speech Genres*, 6.

10. Like Max Weber, from whom I borrow the term "historical accidents," I'm not a determinist. In other words, I don't see "historical stages" as necessary, nor do I believe that history works by an established set of laws. I'm more interested, then, in the "role of possibilities" and "choices in history." For more on "historical accidents," see Weber, *Economy and Society*, 2:1177. Cf. Derrida, *Positions*, 56.

11. For an overview of this subject, see Hayes, *Gentile Impurities and Jewish Identities*. The only time Paul ever accuses Jews of sexually immoral behavior is in Rom 2:22. See Drake, *Slandering the Jew*, 24; and Knust, *Abandoned to Lust*, 63–64.

12. As Ciampa and Rosner, "The Structure and Argument of 1 Corinthians," 207, argue, "It is widely recognized that in early Jewish and Christian thinking, Gentiles were consistently characterized by two particularly abhorrent vices: sexual immorality and idolatry."

13. For the rationale that 1 Thessalonians was written only to men, see Fatum, "Brotherhood in Christ."

14. As Drake, *Slandering the Jew*, 24, points out, "*Porneia*, on Paul's model, is a Gentile problem." Also see Knust, *Abandoned to Lust*, 63.

15. For an important discussion regarding the use of *pornē* to mean prostitution, see Glazebrook, "Prostitution."

16. For a brief overview of Jewish attitudes toward sex during the Second Temple and rabbinic periods, see Finn, *Asceticism in the Graeco-Roman World*, 34–57.

17. For an overview of the various meanings of *porneia*, see Collins, *Studies on the First Letter to the Thessalonians*, 310.

18. Martin, *New Testament History*, 210, writes: "If it refers to [a man's wife], however, it is shocking to see Paul refer to women as seeming to 'belong' to the men. And note that the 'wrong' committed by the man is not against any woman, but against the man whose woman is the object of another's lust. Paul is concerned about men 'cheating' the other men of the community. The language used is that of finances and property." Other interpretations can be found in Malherbe, *The Letters to the Thessalonians*, 226–229.

19. This point is made by Engberg-Pedersen, "The Sinful Body," 51.

20. Martin, *New Testament History,* 209. For a slightly different view, see Engberg-Pedersen, "The Sinful Body," 51–53.

21. For similarities between Paul and the Stoic philosophers on sex without passion, see Martin, "Paul Without Passion." For a different view, see Burridge, *Imitating Jesus,* 126–128.

22. Yarbrough, "Parents and Children in the Letters of Paul," 128.

23. For an overview of early Christian apocalypticism, see Collins, "Early Christian Apocalypticism."

24. To be fair, there are a few passages where Paul identifies himself with those who will be raised from the dead: 1 Cor 6:14; 2 Cor 4:14, 5:1; cf. Phil 1:20. It's also possible that Paul's eschatology evolved as he faced new circumstances. For more on Paul's eschatological evolution, see Dodd, *New Testament Studies,* 108–111. Patristic commentators struggled mightily with Paul's eschatological views. John Chrysostom, for example, held that Paul was not speaking of himself in 4:15 but of those who would be alive at the parousia (*Homilies on 1 Thessalonians* 7). For a more extensive discussion, see Malherbe, *The Letters to the Thessalonians,* 270.

25. For more on *pornē,* see Kline, *God, Heaven, and Har Magedon,* 193.

26. Cardman, "Women, Ministry, and Church Order," 300.

27. See, for example, Malina and Pilch, *Social-Science Commentary on the Letters of Paul,* 85.

28. See, for example, Héring, *The First Epistle of Saint Paul to the Corinthians,* 48. May, "The Body for the Lord," 165, writes, "Precisely because it concerns marriage, 1 Cor 7 is key to understanding the sexual and social implications of Christian identity."

29. Martin, *Sex and the Single Savior,* 138, writes, "In fact, the fuller context of 1 Corinthians 7 ends up implicating Paul in inherent contradictions in his teaching on marriage, divorce, and remarriage." Wire, *The Corinthian Women Prophets,* 229, declares, "Apology on Paul's behalf is unnecessary."

30. See Fee, *The First Epistle to the Corinthians,* 270–271; Hurd, *The Origin of 1 Corinthians,* 67; Phipps, "Is Paul's Attitude Toward Sexual Relations"; and Schrage, "Zur Frontstellung der paulinischen Ehebewertung." A different, slightly dissenting position, is taken by Mitchell, "Concerning *peri de* in 1 Corinthians."

31. Zeller, *Der erste Brief an die Korinther,* 237–238. Martin, *Sex and the Single Savior,* 100, points to the similarities between 1 Cor 7:1 and John 20:17: "When Mary later wants a hug, Jesus won't let her even touch him (John 20:17). (Jesus' *noli me tangere* is the Gospel version of Paul's homosocial slogan 'It is better for a man not to touch a woman'; 1 Cor 7:1)."

32. Fitzmyer, *First Corinthians,* 274, writes, "Whether it is a Corinthian slogan or not, Paul enunciates it at the very beginning of his discussion in this chapter and gives the impression that he is per se in favor of the idea that it expresses, although some interpreters claim that he is rejecting the Corinthian slogan."

33. Martin, *Sex and the Single Savior,* 65.

34. See Castelli, "Paul on Women and Gender," 228, who queries, "Does the delivery of one's physical obligation to one's partner mean the same thing for women and men?"

35. Payne, *Man and Woman,* 106–107.

36. Weiss, *Der erste Korintherbrief,* 172, was one of the first scholars to note the similarities between Paul's directives in 1 Corinthians 7 and the fragments of Musonius Rufus. More recent treatments include Fitzmyer, *First Corinthians,* 276; and Zeller, *Der erste Brief an die Korinther,* 239. For important cautionary remarks regarding the use of Musonius to interpret Paul, see Bowen, "Musonius and Paul on Marriage."

37. Of particular importance on this text is Kloppenborg, "Egalitarianism."

38. Some scholars, such as L. Ann Jervis, "'But I Want You to Know,'" argue that Paul's language doesn't present a "chain of command," which implies that Paul's language doesn't promote gender hierarchy. See, however, the critique of this view by Martin, *The Corinthian Body,* 232–233.

39. Boyarin, "Gender," 123.

40. Knust, "Paul and the Politics of Virtue and Vice," 155, writes, "However pointed Paul's critique may have been, when he adopted sexual virtue and vice as his anti-imperial code language, he reconfirmed a gendered hierarchy that assumes woman is derived from man and identifies desire with 'slavishness.'"

41. "Burning" is a common motif in the ancient world. It appears frequently in the *Epigrams* of Philodemos as *pothos* and *typhomenē,* where it's a well-known characteristic of sexual passion (1.2, 4.6, 11.1, 16.4).

42. Troels Engberg-Pedersen, "The Sinful Body," 55–56, correctly notes, in my opinion, that Paul's apocalyptic beliefs inform this statement. For a recent treatment of 1 Cor 7:17–24, see, Hansen, *"All of You Are One,"* 105–157.

43. For recent comments on whether or not 1 Cor 7 reflects an imminent eschatology, see, Garland, *1 Corinthians,* 328–329; Rosner, *Paul, Scripture and Ethics,* 161–163; and Thiselton, *The First Epistle to the Corinthians,* 575.

44. Zeller, *Der erste Brief an die Korinther,* 264, provides an extensive list of parallels. For a different interpretation of "anxiety" in 1 Cor 7:32–34, see Gundry, "Anxiety or Care for People?" The most recent treatment of these issues is Barnes, *Reading 1 Corinthians,* 223–250.

45. Martin, *Sex and the Single Savior,* 139, writes, "Paul's *preference* is the avoidance of marriage" (italics in the original).

46. For Cynic views of sexuality, see Goulet-Cazé, "Le cynisme ancient et la sexualité."

47. In my opinion, Antoinette Clark Wire, *The Corinthian Women Prophets,* 91, reads far too much into 1 Cor 7:14, when she writes, "Paul's reference to children shows that many women have children and must care for them." This seems to be an overstatement that doesn't fit the available data.

48. A similar point is made by Martin, *Sex and the Single Savior,* 146.

49. For the date of Mark, see Marcus, *Mark 1–8,* 37–39.

50. On the author of Mark, see Marcus, *Mark 1–8,* 17–24.

51. Corley, *Women and the Historical Jesus,* 71.

52. When the Jesus Seminar, for example, voted on these texts they concluded Mark 10:5–10, grey; Matt 5:32, black, 19:3–8, grey; 19:9, black; Luke 16:18, grey.

53. This translation is from Robinson and Kloppenborg, eds., *The Sayings Gospel Q.* It's important to note that most of Q's material on the family is about disrupting the family in order to follow Jesus. (I'm indebted to Sarah Rollens for this insight.)

54. For later rabbinic parallels to this debate, see Luck, *Divorce and Remarriage*, 133–134.

55. Alluding to Genesis in order to support the sanctity of the marriage bond is also found in the Dead Sea Scrolls. For the various references, see Fitzmyer, "Divorce Among First-Century Palestinian Jews."

56. Jesus's views here are reminiscent of Mal 2:10–16. See Collins, "Marriage, Divorce and Family," 149.

57. Corley, *Women and the Historical Jesus*, 70. Though some scholars argue that Jesus's saying assumes Roman and not Jewish law, Corley convincingly argues that some Jewish women did sue for divorce in first-century Palestine.

58. This addition is universally accepted as a product of the author of the Gospel of Matthew. See, for example, Gundry, *Matthew*, 90.

59. Martin, *Sex and the Single Savior*, 105.

60. Antihousehold ideology is also present in Luke-Acts and Revelation. See Martin, *Sex and the Single Savior*, 106–111.

61. In my opinion, the deutero-Pauline authorship of Colossians and Ephesians was settled long ago by Bujard, *Stilanalytische Untersuchungen zum Kolosserbrief als Beitrag zur Methodik von Sprachvergleichen.*

62. This point is made by Krause, *1 Timothy*, 1–26; and Borg and Crossan, *The First Paul*, 1–28.

63. See, for example, Osiek and Balch, *Families in the New Testament World*, 5–35.

64. For an overview of what it means to be "submissive" in the New Testament literature, see Balch, *Let Wives Be Submissive*, 97–98.

65. For more on the connections between the New Testament codes and the Aristotelean code, see Delling, "Zur Taufe von 'Häusern' im Urchristentum," 289; and Voelke, *Les rapports avec autrui dans la philosophie grecque d'Aristote à Panetius*, 52–59.

66. Balch, *Let Wives Be Submissive*, 96–97.

67. For a brief discussion regarding development in Pauline eschatology, see Plevnik, *Paul and the Parousia*, 272–281.

68. Grant, *Paul in the Roman World*, 118.

69. This position is taken, in particular, by Meggitt, *Paul, Poverty and Survival.* On page 118, Meggitt argues that if Pauline scholars would take the social makeup of Roman Corinth seriously, they would end up analyzing Paul's remarks on marriage in 1 Corinthians 7 in light of the Augustan legislation. He contends that if this kind of exercise were done, Pauline scholars would discover that Paul's directives in 1 Corinthians 7 are some sort of first-century political remark against the Roman Empire instead of an endorsement of asceticism.

70. See Martin, "The Construction of the Ancient Family," 40–46.

71. Furthermore, Roman family law would apply only to Roman citizens.

72. Weber, *The Theory of Social and Economic Organization,* 234–363.

73. Martin, *Sex and the Single Savior,* 113.

74. See Cardman, "Women, Ministry, and Church Order," 302–305.

75. Cardman, "Women, Ministry, and Church Order," 303.

76. For a recent attempt to defend the Pauline authorship of 1 and 2 Timothy, see Johnson, *The First and Second Letters to Timothy,* 55–90.

77. See, for example, MacDonald, *The Legend and the Apostle,* 54–89; and Pervo, *The Making of Paul,* 63–118.

78. For an overview of this text, see Marshall, *The Pastoral Epistles,* 467–471.

79. For an overview of widows in the Pastoral Epistles, see Bassler, *1 Timothy, 2 Timothy, Titus,* 92–98, and her article "The Widows' Tale."

80. Martin, *Sex and the Single Savior,* 114.

81. Deleuze, *Foucault,* 70.

82. Cardman, "Women, Ministry, and Church Order," 305.

83. For more on this cycle, see Martin, *New Testament History and Literature,* 301–303.

84. Cooper, *The Virgin and the Bride,* 55.

85. Cooper, *The Virgin and the Bride,* 55.

86. Cardman, "Women, Ministry, and Church Order," 301.

87. Martin, *New Testament History and Literature,* 304.

4. Early Church

1. Martin, *New Testament History and Literature,* 290–291.

2. Heine, *Women and Early Christianity,* 138. Also see Castelli, "Virginity and Its Meaning."

3. For an overview of second- and third-generation Christian ethics, see Meeks, *The Origins of Christian Morality.*

4. See Brown, *The Body and Society,* 202–209.

5. Lévi-Strauss, *Structural Anthropology,* 61–62.

6. For various examples, see Forehlich, *Biblical Interpretation in the Early Church.*

7. Foucault, "The Battle for Chastity."

8. Cf. Hunter, *Marriage, Celibacy, and Heresy in Ancient Christianity.*

9. For an overview of Tatian's life, see Petersen, "Tatian the Assyrian," 129–134. Frend, *The Rise of Christianity,* 175, notes that the title "the Assyrian" describes one "born in the frontier district between the Roman Empire and Parthia."

10. For a different take on Tatian, see Koltun-Fromm, "Re-imagining Tatian."

11. Frend, *The Rise of Christianity,* 174–175.

12. This translation is from Petersen, "Tatian the Assyrian," 125, who uses Chabot, ed. *Chronique de Michel le Syrien,* 4:108–109.

13. Tatian's *On Perfection According to the Savior* (fr. 5) and his *Oratio ad Graecos* provide the only direct testimony of "encratite" theology available today.

14. Hunter, "The Language of Desire," 98, suggests "celibacy" as the best definition.

15. Blond, "L' 'Héresie' encratite vers la fin du quatrième siècle"; and Chadwick, "Encratism." For an overview of Tatian's rejection of meat and wine, see Finn, *Asceticism in the Graeco-Roman World*, 74–78; and McGowan, *Ascetic Eucharist*, 157. Ascetics usually reject wine because they think that too much of it leads to sexual intercourse. This idea is common in the Nag Hammadi literature. *Authoritative Teaching* condemns wine as "the debaucher" (24), while *On the Origin of the World* suggests that the grapevine sprouted up together with Eros from the first blood shed over the earth, with the result that "those who drink of it conceive the desire of sexual union" (109).

16. Petersen, "Tatian the Assyrian," 139.

17. As Peter Brown, *The Body and Society*, 92, points out, it isn't so much that Tatian calls himself an "encratite" as it is his contemporaries who assign him the term. Eusebius seems to be the first one to call Tatian Encratism's "first leader." In his Latin translation of Eusebius's *Ecclesiastical History*, Rufinus repeats Eusebius's assertion that Tatian is in fact Encratism's "first leader" (cf. Jerome, *Vir. ill.* 29; Michael the Syrian, *Chronicle* 6.5). Most scholars, however, assume that the claim is erroneous. For more on this, see Gasparro, *Enkrateia e antropologia*, 23–55, 78.

18. For a helpful overview of Tatian's views on sex, see Gaca, "Driving Aphrodite from the World." All quotations from Tatian's *Address to the Greeks* come from Whittaker, *Tatian*.

19. Bernadette J. Brooten, *Love Between Women*, 38, writes, "Discrediting the intellectual achievements of Sappho by attacking her sexual life may well have contributed to the loss of nearly all of Sappho's writings, as well as those of other women associated with her in any way."

20. As Elizabeth A. Clark, *Reading Renunciation*, 31–32, notes, Tatian equates marriage with *porneia*.

21. Cf. Epiphanius, *Refutation of All Heresies* 46.2; Jerome, *Comm. Gal.* 3 (6:8); Hippolytus, *Refutation of All Heresies* 8.16; Clement of Alexandria, *Miscellanies* 3.12.81.

22. Gaca, *The Making of Fornication*, 241.

23. As Brown, *The Body and Society*, 91, notes, Tatian is more interested in the soul being married to the Spirit than two souls suffusing during the sex act.

24. *On Perfection*, fr. 5 = Clement, *Miscellanies* 3.81.1–2. For the link between *gamos* and *porneia* in encratite thought, see Bianchi, ed., *La tradizione dell'enkrateia*, xxv; and Spada, "Un' omelia greca anonima 'sulla verginità,'" 604 n. 3.

25. Hunter, "The Language of Desire," 98.

26. In his *Diatessaron*, Tatian makes John the Baptist a more extreme ascetic by removing locusts from his diet.

27. Felix refused permission, upon which Justin relates, "the youth remained single." One is reminded, of course, of Origen's reportedly successful attempt to castrate himself in 198 C.E. Coincidentally, Origen was also in Alexandria.

28. Vööbus, *Celibacy*, 17.

29. Frend, *The Rise of Christianity*, 175.

30. Frend, *The Rise of Christianity*, 175.

31. Frend, *The Rise of Christianity*, 175.

32. For an overview of Clement's life and works, see Osborn, *Clement of Alexandria*, 1–28. For a general overview of Clement's views on marriage, see Reydams-Schils, "Clement of Alexandria," and "Musonius Rufus."

33. Wood, *Clement of Alexandria*, xiv.

34. Broudéhoux, *Mariage et famille*, provides the most comprehensive study of Clement's views on marriage. Also see Mees, "Clemens von Alexandrien über Ehe und Familie."

35. Bernadette J. Brooten, *Love Between Women*, 323, notes, "For him, the Genesis creation narratives lay the framework for understanding nature as gendered, while Christ's maleness further helps to delineate human nature." Clement's interpretation of Genesis follows Philo, who understood the Septuagint Pentateuch as endorsing Procreationism. For an overview, see Runia, *Philo in Early Christian Literature*, 132–156; and van den Hoek, *Clement of Alexandria*, 23–230.

36. Boswell, *Christianity, Social Tolerance, and Homosexuality*, 147. Also see Brooten, *Love Between Women*, 326.

37. Like Musonius, Clement views the production of large families as a patriotic duty: "One must marry on behalf of the fatherland, the succession of children, and to fulfill our obligation to the cosmos (*kosmos*) so far as we are able" (*Miscellanies* 2.140.1). He also cites Musonius in support of Procreationism (*Christ the Educator* 2.92.2). For Clement's use of Musonius, see Wendland, *Quaestiones Musonianae*, 31–32.

38. Clement exceeds Philo's strictures by noting that the two-word tenth commandment in the Septuagint, *ouk epithumēsis*, declares that any instance of sex for pleasure rather than procreation, even within a Christian marriage, implicates its agents in apostasy. Clement refers to this commandment at *An Exhortation to the Greeks* 108.5; and *Miscellanies* 3.71.3, 3.76.1, and 3.57.1–2 (where he describes it in some detail).

39. Animals would best conform to Clement's view of nature if they didn't engage in any unnatural sexual behaviors. For more on animals and sexuality in early Christian texts, see Pendergraft, "'Thou Shalt Not Eat the Hyena,'" 142, for the influence of these ancient views on medieval discussions of same-sex love. Other ancient references to the hare and the hyena include Pliny, *Natural History* 8.81.217–220, and Claudius Aelian, *De natura animalium* 1.25.

40. Hunter, "The Language of Desire," 97.

41. For an overview of Clement's (re)reading of 1 Corinthians 7, see Clark, *Reading Renunciation*, 316–328.

42. Gaca, *The Making of Fornication*, 269.

43. Brooten, *Love Between Women*, 325–326.

44. Matthew 5:27–28 provides Clement with the proof text he needs for labeling *epithumia* as adultery (*An Exhortation to the Greeks* 108.5; cf. *Miscellanies* 3.71.3; *Christ the Educator* 3.82.5–83.4). He falls just short of calling sexual desire within marriage *porneia*.

45. Gaca, *The Making of Fornication*, 260.

46. For an overview of *sōphrosynē*, see North, *SOPHROSYNE*.

47. Broudéhoux, *Mariage et famille*, 91–94. In support of his views on remarriage, Clement greatly elaborates the New Testament teaching that married Christians must not divorce (Mark 10:11–12, Luke 16:18, 1 Cor 7:10, Eph 5:22–33).

48. Hunter, "The Language of Desire," 107, claims, "Clement proposes a rival, more moderate ideal of *enkrateia*." Also see Karavites, *Evil, Freedom, and the Road to Perfection in Clement of Alexandria*, 89.

49. Gaca, *The Making of Fornication*, 247.

50. Gaca, *The Making of Fornication*, 259.

51. For an overview of Clement's asceticism, see Finn, *Asceticism in the Graeco-Roman World*, 94–97.

52. Ferguson, *Clement of Alexandria*, 131.

53. Oulton and Chadwick, eds., *Alexandrian Christianity*, 34.

54. For a basic introduction to Epiphanes, see Oulton and Chadwick, eds., *Alexandrian Christianity*, 25–29; and Smith and Wace, "Epiphanes." For the possible connection between Epiphanes and the Carpocratians, see Liboron, *Die karpokratianische Gnosis*, 15–18.

55. For an overview, see Bluestone, *Women and the Ideal Society*, 3–20; and Hill, "The First Wave of Feminism."

56. For an overview of this text, see Hengel, *Property and Riches in the Early Church*, 23–34; Judge, *The Social Pattern of Christian Groups*, 30–52; and Theissen, *Social Reality and the Early Christians*, 33–93.

57. Gaca, *The Making of Fornication*, 275.

58. Gaca, *The Making of Fornication*, 285.

59. For a more recent overview of Cassian's life, see Stewart, *Cassian the Monk*, 4–24. I borrow the phrase "battle for chastity" from Foucault, "The Battle for Chastity," 188.

60. For the date, see Stewart, *Cassian the Monk*, 16. Also see Leyser, *Authority and Asceticism*, 42.

61. Rousseau, *Ascetics, Authority, and the Church*, 182.

62. For an overview of these two works, see Finn, *Asceticism in the Graeco-Roman World*, 125–129.

63. Foucault, "The Battle for Chastity," 196.

64. Stewart, *Cassian the Monk*, 67.

65. For more on this theme, see Cloke, *This Female Man of God*, 121–133.

66. Stewart, *Cassian the Monk*, 67. For an overview of ecclesiastic condemnation of marital virginity, see the insightful comments of Elm, *Virgins of God*, 48–51.

67. Stewart, *Cassian the Monk*, 69. Cf. Evagrius, *Rerum mon. rat.* 1–2 (cols. 1252D–1253C) on marriage and monks.

68. Stewart, *Cassian the Monk*, 68. Also see Brown, *The Body and Society*, 231–232, 420–422.

69. Kelly, *Jerome*, 102.

70. For an introduction to these issues, see Hunter, "Resistance to the Virginal Ideal," and more recently *Marriage, Celibacy and Heresy in Ancient Christianity*.

71. Martin, *Sex and the Single Savior*, 116.

72. I'm quoting the translation of the letter given in Hunter, "Rereading the Jovinianist Controversy."

73. Hunter, "Rereading the Jovinianist Controversy," 453.

74. Hunter, "Resistance to the Virginal Ideal," 61.

75. Hunter, " 'On the Sin of Adam and Eve,' " 290.

76. Clark, "Anti-familial Tendencies in Ancient Christianity," 373–375.

77. Brown, *The Body and Society*, 265.

5. Then and Now

1. McCabe, *Law, Love and Language*, 156.

2. McCabe, *Law, Love and Language*, 156.

3. Quoted in Dreyfus and Rabinow, *Michel Foucault*, 128.

4. Foucault, *The Archaeology of Knowledge*, 9–10.

5. Foucault, *An Introduction*, 106. Foucault coined the term "biopower" (*biopouvoir*), which relates to the practice of modern nation-states and their regulation of their subjects through "an explosion of numerous and diverse techniques for achieving the subjugations of bodies and the control of populations." See Foucault, *An Introduction*, 140.

6. Indeed, Edelman, *No Future*, 58, is right to point out that procreation in modern American society is really all about "heteroreproductivity."

7. As Runions, *The Babylon Complex*, 197, states: "Sexuality is regulated according to Christian values in order to save the nation and humanity. Universal humanity is particularized as Christian and safeguarded by the United States. Since the nation and humanity are ultimately preserved by heterosexuality, 'true' humanity is 'saved,' affiliated with the United States, and heterosexual."

8. Foucault, *An Introduction*, 86.

9. Dreyfus and Rabinow, *Michel Foucault*, 130.

10. In my opinion, Jakobsen and Pellegrini, *Love the Sin*, 31, are right to maintain, "Whether or not 'Judaism' and 'Christianity' agree on questions of sexual ethics depends entirely on which Judaism and which Christianity are being considered, and even Orthodox Judaism and conservative Christianity do not agree on all issues regarding sex."

11. Clark, "Antifamilial Tendencies in Ancient Christianity," 380.

12. I agree with Foucault, who in "Discourse on Power" (interview from 1978) said: "[Here] is an observation that people often make of my thought: you do not ever say what the concrete solutions to the problems you pose could be; you do not make proposals . . . I absolutely will not play the part of one who prescribes solutions . . . My role is to address problems effectively, really: and to pose them with the greatest possible rigor, with the maximum complexity and difficulty so that a solution does not arise all at once because of the thought of some reformer or even in the brain of a political party. The problems that I try to address, these perplexities of crime, madness, and sex which involve daily life, cannot be

easily resolved. It takes years, decades of work carried out at the grassroots level with the people directly involved; and the right to speech and political imagination must be returned to them." Quoted in Foucault, *Remarks on Marx*, 157–159.

13. Turner, *Thomas Aquinas*, 142–143.

14. See, for example, Girgis, George, and Anderson, "What Is Marriage?"

15. Girgis et al., "What Is Marriage?," 246.

16. Girgis et al., "What Is Marriage?," 246.

17. Girgis et al., "What Is Marriage?," 246.

18. Girgis et al., "What Is Marriage?," 246.

19. Girgis et al., "What Is Marriage?," 246–247.

20. Girgis et al., "What Is Marriage?," 247.

21. Patrick Fagan, "The Wealth of Nations Depends on the Health of Families," Witherspoon Institute, Public Discourse, unpaginated, 6 February 2013, http://www.thepublicdiscourse.com/2013/02/7821/. Quotations from Fagan in the text are from this document.

22. See the analysis of Fineman, *The Neutered Mother*, 104, who points out that many conservatives view singleness as deviant.

23. Fineman, *The Neutered Mother*, 104.

24. Interestingly, in *Amoris Laetitia*, 30, Pope Francis suggests that the story of Herod ordering the murder of Jewish babies says more about modern "refugee families" than it does about abortion. As he relates: "Every family should look to the icon of the Holy Family of Nazareth. Its daily life had its share of burdens and even nightmares, as when they met with Herod's implacable violence. This last was an experience that, sad to say, continues to afflict the many refugee families who in our day feel rejected and helpless."

25. Heritage Foundation, "What You Need to Know About Marriage: Questions and Answers Driving the Debate," available at http://www.heritage.org/marriage/.

26. Unfortunately, the Heritage Foundation seems unaware of the fact that before DOMA, the federal government accepted variant state definitions of marriage. As Nancy Cott and others point out in the *Amicus Curiae on Same-Sex Marriage*: "States have taken seriously their responsibility for marriage definition. In every state, marriage has been defined as a voluntary bond between a couple—and a couple only—who share sexual intimacy and mutual economic support. States' additional requirements have varied, often significantly, sometimes in ways obnoxious to their sister states. More than once in U.S. history, the level of contention and division over marital policy rose alarmingly when one or more states innovated, and others disapproved" (23). The brief is available at https://www.glad.org/uploads/docs/cases/windsor-v-united-states/amicus-brief-of-american-historical-association-and-historians.pdf.

27. Heritage Foundation, "What You Need to Know About Marriage," n.p.

28. Heritage Foundation, "What You Need to Know About Marriage," n.p.

29. Wilson, "In Defense of Traditional Marriage."

30. Wilson, "In Defense of Traditional Marriage," 4.

31. Wilson, "In Defense of Traditional Marriage," 2.

32. Wilson, "In Defense of Traditional Marriage," 2. In *Amoris Laetitia*, 67, Pope Francis writes: "The Second Vatican Council, in its Pastoral Constitution Gaudium et Spes, was concerned 'to promote the dignity of marriage and the family (cf. Nos. 47–52).' The Constitution 'defined marriage as a community of life and love (cf. 48), placing love at the center of the family' . . . 'True love between husband and wife' (49) involves mutual self-giving, includes and integrates the sexual and affective dimensions, in accordance with God's plan (cf. 48–49)."

33. She points to Paul VI, *Gaudium et Spes* 48, which reads, "For God himself is the author of matrimony and has endowed it with various values and purposes." From the *Catechism of the Catholic Church* she refers to no. 1959, which says, "The natural law . . . provides the necessary basis for the civil law with which it is connected." See as well Pontifical Council for the Family, *The Truth and Meaning of Human Sexuality*, nos. 32–33.

34. Wilson, "In Defense of Traditional Marriage," 3.

35. Wilson, "In Defense of Traditional Marriage," 4.

36. For an important discussion about the differences between "construction" and "reconstruction," see Martin, *New Testament History and Literature*, 182–184.

37. United States Conference of Catholic Bishops, "Between Man and Woman: Questions and Answers About Marriage and Same-Sex Unions," unpaginated, 2003, http://www.usccb.org/issues-and-action/marriage-and-family/marriage/promotion-and-defense-of-marriage/questions-and-answers-about-marriage-and-same-sex-unions.cfm. The discussion and quotations in the text refer to this document.

38. Elsewhere in the document, the U.S. bishops proclaim: "They are equal as human beings but different as man and woman, fulfilling each other through this natural difference. This unique complementarity makes possible the conjugal bond that is the core of marriage."

39. The transcript of the hearings can be found at http://www.supremecourt.gov /oral_arguments/argument_transcripts/14–556q1_7l48.pdf. Throughout, I refer to the page numbers provided in the electronic document.

40. For a discussion of the classical roots of Christian marriage as defined by Anglicanism, see Treggiari, *Roman Marriage*, 11–13. Procreation is also the central purpose of marriage in Eastern Orthodox churches. For an overview, see McGuckin, *The Orthodox Church*, 309–323. For an analysis of how this works in liberal U.S. politics, see Runions, *The Babylon Complex*, 118–119, 146.

41. Joseph Wolff was a Christian missionary to the Jews, and his journal and memoir was first published in 1824 (*Missionary Journal and Memoir, of the Rev. Joseph Wolf* [sic] *Missionary to the Jews*). According to Silk, "The Abrahamic Religions as a Modern Concept," 73, Wolff was "advised 'to establish a Judeo-christian church,' by which he meant one that permitted Jews to maintain such practices as circumcision and Saturday worship." The term may have been used earlier but without the hyphen by Alexander M'Caul in 1821.

42. Eisenhower quoted in Henry, "'And I Don't Care What It Is,'" 41.

43. Dennis Prager, WND, "The Case for Judeo-Christian Values, Part 5," 15 February 2005, http://www.wnd.com/2005/02/28929/.

44. Tocqueville, *Democracy in America*, 287, 14.

45. Adelle M. Banks, *Washington Post*, "Southern Baptist President: God, Not Supreme Court, Has 'Final Authority,'" https://www.washingtonpost.com/national/southern-baptist-president-god-not-supreme-court-has-final-authority/2015/06/16/e026314a-146e-11e5-8457-4b431bf7ed4c_story.html?utm_term=.4100bb39eadc.

46. Ronnie Floyd, Southern Baptist Convention, "On the Call to Public Witness on Marriage," Columbus, OH, 2015, http://www.sbc.net/resolutions/2255/on-the-call-to-public-witness-on-marriage.

47. Richard Lee, Sermon Central, "Seven Principles of the Judeo-Christian Ethic," http://www.sermoncentral.com/content/Richard-Lee-7-Principles-Judeo-Christian-Ethic?Page=1&ac&csplit=9060.

48. Lyotard and Gruber, *The Hyphen*, 14.

49. Althusser, "Ideology and Ideological State Apparatuses," 96.

50. McLean, *Biblical Interpretation and Philosophical Hermeneutics*, 209.

51. Butler, *Gender Trouble*, 153.

52. Butler, *Gender Trouble*, 157.

53. Irigaray, *This Sex Which Is Not One*, 165.

54. Cf. Sedgwick, *Epistemology of the Closet*, 228–229.

55. For an analysis of the effect of capitalism on marriage and sexuality, see Hennessy, *Profit and Pleasure*.

56. Ingraham, *White Weddings*, 32.

BIBLIOGRAPHY

AYB   Anchor Yale Bible
DSD   *Dead Sea Discoveries*
JBL   *Journal of Biblical Literature*
JECS   *Journal of Early Christian Studies*
JRS   *Journal of Roman Studies*
NovT   *Novum Testamentum*
NTS   *New Testament Studies*

Africa, T. "The Mask of an Assassin." *Journal of Interdisciplinary History* 8 (1978): 499–626.

Agamben, Giorgio. *The Time That Remains: A Commentary on the Letter to the Romans.* Stanford, CA: Stanford University Press, 2005.

Althusser, Louis. *Essays in Self-Criticism.* London: NLB, 1976.

———. "Ideology and Ideological State Apparatuses." Pages 127–186 in *Lenin and Philosophy and Other Essays.* Translated by Ben Brewster. New York: Monthly Review Press, 1971.

Arthur, Marylin B. "Early Greece: The Origins of the Western Attitude Toward Women." Pages 1–58 in *Women in the Ancient World: The Arethusa Papers.* Edited by John Peradotto and J. P. Sullivan. Albany, NY: SUNY Press, 1984.

Asmis, Elizabeth. "The Stoics on Women." Pages 68–92 in *Feminism and Ancient Philosophy*. Edited by Julie K. Ward. London: Routledge, 1996.

Bailey, Kenneth E. "Women in the New Testament: A Middle Eastern Cultural View." *Anvil* March (1994): 7–24.

Bakhtin, M. M. *Speech Genres and Other Late Essays*. Austin: University of Texas Press, 1996.

Balch, David L. *Let Wives Be Submissive: The Domestic Code in I Peter*. Society of Biblical Literature Monograph Series 26. Atlanta: Scholars Press, 1981.

Balsdon, J. P. V. D. *Roman Women: Their History and Habits*. New York: Barnes & Noble, 1962.

Barclay, John M. G. *Jews in the Mediterranean Diaspora: From Alexandria to Trajan (323 BCE-117 CE)*. Edinburgh: T&T Clark, 1996.

Barnes, Nathan. *Reading 1 Corinthians with Philosophically Educated Women*. Eugene, OR: Pickwick, 2014.

Bassler, Jouette. *1 Timothy, 2 Timothy, Titus*. New Testament Commentaries. Nashville, TN: Abingdon, 1996.

———. "The Widows' Tale: A Fresh Look at 1 Tim 5:3–16." *JBL* 103 (1984): 23–41.

Benjamin, Walter. "Goethe's Elective Affinities." Pages 297–362 in *Selected Writings Volume 1, 1913–1926*. Edited by Marcus Bullock and Michael W. Jennings. Cambridge, MA: Belknap Press of Harvard University Press, 1996.

Belkin, Samuel. *Philo and the Oral Law: The Philonic Interpretation of Biblical Law in Relation to Palestinian Halakah*. Cambridge, MA: Harvard University Press, 1940.

Bianchi, Ugo, ed. *La tradizione dell'enkrateia: motivazioni ontologiche e protologiche*. Atti del Colloquio Internazionale Milano, 20–23 April 1982. Rome: Edizioni dell'Ateneo, 1985.

Blond, Georges. "L' 'Hérésie' encratite vers la fin du quatrième siècle." *Recherches de science religieuse* 31 (1944): 157–210.

Bluestone, Natalie Harris. *Women and the Ideal Society: Plato's Republic and Modern Myths of Gender*. Amherst: University of Massachusetts Press, 1987.

Borg, Marcus J., and John Dominic Crossan. *The First Paul: Reclaiming the Radical Visionary Behind the Church's Conservative Icon*. New York: HarperOne, 2010.

Boswell, John. *Christianity, Social Tolerance, and Homosexuality: Gay People in Western Europe from the Beginning of the Christian Era to the Fourteenth Century*. Chicago: University of Chicago Press, 1980.

Bourdieu, Pierre, and Loïc J. D. Wacquant. *An Invitation to Reflexive Sociology*. Chicago: University of Chicago Press, 1992.

Bowen, Roy Ward. "Musonius and Paul on Marriage." *NTS* 36 (1990): 281–289.

Boyarin, Daniel. *Carnal Israel: Reading Sex in Talmudic Culture.* Berkley: University of California Press, 2005.

———. "Gender." Pages 117–135 in *Critical Terms for Religious Studies.* Edited by Mark C. Taylor. Chicago: University of Chicago Press, 1998.

Brooten, Bernadette J. *Love Between Women: Early Christian Responses to Female Homoeroticism.* Chicago: University of Chicago Press, 1996.

Broudéhoux, Jean-Paul. *Mariage et famille chez Clément d'Alexandria.* Théologie Historique 11. Paris: Beauchesne, 1970.

Brown, Peter. *The Body and Society: Men, Women, and Sexual Renunciation in Early Christianity.* New York: Columbia University Press, 2008.

Bujard, Walter. *Stilanalytische Untersuchungen zum Kolosserbrief als Beitrag zur Methodik von Sprachvergleichen.* Studien zur Umwelt des Neuen Testaments 11. Göttingen: Vandenhoeck & Ruprecht, 1973.

Bunch, Charlotte. "Not for Lesbians Only." Pages 54–58 in *Materialist Feminism: A Reader in Class, Difference, and Women's Lives.* Edited by Rosemary Hennessy and Chrys Ingraham. New York: Routledge, 1997.

Burridge, Richard A. *Imitating Jesus: An Inclusive Approach to New Testament Ethics.* Grand Rapids, MI: Eerdmans, 2007.

Butler, Judith. *Gender Trouble.* New York: Routledge, 1990.

Cardman, Francine. "Women, Ministry, and Church Order in Early Christianity." Pages 300–329 in *Women and Christian Origins.* Edited by Ross Shepard Kraemer and Mary Rose D'Angelo. Oxford: Oxford University Press, 1999.

Castelli, Elizabeth A. "Paul on Women and Gender." Pages 221–235 in *Women and Christian Origins.* Edited by Ross Shepard Kraemer and Mary Rose D'Angelo. Oxford: Oxford University Press, 1999.

———. "Virginity and Its Meaning for Women's Sexuality in Early Christianity." *Journal of Feminist Studies in Religion* 2 (1986): 61–88.

Chabot, J.-B., ed. *Chronique de Michel le Syrien.* Volume 4. Paris: Leroux, 1910.

Chadwick, Henry. "Encratism." Pages 343–365 in *Reallexikon für Antike und Christentum.* Volume 5. Edited by Theodor Klauser et al. Stuttgart: Hiersemann, 1950–.

Chepey, Stuart. *Nazarites in Late Second Temple Judaism.* Leiden: Brill, 2005.

Ciampa, Roy E., and Brian S. Rosner. "The Structure and Argument of 1 Corinthians: A Biblical/Jewish Approach." *NTS* 52 (2006): 205–218.

Clark, Elizabeth A. "Anti-familial Tendencies in Ancient Christianity." *Journal of the History of Sexuality* 5 (1995): 356–380.

———. *Reading Renunciation: Asceticism and Scripture in Early Christianity.* Princeton, NJ: Princeton University Press, 1999.

Cloke, Gillian. *This Female Man of God: Women and Spiritual Power in the Patristic Age, 350–450 AD*. London: Routledge, 1995.

Cohen, Jeremy. *"Be Fertile and Increase, Fill the Earth and Master It": The Ancient and Medieval Career of a Biblical Text*. Ithaca, NY: Cornell University Press, 1989.

Collins, Adela Y. "Early Christian Apocalypticism." Pages 288–292 in *The Anchor Bible Dictionary*. Volume 1. Edited by David Noel Freedman. New Haven, CT: Yale University Press, 1992.

Collins, John J. "Marriage, Divorce and Family in Second Temple Judaism." Pages 104–162 in *Families in Ancient Israel*. Edited by Leo Perdue, Joseph Blenkinsopp, John J. Collins, and Carol Meyers. Louisville, KY: Westminster John Knox, 1997.

———. "Watchers." Pages 893–895 in *Dictionary of Deities and Demons in the Bible*. Edited by K. van der Toorn, B. Becking, and P. W. van der Horst. 2nd ed. Leiden: Brill, 1999.

Collins, Raymond F. *Studies on the First Letter to the Thessalonians*. Bibliotheca Ephemeridum Theologicarum Lovaniensium 66. Leuven: Leuven University Press, 1984.

Cooley, Alison E., ed. *Res Gestae Divi Augusti: Text, Translation, and Commentary* Cambridge: Cambridge University Press, 2009.

Coontz, Stephanie. *The Way We Never Were: American Families and the Nostalgia Trap*. New York: Basic Books, 1992.

Cooper, Kate. *The Virgin and the Bride: Idealized Womanhood in Late Antiquity*. Cambridge, MA: Harvard University Press, 1996.

Corbett, Percy E. *The Roman Law of Marriage*. Oxford: Clarendon, 1969.

Corley, Kathleen E. *Women and the Historical Jesus: Feminist Myths of Christian Origins*. Santa Rosa, CA: Polebridge, 2002.

Çsillag, Pál. *The Augustan Laws on Family Relations*. Budapest: Akadémiai Kiadó, 1976.

Cudjoe, R. V. *The Social and Legal Position of Widows and Orphans in Classical Athens*. Symboles 3. Athens: Centre for Ancient Greek and Hellenistic Law, 2010.

D'Angelo, Mary Rose. "Gender and Geopolitics in the Work of Philo of Alexandria: Jewish Piety and Imperial Family Values." Pages 63–88 in *Mapping Gender in Ancient Religious Discourses*. Edited by Todd Penner and Caroline Vander Stichele. Leiden: Brill, 2007.

Daube, David. *The Duty of Procreation*. Eugene, OR: Wipf & Stock, 2011.

Dean, Mitchell. *Critical and Effective Histories: Foucault's Methods and Historical Sociology*. London: Routledge, 1994.

Degrassi, A. *Inscriptiones Italiae* 13.2. Rome: Istituto Poligrafico dello Strato, 1963.

Deleuze, Gilles. *Foucault*. London: Althone, 1986.

Delling, Gerhard. "Zur Taupe von 'Häusern' im Urchristentum." *NovT* 7 (1965): 285–311.

Deming, Will. *Paul on Marriage and Celibacy: The Hellenistic Background of 1 Corinthians 7.* Grand Rapids, MI: Eerdmans, 2004.

Derrida, Jacques. *Positions.* Chicago: University of Chicago Press, 1981.

Dixon, Suzanne. *Reading Roman Women: Sources, Genres and Real Life.* London: Duckworth, 2001.

———. *The Roman Mother.* Norman, OK: University of Oklahoma Press, 1988.

Dodd, C. H. *New Testament Studies.* Manchester: Manchester University Press, 1963.

Drake, Susanna. *Slandering the Jew: Sexuality and Difference in Early Christian Texts.* Philadelphia: University of Pennsylvania Press, 2013.

Dreyfus, Herbert L., and Paul Rabinow. *Michel Foucault: Beyond Structuralism and Hermeneutics.* Chicago: University of Chicago Press, 1983.

Edelman, Lee. *No Future: Queer Theory and the Death Drive.* Durham, NC: Duke University Press, 2004.

Edwards, Catherine. *The Politics of Immorality in Ancient Rome.* Cambridge: Cambridge University Press, 1993.

Eidinow, Esther. "Sex, Religion, and the Law." Pages 87–106 in *A Cultural History of Sexuality in the Classical World.* Edited by Mark Golden and Peter Toohey. New York: Bloomsbury, 2014.

Elm, Susanna. *Virgins of God: The Making of Asceticism in Late Antiquity.* Oxford: Clarendon, 1994.

Elster, Jon, ed. *Karl Marx: A Reader.* Cambridge: Cambridge University Press, 1986.

Engberg-Pedersen, Troels. "The Sinful Body: Paul on Marriage and Sex." Pages 41–60 in *Ehe—Familie—Gemeinde: Theologische und soziologische Perspektiven auf frühchristliche Lebenswelten.* Arbeiten zur Bibel und ihrer Geschichte. Edited by Dorothee Dettinger and Christof Landmesser. Leipzig: Evangelische Verlagsanstalt, 2014.

Engel, David M. "The Gender Egalitarianism of Musonius Rufus." *Ancient Philosophy* 20 (2000): 377–391.

———. "Women's Role in the Home and State: Stoic Theory Reconsidered." *Harvard Studies in Classical Philology* 101 (2003): 267–288.

Eschel, Hanan, Magen Broshi, Richard Freund, and Brian Schultz. "New Data on the Cemetery East of Khirbet Qumran." *DSD* 9/2 (2002): 135–165.

Fatum, Lone. "Brotherhood in Christ: A Gender Hermeneutical Reading of 1 Thessalonians." Pages 183–197 in *Constructing Early Christian Families: Family as Social Reality and Metaphor.* Edited by Halvor Moxnes. London: Routledge, 1997.

Fee, Gordon D. *The First Epistle to the Corinthians.* New International Commentary on the New Testament. Grand Rapids, MI: Eerdmans, 1987.

Ferguson, John. *Clement of Alexandria.* New York: Twayne, 1974.

Fineman, Martha Albertson. *The Neutered Mother: The Sexual Family and Other Twentieth Century Tragedies.* New York: Routledge, 1995.

Finn, Richard. *Asceticism in the Graeco-Roman World.* Key Themes in Ancient History. Cambridge: Cambridge University Press, 2009.

Fitzgerald, John T. "Cynics." Page 160 in *Encyclopedia of the Dead Sea Scrolls.* Volume 1. Edited by Lawrence H. Schiffman and James C. VanderKam. New York: Oxford University Press, 2000.

——. "Epicureans." Pages 254–255 in *Encyclopedia of the Dead Sea Scrolls.* Volume 1. Edited by Lawrence H. Schiffman and James C. VanderKam. New York: Oxford University Press, 2000.

——. "Orphans in Mediterranean Antiquity and Early Christianity." *Acta Theologica* Supplement 23 (2016): 29–48.

——. "Pythagoreans." Pages 728–729 in *Encyclopedia of the Dead Sea Scrolls.* Volume 2. Edited by Lawrence H. Schiffman and James C. VanderKam. New York: Oxford University Press, 2000.

Fitzmyer, Joseph. "Divorce Among First-Century Palestinian Jews." *Eretz-Israel* 14 (1978): 103–110.

——. *First Corinthians.* AYB 32. New Haven, CT: Yale University Press, 2008.

——. *Tobit: Commentaries on Early Jewish Literature.* Berlin: Walter de Gruyter, 2003.

Flemming, Rebecca. "Gendering Medical Provision in the Cities of the Roman West." Pages 275–294 in *Women and the Roman City in the Latin West.* Edited by Emily Hemelrijk and Greg Woolf. Leiden: Brill, 2013.

——. *Medicine and the Making of Roman Women: Gender, Nature, and Authority from Celsus to Galen.* Oxford: Oxford University Press, 2000.

Foucault, Michel. *The Archaeology of Knowledge.* New York: Vintage, 2010.

——. "The Battle for Chastity." Pages 188–197 in *Religion and Culture: Michel Foucault.* Edited by Jeremy R. Carrette. New York: Routledge, 1999.

——. *The History of Sexuality. Volume 1: An Introduction.* New York: Vintage, 1990.

——. *The History of Sexuality. Volume 2: The Use of Pleasure.* New York: Vintage, 1990.

——. *The History of Sexuality. Volume 3: The Care of the Self.* New York: Vintage, 1988.

——. *Remarks on Marx: Conversations with Duccio Trombardori.* New York: Semiotext(e), 1991.

——. "Sexuality and Solitude." Pages 182–187 in *Religion and Culture: Michel Foucault.* Edited by Jeremy Carrette. New York: Routledge, 1999.

Fraenkel, Eduard. *Horace.* 1957. Reprint, Oxford: Clarendon, 1997.

Francis (pope). *Amoris Laetitia: On Love in the Family.* Huntington, IN: Our Sunday Visitor, 2016.

Frend, W. H. C. *The Rise of Christianity.* Philadelphia: Fortress, 1984.

Forehlich, Karlfried. *Biblical Interpretation in the Early Church.* Philadelphia: Fortress, 1984.

Gaca, Kathy L. "Driving Aphrodite from the World: Tatian's Encratite Principles of Sexual Renunciation." *Journal of Theological Studies* 53:1 (2002): 28–52.

———. *The Making of Fornication: Eros, Ethics, and Political Reform in Greek Philosophy and Early Christianity.* Berkeley: University of California Press, 2003.

Galinsky, Karl. *Augustus: Introduction to the Life of an Emperor.* Cambridge: Cambridge University Press, 2012.

Gardner, Jane F. *Women in Roman Law and Society.* Bloomington: Indiana University Press, 1991.

Garland, David E. *1 Corinthians.* Baker Exegetical Commentary on the New Testament. Grand Rapids, MI: Baker Academic, 2003.

Gasparro, Giulia Sfameni. *Enkrateia e antropologia: le motivazioni protologiche della continenze e della verginità nel cristianesimo dei primi secoli e nello gnosticismo.* Studie Ephemeridis "Augustinianum" 20. Rome: Institutum Patristicum "Augustinianum," 1984.

Gimenez, Martha. "The Oppression of Women: A Structuralist Marxist View." Pages 71–82 in *Material Feminism: A Reader in Class, Difference, and Women's Lives.* Edited by Rosemary Hennessy and Chrys Ingraham. New York: Routledge, 1997.

Girgis, Sherif, Robert P. George, and Ryan T. Anderson, "What Is Marriage?" *Harvard Journal of Law and Public Policy* 34 (2010): 245–287.

Glancy, Jennifer. "The Sexual Use of Slaves: A Response to Kyle Harper on Jewish and Christian *Porneia*." *JBL* 134 (2015): 215–229.

Glazebrook, Allison. "Prostitution." Pages 145–168 in *A Cultural History of Sexuality in the Classical World.* Edited by Mark Golden and Peter Toohey. London: Bloomsbury, 2011.

Goff, Matthew J. *Discerning Wisdom: The Sapiential Literature of the Dead Sea Scrolls.* Supplements to Vetus Testamentum 116. Leiden: Brill, 2007.

———. *4QInstruction.* Wisdom Literature from the Ancient World. Atlanta: SBL Press, 2013.

Golden, Mark, and Peter Toohey. "Introduction." Pages 1–16 in *A Cultural History of Sexuality in the Classical World.* Edited by Mark Golden and Peter Toohey. New York: Bloomsbury, 2014.

Goldhill, Simon. *Foucault's Virginity: Ancient Erotic Fiction and the History of Sexuality.* Cambridge: Cambridge University Press, 1995.

Goodman, Martin. *The Ruling Class of Judaea: The Origins of the Jewish Revolt Against Rome A.D. 66–70.* Cambridge: Cambridge University Press, 1987.

Goulet-Cazé, Marie-Odile. "Le cynisme ancient et la sexualité." *Clio. Femmes, Genre, Histoire* (2005): 17–35.

Grant, Robert M. *Paul in the Roman World: The Conflict at Corinth.* Louisville, KY: Westminster John Knox, 2001.

Green, P. "Carmen et error: *Prophasis* and *aitia* in the manner of Ovid's exile." *Classical Antiquity* 1 (1982): 202–220.

Griffin, Miriam. "*Urbs Roma, Plebs,* and *Princeps.*" Pages 19–46 in *Images of Empire.* Edited by Loveday Alexander. Sheffield: JSOT Press, 1991.

Groen-Vallinga, Miriam J. "Female Participation in the Roman Urban Labour Market." Pages 295–312 in *Women and the Roman City in the Latin West.* Edited by Emily Hemelrijk and Greg Woolf. Leiden: Brill, 2013.

Gundry, Judith M. "Anxiety or Care for People? The Theme of 1 Corinthians 7:32–34 and the Relation Between Exegesis and Theology." Pages 109–130 in *Reconsidering the Relationship Between Biblical and Systematic Theology in the New Testament.* Edited by Brian Lugioyo, Benjamin E. Reynolds, and Kevin J. Vanhoozer. Tübingen: Mohr Siebeck, 2014.

Gundry, Robert. *Matthew: A Commentary on His Literary and Theological Art.* Grand Rapids, MI: Eerdmans, 1982.

Hall, Stuart. "The Problem of Ideology: Marxism Without Guarantees." Pages 24–44 in *Stuart Hall: Critical Dialogues in Cultural Studies.* Edited by David Morley and Kuan-Hsing Chen. London: Routledge, 1996.

Hankinson, R. J. "The Man and His Work." Pages 1–33 in *The Cambridge Companion to Galen.* Edited by R. J. Hankinson. Cambridge: Cambridge University Press, 2008.

Hansen, Bruce. *"All of You Are One": The Social Vision of Gal 3.28, 1 Cor 12.13 and Col 3.11.* London: T&T Clark, 2010.

Harper, Kyle. *From Shame to Sin: The Christian Transformation of Sexual Morality in Late Antiquity.* Cambridge, MA: Harvard University Press, 2013.

———. "*Porneia:* The Making of a Christian Sexual Norm. *JBL* 134 (2013): 363–383.

Harrington, H. K. *Holiness: Rabbinic Judaism and the Graeco-Roman World.* London: Routledge, 2001.

———. *The Purity Texts.* Companion to the Qumran Scrolls. London: T&T Clark, 2004.

Hayes, Christine. *Gentile Impurities and Jewish Identities: Intermarriage and Conversion from the Bible to the Talmud.* Oxford: Oxford University Press, 2002.

Heine, Susanne. *Women and Early Christianity: Are Feminist Scholars Right?* London: SCM-Canterbury, 1987.

Heinemann, Isaak. *Philons griechische und jüdische Bildung: Kulturvergleichende Untersuchungen zu Philons Darstellung der jüdische Gesetze.* Hildersheim: Georg Olms, 1962.

Hengel, Martin. *Property and Riches in the Early Church: Aspects of a Social History of Early Christianity.* Translated by John Bowden. Philadelphia: Fortress, 1974.

Hennessy, Rosemary. *Profit and Pleasure: Sexual Identities in Late Capitalism.* New York: Routledge, 2000.

Henry, Patrick. "'And I Don't Care What It Is': The Tradition-History of a Civil Religion Proof-Text." *Journal of the American Academy of Religion* 49 (1981): 35–47.

Herbert-Brown, Geraldine. "Fasti: The Poet, the Prince, and the Plebs." Pages 120–139 in *A Companion to Ovid.* Edited by Peter E. Knox. Oxford: Blackwell, 2009.

Héring, Jean. *The First Epistle of Saint Paul to the Corinthians.* London: Epworth, 1961.

Hill, Lisa. "The First Wave of Feminism: Were the Stoics Feminists?" *History of Political Thought* 22 (2001): 12–40.

Hirsch, E. D. *Validity in Interpretation.* New Haven, CT: Yale University Press, 1967.

Hunter, David G. "The Language of Desire: Clement of Alexandria's Transformation of Ascetic Discourse." *Semeia* 57 (1992): 95–111.

———. *Marriage, Celibacy and Heresy in Ancient Christianity: The Jovinianist Controversy.* Oxford Early Christian Studies. Oxford: Oxford University Press, 2009.

———. "'On the Sin of Adam and Eve': A Little-Known Defense of Marriage and Childbearing by Ambrosiaster." *Harvard Theological Review* 82 (1989): 283–299.

———. "Rereading the Jovinianist Controversy: Asceticism and Clerical Authority in Late Ancient Christianity." *Journal of Medieval and Early Modern Studies* 33 (2003): 453–470.

———. "Resistance to the Virginal Ideal in Late-Fourth-Century Rome: The Case of Jovinian." *Theological Studies* 48 (1987): 45–64.

Hunter, Ian. "Michel Foucault: Discourse Versus Language." Unpublished manuscript. Griffith University, Brisbane, 1988.

Hurd, John C. *The Origin of 1 Corinthians.* Macon, GA: Mercer University Press, 1983.

Ingraham, Chrys. *White Weddings: Romancing Heterosexuality in Popular Culture.* New York: Routledge, 1999.

Irigaray, Luce. "Interview 1." Pages 43–58 in *Les femmes, la pornographie, l'éroticisme.* Edited by Marie-Françoise Hans and Gilles Lapouge. Paris: Seuil, 1978.

——. *This Sex Which Is Not One.* Ithaca, NY: Cornell University Press, 1985.

Jacobs, Andrew. "Dialogical Differences: (De)Judaizing Jesus' Circumcision." *JECS* (2007): 291–335.

Jakobsen, Janet R., and Ann Pellegrini. *Love the Sin: Sexual Regulation and the Limits of Religious Tolerance.* Boston: Beacon, 2004.

Jensen, Joseph. "Does *porneia* Mean Fornication? A Critique of Bruce Malina." *Novum Testamentum* 20 (1978): 161–184.

Jervis, L. Ann. "'But I Want You to Know . . .': Paul's Midrashic Intertextual Response to the Corinthian Worshipers (1 Cor 11:2–16)." *JBL* 112 (1993): 231–246.

Johns, Catherine. *Sex or Symbol: Erotic Images of Greece and Rome.* London: British Museum Press, 1982.

Johnson, Luke Timothy. *The First and Second Letters to Timothy.* AYB 35A. New Haven, CT: Yale University Press, 2001.

Johnson, W. A. *Readers and Reading Culture in the High Roman Empire.* Oxford: Oxford University Press, 2010.

Jörs, P. "Ueber das Verhältnis der *Lex Iulia de maritandis ordinibus* zur *Lex Papia Poppaea.*" PhD diss., University of Bonn, 1882.

Judge, Edwin A. *The Social Pattern of Christian Groups in the First Century: Some Prolegomena to the Study of New Testament Ideas of Social Obligation.* London: Tyndale, 1960.

Kampen, Natalie Boymel. "Gender Theory in Roman Art." Pages 14–25 in *I CLAVDIA: Women in Ancient Rome.* Edited by D. E. E. Kleiner and Susan B. Matheson. New Haven, CT: Yale University Press, 1996.

Karavites, Peter. *Evil, Freedom, and the Road to Perfection in Clement of Alexandria.* Leiden: Brill, 1999.

Kelly, J. N. D. *Jerome: His Life, Writings, and Controversies.* New York: Harper & Row, 1975.

Kendall, Gavin, and Gary Wickman. *Using Foucault's Methods.* Introducing Qualitative Methods. London: SAGE, 1999.

Klassen, William. "Musonius Rufus, Jesus, and Paul: Three First-Century Feminists." Pages 167–186 in *From Jesus to Paul: Studies in Honour of Francis Wright Beare.* Edited by Peter Richardson and John C. Hurd. Waterloo, Ontario: Wilfrid Laurier University Press, 1984.

Kline, Meredith G. *God, Heaven, and Har Magedon: A Covenantal Tale of Cosmos and Telos.* Eugene, OR: Wipf & Stock, 2006.

Kloppenborg, John S. "Egalitarianism in the Myth and Rhetoric of Pauline Churches." Pages 247–263 in *Reimagining Christian Origins: A Colloquium Honoring Burton L. Mack*. Edited by Elizabeth A. Castelli and Hal Taussig. Valley Forge, PA: Trinity Press International, 1996.

Knust, Jennifer Wright. *Abandoned to Lust: Sexual Slander and Ancient Christianity*. New York: Columbia University Press, 2006.

——. "Paul and the Politics of Virtue and Vice." Pages 155–174 in *Paul and the Roman Imperial Order*. Edited by Richard A. Horsley. Harrisburg, PA: Trinity Press International, 2004.

Koltun-Fromm, Naomi. "Re-imagining Tatian: The Damaging Effects of Polemical Rhetoric." *JECS* 16:1 (2008): 1–30.

Konstan, David. *Sexual Symmetry: Love in the Ancient Novel and Related Genres*. Princeton, NJ: Princeton University Press, 1994.

Kraemer, Ross S. "Jewish Women and Christian Origins: Some Caveats." Pages 35–49 in *Women and Christian Origins*. Edited by Ross Shepard Kraemer and Mary Rose D'Angelo. Oxford: Oxford University Press, 1999.

Krause, Deborah. *1 Timothy*. London: T&T Clark, 2004.

Kuefler, Matthew. *The Manly Eunuch: Masculinity, Gender Ambiguity, and Christian Ideology in Late Antiquity*. Chicago Series on Sexuality, History, and Society. Chicago: University of Chicago Press, 2001.

Kugel, James L. *How to Read the Bible: A Guide to Scripture, Then and Now*. New York: Free Press, 2007.

——. *A Walk Through Jubilees: Studies in the Book of Jubilees and the World of Its Creation*. Leiden: Brill, 2012.

Lape, Susan. "Heterosexuality." Pages 17–36 in *A Cultural History of Sexuality in the Classical World*. Edited by Mark Golden and Peter Toohey. London: Bloomsbury, 2014.

Laqueur, Thomas. *Making Sex: Body and Gender from the Greeks to Freud*. Cambridge, MA: Harvard University Press, 1990.

Levin, Susan B. "Women's Nature and Role in the Ideal *POLIS: Republic* V Revisited." Pages 13–30 in *Feminism and Ancient Philosophy*. Edited by Julie K. Ward. London: Routledge, 1996.

Levine, Amy-Jill. "Judith." Pages 632–641 in *The Oxford Bible Commentary*. Edited by John Barton and John Muddiman. Oxford: Oxford University Press, 2001.

——. "Sacrifice and Salvation: Otherness and Domestication in the Book of Judith." Pages 17–30 in *"No One Spoke Ill of Her": Essays on Judith*. Edited by James C. VanderKam. Atlanta: Scholars Press, 1992.

Levine, Baruch A. *Leviticus*. JPS Torah Commentary. Philadelphia: Jewish Publication Society, 1989.

Lévi-Strauss, Claude. *Structural Anthropology*. New York: Basic Books, 1963.

Leyser, Conrad. *Authority and Asceticism from Augustine to Gregory the Great*. Oxford: Clarendon, 2000.

Liboron, Herbert. *Die karpokratianische Gnosis: Untersuchungen zur Geschichte und Anschauungswelt eines spätgnostischen Systems*. Leipzig: Komissionsverlag von Jordan & Gramberg, 1938.

Lintott, A. W. *The Constitution of the Roman Republic*. Oxford: Clarendon, 1999.

Loader, William. *Making Sense of Sex: Attitudes Towards Sexuality in Early Jewish and Christian Literature*. Grand Rapids, MI: Eerdmans, 2013.

Luck, William F. *Divorce and Remarriage: Recovering the Biblical View*. San Francisco: Harper and Row, 1987.

Lyotard, Jean-François, and Ebehard Gruber. *The Hyphen: Between Judaism and Christianity*. Philosophy and Literary Theory. Amherst, NY: Humanity Books, 1999.

MacDonald, Dennis R. *The Legend and the Apostle: The Battle for Paul in Story and Canon*. Louisville, KY: Westminster John Knox, 1983.

MacDonald, Margaret Y. "Reading Real Women Through the Undisputed Letters of Paul." Pages 199–220 in *Women and Christian Origins*. Edited by Ross Shepard Kraemer and Mary Rose D'Angelo. Oxford: Oxford University Press, 1999.

Mack, Burton L. *A Myth of Innocence: Mark and Christian Origins*. Philadelphia: Fortress, 1988.

Malherbe, Abraham J. *The Letters to the Thessalonians*. AYB 32B. New Haven, CT: Yale University Press, 2000.

Malina, Bruce J., and John J. Pilch. *Social-Science Commentary on the Letters of Paul*. Minneapolis: Fortress, 2006.

Marcus, Joel. *Mark 1–8*. AYB 27. New York: Doubleday, 1999.

Marshall, I. Howard. *The Pastoral Epistles*. International Critical Commentary. Edinburgh: T&T Clark, 1999.

Martin, Dale. "The Construction of the Ancient Family: Methodological Considerations." *JRS* 86 (1996): 40–60.

———. *The Corinthian Body*. New Haven, CT: Yale University Press, 1995.

———. *New Testament History and Literature*. New Haven, CT: Yale University Press, 2012.

———. "Paul Without Passion: On Paul's Rejection of Desire in Sex and Marriage." Pages 201–215 in *Constructing Early Christian Families: Family as Social*

Reality and Metaphor. Edited by Halvor Moxnes. London: Routledge, 1997.

———. *Sex and the Single Savior: Gender and Sexuality in Biblical Interpretation.* Louisville, KY: Westminster John Knox, 2006.

Mattern, Susan. *Galen and the Rhetoric of Healing.* Baltimore: Johns Hopkins University Press, 2008.

May, Alistair Scott. "The Body for the Lord: Sex and Identity in 1 Corinthians 5–7." PhD diss., University of Glasgow, 2001.

McCabe, Herbert. *Law, Love and Language.* London: Sheed and Ward, 1968.

McGinn, T. A. J. *Prostitution, Sexuality, and the Law in Ancient Rome.* Oxford: Oxford University Press, 1998.

McGowan, Andrew. *Ascetic Eucharist: Food and Drink in Early Christian Ritual Meals.* Oxford: Clarendon, 1999.

McGuckin, John Anthony. *The Orthodox Church: An Introduction to Its History, Doctrine, and Spiritual Culture.* Oxford: Wiley-Blackwell, 2011.

McLean, B. H. *Biblical Interpretation and Philosophical Hermeneutics.* Cambridge: Cambridge University Press, 2012.

Meeks, Wayne A. *The Origins of Christian Morality.* New Haven, CT: Yale University Press, 1995.

Mees, Michael. "Clemens von Alexandrien über Ehe und Familie." *Augustinianum* 17 (1977): 113–131.

Meggitt, Justin J. *Paul, Poverty and Survival.* Edinburgh: T&T Clark, 1998.

Milgrom, Jacob. *Numbers.* Jewish Publication Society Torah Commentary. Philadelphia: Jewish Publication Society, 1990.

Mitchell, Margaret M. "Concerning *peri de* in 1 Corinthians." *NovT* 31 (1989): 229–256.

Moore, Carey A. *Tobit.* AYB 40A. New York: Doubleday, 1996.

Moore, George Foot. *Judaism in the First Centuries of the Christian Era: The Age of the Tannaim.* 2 volumes. Cambridge, MA: Harvard University Press, 1944.

Morales, Helen. *Vision and Narrative in Achilles Tatius' Leucippe and Clitophon.* Cambridge Classical Studies. Cambridge: Cambridge University Press, 2004.

Muddiman, J. "Fast, Fasting." Pages 773–776 in *The Anchor Bible Dictionary.* Volume 2. Edited by David Noel Freedman. New Haven, CT: Yale University Press, 1992.

Myers, Jacob M. *I and II Esdras.* AYB 42. Garden City, NY: Doubleday, 1974.

Nörr, D. "The Matrimonial Legislation of Augustus: An Early Instance of Social Engineering." *Irish Jurist* 16 (1981): 350–364.

North, Helen. *SOPHROSYNE: Self-Knowledge and Self-Restraint in Greek Literature.* Ithaca, NY: Cornell University Press, 1966.

Osborn, Eric. *Clement of Alexandria.* Cambridge: Cambridge University Press, 2005.

Osiek, Carolyn A., and David L. Balch. *Families in the New Testament World: Households and House Churches.* Louisville, KY: Westminster John Knox, 1997.

Oulton, J. E. L, and Henry Chadwick, eds. *Alexandrian Christianity: Selected Translations of Clement and Origen.* Library of Christian Classics 2. Philadelphia: Westminster, 1954.

Parker, Holt. "Women and Medicine." Pages 107–124 in *A Companion to Women in the Ancient World.* Edited by Sharon L. James and Shelia Dillon. Oxford: Blackwell, 2012.

Paul VI (pope). *Gaudium et Spes.* Online: http://www.vatican.va/archive/hist_ councils/ii_vatican_council/documents/vat-ii_const_19651207_gaudium-et-spes_en.html.

———. *Lumen Gentium.* Online: http://www.vatican.va/archive/hist_councils/ii _vatican_council/documents/vat-ii_const_19641121_lumen-gentium_en.html.

Payne, Philip B. *Man and Woman, One in Christ: An Exegetical and Theological Study of Paul's Letters.* Grand Rapids, MI: Zondervan, 2009.

Pêcheux, Michel. "The Mechanism of Ideology (Mis)recognition." Pages 141–151 in *Mapping Ideology.* Edited by Slavoj Žižek. London: Verso, 2012.

Pendergraft, Mary. "'Thou Shalt Not Eat the Hyena': A Note on 'Barnabas' *Epistle* 10.7." *Vigiliae Christianae* 46 (1992): 75–79.

Pervo, Richard I. *The Making of Paul: Constructions of the Apostle in Early Christianity.* Minneapolis: Fortress, 2010.

Petersen, William L. "Tatian the Assyrian." Pages 125–158 in *A Companion to Second-Century Christian Heretics.* Edited by Antti Marjanen and Petri Luomanen. Leiden: Brill, 2008.

Phipps, W. E. "Is Paul's Attitude Toward Sexual Relations Contained in 1 Cor. 7.1?" *NTS* 28 (1982): 125–131.

Plevnik, Joseph. *Paul and the Parousia: An Exegetical and Theological Investigation.* Peabody, MA: Hendrickson, 1997.

Pontifical Council for the Family. *The Truth and Meaning of Human Sexuality: Guidelines for Education Within the Family.* Boston: Pauline Books, 1996.

Posner, Sarah. *God's Profits: Faith, Fraud, and the Republican Crusade for Values Voters.* Sausalito, CA: PoliPointPress, 2008.

Propp, William H. C. *Exodus 19–40.* AYB 2A. New York: Doubleday, 2006.

Rabinow, Paul, ed. *The Foucault Reader.* New York: Vintage, 2010.

Raditsa, Leo Ferrero. "Augustus' Legislation Concerning Marriage, Procreation, Love Affairs and Adultery." Pages 13:278–339 in *Aufstieg und Niedergang der römischen Welt: Geschichte und Kultur Roms im Spiegel der neueren Forschung.* Part 2,

Principat. Edited by Hildegard Temporini and Wolfgang Haase. Berlin: de Gruyter, 1972–.

Ramelli, Illaria. *Hierocles the Stoic: Elements of Ethics, Fragments, and Excerpts.* Writings from the Greco-Roman World 28. Translated by David Konstan. Atlanta: Society of Biblical Literature, 2009.

Rancière, Jacques. *Hatred of Democracy.* London: Verso, 2014.

Rawson, Beryl. "Adult-Child Relationships in Roman Society." Pages 7–30 in *Marriage, Divorce, and Children in Ancient Rome.* Edited by Beryl Rawson. Oxford: Oxford University Press, 2004.

Reed, David A. "How Semitic Was John? Rethinking the Hellenistic Background to John 1:1." *Australian Theological Review* (2003): 709–726.

Rehmann, Jan. *Theories of Ideology: The Powers of Alienation and Subjection.* Historical Materialism 54. Leiden: Brill, 2013.

Rey, Jean-Sébastien. *4QInstruction: sagesse et eschatologie.* Studies on the Texts of the Desert of Judah. Leiden: Brill, 2009.

Reydams-Schils, Gretchen. "Clement of Alexandria on Women and Marriage in Light of the New Testament Household Codes." Pages 113–134 in *Greco-Roman Culture and the New Testament.* Edited by David E. Aune and Frederick Brenk. Leiden: Brill, 2012.

———. "Musonius Rufus, Porphyry, and Christians in Counter-Point on Marriage and the Good." Pages 153–168 in *Being Good? Metamorphoses of Neoplatonism.* Edited by A. Kijewska. Lublin: Wydawnictwo KUL, 2004.

Riccobono, Salvatore. *Acta divi Augusti.* Rome: Ex officinal typographica R. Academiae italicae, 1945.

Robinson, James M., and John S. Kloppenborg, eds. *The Sayings Gospel Q in Greek and English.* Minneapolis: Fortress, 2002.

Rose, Nikolas. "Of Madness Itself 'Histoire de la Folie' and the Object of Psychiatric History." *History of the Human Sciences* 3 (1990): 373–380.

Rosner, Brian S. *Paul, Scripture and Ethics: A Study of 1 Corinthians 5–7.* Grand Rapids, MI: Baker, 1994.

Rotondi, Giovanni. *Leges publicae populi Romani.* Hildersheim: G. Olms, 1966.

Rousseau, Philip. *Ascetics, Authority, and the Church in the Age of Jerome and Cassian.* Oxford: Oxford University Press, 1978.

Runia, David T. *Philo in Early Christian Literature: A Survey.* Minneapolis: Fortress, 1993.

Runions, Erin. *The Babylon Complex: Theopolitical Fantasies of War, Sex, and Sovereignty.* New York: Fordham University Press, 2014.

Sanders, H. "A Birth Certificate of the Year 145 A.D." *American Journal of Archaeology* 32 (1928): 309–329.

Sarna, Nahum. *Genesis*. JPS Torah Commentary. Philadelphia: Jewish Publication Society, 1989.

Schrage, Wolfgang. "Zur Frontstellung der paulinischen Ehebewertung in 1 Kor 7 1–7." *Zeitschrift für die neutestamentliche Wissenschaft und die Kunde der älteren Kirche* 67 (1976): 214–234.

Sedgwick, Eve Kosofsky. *Epistemology of the Closet*. Berkeley: University of California Press, 2008.

Sharrock, Alison. "Ovid and the Discourses of Love: The Amatory Works." Pages 150–162 in *Cambridge Companion to Ovid*. Edited by Philip Hardie. Cambridge: Cambridge University Press, 2002.

Shaw, B. S. "The Age of Roman Girls at Marriage: Some Reconsiderations." *JRS* 77 (1987): 30–46.

Silk, Mark. "The Abrahamic Religions as a Modern Concept." Pages 71–87 in *The Oxford Handbook of Abrahamic Religions*. Edited by Adam J. Silverstein and Guy G. Stroumsa. Oxford: Oxford University Press, 2015.

Skinner, Marilyn B. *Sexuality in Greek and Roman Culture*. 2nd ed. Malden, MA: Wiley Blackwell, 2014.

Smith, Jonathan Z. *Drudgery Divine: On the Comparison of Early Christianities and the Religions of Late Antiquity*. Chicago: Chicago University Press, 1990.

Smith, William, and Henry Wace. "Epiphanes." Pages 2:147–148 in *A Dictionary of Christian Biography, Literature, Sects and Doctrines*. London: J. Murray, 1880–1900. Repr., New York: AMS Press, 1984.

Spada, Concetta Aloe. "Un' omelia greca anonima 'sulla verginità." Pages 603–623 in *La tradizione dell'enkrateia: motivazioni ontologice e protologiche*. Edited by Ugo Bianchi. Rome: Edizioni dell'Ateneo, 1985.

Stewart, Columba. *Cassian the Monk*. Oxford Studies in Historical Theology. Oxford: Oxford University Press, 1999.

Swain, Simon. *Economy, Family, and Society from Rome to Islam: A Critical Edition, English Translation, and Study of Bryson's Management of the Estate*. Cambridge: Cambridge University Press, 2013.

Syme, Ronald. *The Roman Revolution*. Oxford: Clarendon, 2002.

Taylor, Joan E. *The Essenes, the Scrolls, and the Dead Sea*. Oxford: Oxford University Press, 2012.

Taylor, Mark C. "Introduction." Pages 1–20 in *Critical Terms for Religious Studies*. Edited by Mark C. Taylor. Chicago: University of Chicago Press, 1998.

Tempkin, Owsei. *Galenism: Rise and Decline of a Medical Philosophy*. Ithaca, NY: Cornell University Press, 1973.

Theissen, Gerd. *Social Reality and the Early Christians: Theology, Ethics, and the World of the New Testament*. Translated by Margaret Kohl. Minneapolis: Fortress, 1992.

Thiselton, Anthony C. *The First Epistle to the Corinthians: A Commentary on the Greek Text*. New International Greek Testament Commentary. Grand Rapids, MI: Eerdmans, 2000.

Tocqueville, Alexis de. *Democracy in America*. 1838. Facsimile reprint edition. Clark, NJ: Lawbook Exchange, 2003.

Tougher, Shaun. *Eunuchs in Antiquity and Beyond*. Swansea: Classical Press of Wales, 2002.

Treggiari, Susan. *Roman Marriage: "Iusti Conigues" from the Time of Cicero to the Time of Ulpian*. Oxford: Clarendon, 1991.

———. "Social Status and Social Legislation" Pages 873–904 in *The Cambridge Ancient History*. Volume 10. Edited by Alan K. Bowman. Cambridge: Cambridge University Press, 1996.

———. "Women in Roman Society." Pages 116–125 in *I CLAVDIA: Women in Ancient Rome*. Edited by D. E. E. Kleiner and Susan B. Matheson. New Haven, CT: Yale University Press, 1996.

Turner, Denys. *Thomas Aquinas: A Portrait*. New Haven, CT: Yale University Press, 2013.

van den Hoek, A. *Clement of Alexandria and His Use of Philo in the* Stromateis: *An Early Christian Reshaping of a Jewish Model*. Leiden: Brill, 1988.

van der Horst, P. W. *The Sentences of Pseudo-Phocylides*. Leiden: Brill, 1978.

VanderKam, James C. *The Book of Jubilees*. Sheffield: Sheffield Academic Press, 2001.

van Geytenbeek, A. C. *Musonius Rufus and the Greek Diatribe*. Assen: VanGorcum, 1962.

Veyne, Paul. *The Roman Empire*. Cambridge, MA: Belknap Press of Harvard University Press, 1987.

Visotzky, Burton L. *Reading the Book: Making the Bible a Timeless Text*. Philadelphia: Jewish Publication Society, 2005.

Voelke, André Jean. *Les rapports avec autrui dans la philosophie grecque d'Aristote à Panetius*. Paris: J. Vrin, 1961.

von Staden, Heinrich. *Herophilus: The Art of Medicine in Early Alexandria*. Cambridge: Cambridge University Press, 1989.

Vööbus, Arthur. *Celibacy: A Requirement for Admission to Baptism in the Early Syrian Church*. Papers of the Estonian Theological Society in Exile 1. Stockholm: Estonian Theological Society in Exile, 1951.

Wallace-Hadrill, Andrew. "Family and Inheritance in the Augustan Marriage Laws." *Proceedings of the Cambridge Philological Society* 27 (1981): 58–80.

———. "The Golden Age and Sin in Augustan Ideology." *Past and Present* 95 (1982): 19–36.

Weber, Max. *Economy and Society: An Outline of Interpretive Sociology.* 2 volumes. Berkeley: University of California Press, 1978.

———. *The Theory of Social and Economic Organization.* New York: Free Press, 2012.

Weiss, Allen. "Offred's Complicity and the Dystopian Tradition in Margaret Atwood's *The Handmaid's Tale.*" *Studies in Canadian Literature / Études en littérature canadienne* 34 (2009): 120–141.

Weiss, Johannes. *Der erste Korintherbrief.* Kritisch-exegetischer Kommentar über das Neue Testament (Meyer-Kommentar). Göttingen: Vandenhoeck & Ruprecht, 1925.

Welborn, L. L. "Paul and Pain: Paul's Emotional Therapy in 2 Corinthians 1.1–2.13; 7.5–16 in the Context of Ancient Psychagogic Literature." *NTS* 57 (2011): 547–570.

Wendland, Paul. *Quaestiones Musonianae. De Musonio Stoico Clementis Alexandrini aliorumque auctore.* Berlin: Mayer & Mueller, 1886.

Whitmarsh, Tim. *Greek Literature and the Roman Empire: The Politics of Imitation.* Oxford: Oxford University Press, 2001.

Whittaker, Molly. *Tatian: Oratia ad Graecos and Fragments.* Oxford Early Christian Texts. Oxford: Clarendon, 1982.

Williams, Gordon. "Some Aspects of Roman Marriage Ceremonies and Ideals." *JRS* 48 (1958): 16–29.

Williams, Raymond. *Marxism and Literature.* Oxford: Oxford University Press, 1977.

Wilson, Anne. "In Defense of Traditional Marriage." *Catholic Update* (June 2015): 1–4.

Wire, Antoinette Clark. *The Corinthian Women Prophets: A Reconstruction Through Paul's Rhetoric.* Minneapolis: Fortress, 1990.

Wise, Michael, Martin Abegg, and Edward Cook. *The Dead Sea Scrolls: A New Translation.* New York: HarperOne, 2005.

Wolbert, Werner. *Ethische Argumentation und Paränese in 1 Kor 7.* Düsseldorf: Patmos, 1981.

Wood, Simon P. *Clement of Alexandria: Christ the Educator.* Fathers of the Church. Washington, DC: Catholic University of America Press, 1954.

Yarbrough, Larry. "Parents and Children in the Letters of Paul." Pages 126–141 in *The Social World of the First Christians: Essays in Honor of Wayne A. Meeks.* Edited by L. M. White and L. Yarbrough. Minneapolis: Fortress, 1996.

Zeitlin, Froma. "The Poetics of *Erōs:* Nature, Art and Imitation in Longus' *Daphnis and Chloe.*" Pages 417–464 in *Before Sexuality: The Construction of Erotic Experience in the Ancient Greek World.* Edited by David M. Halperin, John J. Winkler, and Froma I. Zeitlin. Princeton, NJ: Princeton University Press, 1990.

Zeller, Dieter. *Der erste Brief an die Korinther.* Göttingen: Vandenhoeck & Ruprecht, 2010.

Zias, Joe. "The Cemeteries of Qumran and Celibacy—'Confusion Laid to Rest?'" *DSD* 7 (2000): 220–253.

Zimmerman, Frank. *The Book of Tobit.* Dropsie College Series. New York: Harper & Brothers, 1958.

Žižek, Slavoj, ed. *Mapping Ideology.* Mapping Series. London: Verso, 2012.

INDEX OF AUTHORS

INDEX OF SUBJECTS

INDEX OF SCRIPTURE